FUNDAMENTALS OF DATA ANALYTICS

Learn Essential Skills, Embrace The Future, And Catapult Your Career In The Data-Driven World—A Comprehensive Guide To Data Literacy For Beginners

Russell Dawson

Table of Contents

BOOK 1

INTRODUCTION

If you were asked about one of the main pillars that supports businesses worldwide, would you be able to answer? While most people could say the answer to this question is *technology*, this would only be partially correct. Despite technology currently being used for most businesses (When was the last time you saw a company that did not have computers in their office?), there are still a few occupations that don't have the immediate need to incorporate it into their activities. To illustrate this point, think about a street hot dog vendor—you usually don't see these with their computers open while selling their food.

However, there is one resource used by all businesses, from the hot dog vendor or the farmer planting their crops to the big corporations all around the world, with which they cannot work without and can determine their success. Can you guess what it is? If you said "data," then you are correct! Today, data is one of the essential keys to supporting the most diverse businesses. Data is independent of technology, although technology has given us the ability to process it faster and obtain conclusions that could previously take several hours or even days.

When I mention data, I am referring to all the information that can be used to support a business to function, which may or may not be electronic. From the beginning of time, when farmers used to register rainfall or the seasons on a piece of paper, passing through more elaborate records of John Grant keeping track of the number of deaths, the mortality rate, and causes of death of the London population, to a more modern concept of having a place where employees register their information with a company, all of these cases include the use of data (El Shatby, 2022).

If you observe the given examples, you will see that the use of data, in these cases, is not necessarily related to technology. They refer to information people collected and used to help them carry out a task or reach conclusions about a particular topic. All this changed when individuals started noticing that they could store and organize data to carry out deeper and more meaningful analyses that could change and impact their business performance.

The great change in how we viewed and used data arrived in 1997, together with Google and the internet. Not only was data being stored and gathered in real time, but it was also being made available to others. Before the search engines appeared, or even before the internet, data was primarily stored physically, which posed a challenge to those who wanted to analyze a more complex set of information. Can you imagine what it would be like to manually analyze the details of all the patients in a big hospital who suffered from a common disease to try and find the common link? It would take *a lot* of time, dedication, effort, and space to store all this information.

When computers started to gain popularity and become more and more sophisticated, companies and individuals started storing their information in them and using these machines to process, organize, and sort through the incredible volume of information created. Data came in many types: pictures, text, audio, videos, tables, and almost any other type of format that could be supported and processed by a computer. We managed to move from a global data storage of 2.6 exabytes (EB) in 1986 to almost 6,800 EB in 2020, where 1 EB is equal to 1,000,000,000,000,000,000 bytes (1e+18 bytes) or *1 million terabytes* (Bartley, 2020).

As impressive as this number is, you should remember that it refers only to the electronically stored data. According to Bartley (2020), we generate approximately 2.5 quintillion bytes per day, which adds up to 64 zettabytes in 2020. If you are confused about this number, consider that one unique zettabyte is equivalent to "660 billion Blu-ray discs, 33 million human brains, 330 million of the world's largest hard drives" (Bartley, 2020). Can you imagine how much this is? And this is only considering electronic data and leaving aside everything stored and registered in nondigital data.

Every day, when we use our computer to access the internet and carry out a search, buy something online, or even click on a link to read the news, we are generating data. This data that registers everything we do online and is transformed into information to be used by companies is one of the most valuable resources in the world today. However, one critical part of the equation must be considered: It does not matter if you have access to all the data in the world if you do not know how to understand, process, use, and analyze it.

If a business is unable to gather this data and transform it into significant observations and insights that can be used to its advantage, the data is useless. If they can't extract meaning and analyze what the data is saying to reach conclusions that benefit them, these are nothing more than numbers (or any type of data) grouped without meaning. Enter into scene one of the most important, demanded, and valued professions in the market today: the data analyst.

You must be asking yourself, *What does a data analyst do? How does this analysis work, and what will I benefit from this? How is a data analysis carried out?* This book is here to answer these questions and teach you much more on this subject that is considered the present and the future of businesses globally.

WHY DATA ANALYTICS?

Based on the increasing relevance of data in the current world, it is safe to say that knowing how to deal with data, or in other words, data gathering, management, and analysis, will become one of the most sought-after skills in future professionals. Knowing how to manipulate this data will be essential for companies looking to make informed decisions about conducting their businesses and planning future actions. Furthermore, it will enable these decision-making processes to be based on facts that back up the course of action and establish a strategy to move forward.

Because of the results and decisions a data analyst might lead to, it is essential to obtain information from a trustworthy source that can outline how the process should be carried out and its potential effects. Learning the correct and most efficient methods to apply this leads to more effective results while saving resources simultaneously. And it is with this approach that this book was written.

With the information contained herein, you will understand the fundamental techniques of data analysis and the best ways to conduct the process, so optimal results are achieved. You will learn about real-time business techniques and how to develop and establish the mindset of a successful professional oriented toward problem-solving based on data. By applying the information you are about to read in your workplace, you will have a significant competitive advantage compared to other professionals who do not have this background or knowledge.

By approaching the challenges faced with an analytical mindset supported by data, you will be able to propose solutions and propel your career to the next level. Finally, you will be taught how to present the results obtained in your analysis. After all, it is not only about knowing how to understand, manipulate, and "translate" the data but also how to convey this information clearly and efficiently to all stakeholders involved.

If you are ready to start a revolution in your professional life and see how data analytics can make a difference, join me in this journey that will teach you everything you need to know. Once you are done, you will understand the topic comprehensively and be ready to put your newly earned skills into action. Are you ready?

CHAPTER 1:
DATA ANALYTICS IN A DATA-DRIVEN WORLD

Data. Have you ever asked yourself what the role it is currently playing in our lives is? Regardless if you are in a business, a research facility, or even in school, there is a high probability that at one point or the other, the following question will be asked: "What does the data say about this matter?" This is because data has become an essential component in the decision process, much more than it has been in the past and likely less than what it will be in the future.

Looking into the recent past, the use of data was mostly limited to specific purposes such as medical research for illnesses and medicine and targeted surveys that sometimes weren't as comprehensive as necessary. Businesses were mostly run on the beliefs and "feelings" of the C-suite executives or owners, aligned with metrics that could be either objective or subjective depending on the company. If you talk to someone who has been working for the past 20 years and ask them what the criteria used to decide their bonuses or salary increases were, the answer will likely be something subjective.

The same can be said for the reasons as to why a certain company decided to go down a certain path. "It was a management decision," is what you will be told most of the time. Not based on data, not based on information, but rather on what the top leaders thought was appropriate and the best course of action for tackling a certain issue.

This was the norm in most cases until data, and its advantages, came into the picture. The amount and availability of data changed everything.

It is safe to say that we have, for some time now, been in the era of a world that makes data-driven decisions. These decisions have proven, in many cases, to be the correct approach and way of dealing with matters that range from external matters such as product satisfaction and customer service to internal evaluations that include employee performance and machine efficiency. In some cases and many corporate boardrooms, it even goes as far as helping to determine the plan that organizations will follow for the years to come and establishing objectives.

While the increase in the amount of data available is one of the factors that have definitely made us "data-driven," it is also possible to say that it is because we have become "data-driven" that the amount of data available has increased. But technological advancements also cannot be put aside in this equation. In the age of social media and technology which is constantly changing and evolving, it has become crucial for companies to understand what they are doing well and what can be improved. It has become a matter of *corporate survival* being informed almost in real time what is going on or trending on the internet.

This is where data comes in. All this "digital gold" plays a crucial part in determining if a company will thrive or fail. Today, companies that have the C-suite using their "personal beliefs" to make decisions are becoming rarer by the day. Data-driven decisions have taken center stage in almost all aspects of our lives, which has led to another need: understanding how to analyze and use all the data available to the best of its advantage to aid in the decision-making process. That is precisely where data analytics comes in.

WHAT IS DATA ANALYTICS?

The term "data analytics" means exactly what you might imagine: the ability to analyze raw data and obtain conclusions from it. However, it is not only a matter of looking at the data; there is a whole process that needs to be carried out before this can be done. These professionals are "responsible for data collection, organization, and maintenance, as well as for using statistics, programming, and other techniques to gain insights from data" (Burnham, 2021). This means they will use the results of the analysis they carried out to identify if there are any trends and use these to solve potential problems that the company might be facing.

However, it is not uncommon to have many individuals, and even organizations, confuse data analytics with another profession that deals with data—data science. While both of these fields of expertise have many common points between them, some significant differences must be taken into consideration. Let's take a look into what these are and how to differentiate between them.

Data Analytics vs. Data Science

Both fields of data analytics and data science deal with data as the names suggest, and a lot of it is a matter of fact. The amount of data can have as many as millions of data points, and understanding how to establish a relationship between them is essential for both professions. To deal with this data, both data analysts and scientists usually need to have some knowledge of a programming language such as SQL, Python, or R, which are some of the most commonly used by these professionals.

However, the main difference between both these areas is also how they deal with the data. While the data analyst will examine the data, identify trends, and use the tools to find answers to problems, the data scientist is going to use programming languages to design a process that will analyze this data and build the best model for optimal observations to be obtained (Burnham, 2021). To do this, the data scientist will employ mathematical, statistical, and machine learning (ML) techniques that will help build the program.

In addition to this, the data scientist will develop programs to try and identify possible connections between that data that would likely not be seen without analysis, predicting unforeseen trends. In addition to this, the data scientist will help in the process of identifying the question and selecting the best data to answer it. These differences may not seem like much, but they directly impact how the data will be manipulated and how each process will be carried out and presented to the stakeholders.

Finally, it should be mentioned that when considering both professions, different technical skills should be taken into account. A data scientist, for example, will need to have some knowledge of programming languages and statistics to understand the algorithm and the way the machine is processing the data. On the other hand, the data analyst needs to know how to use the tools to carry out the analysis and establish patterns, sometimes also requiring the ability to scrape data from certain sources and be able to present the results to several audiences in an understandable and clear manner.

While it would be possible to go on and on talking about the other differences and approaches, you bought this book to learn more about data analytics. Therefore, as you continue to the next section, you are going to learn about the first important piece of information you should know about the area, which are the types of data analytics, what each of them means, and how they can be applied.

TYPES OF DATA ANALYTICS

If you were to type in the search bar of your browser, "types of data analytics," you would see that there are over 1.5 billion results that match what you are looking for. However, one thing you will notice if you look closely into those that are shown within the first 20 results is that most of them mention that there are 4 types of data analysis. Some articles mention five and others divide these four into two categories, but they are predominantly the same regardless of where you look. These four different types of analysis are descriptive, diagnostic, predictive, and prescriptive. Let's look at what each of them means and their main characteristics.

- **Descriptive analytics:** Suppose you work for a newspaper and are asked to inform management about subscriber numbers of the daily update email sent every morning. You will gather this information and place it on a graph or other visual tool that will illustrate the result of what you were asked to do. In the visual representation of the data, one of the possibilities is that there has been a decrease in the number of subscribers over the past 2 months.

What you have just read in the previous paragraph is an example of descriptive analytics. This means that the only question you are going to answer is, "What happened?" When carrying out this type of analysis, you are not looking for motives, possible action plans, or solutions to problems. You are stating a fact based on the data by giving a snapshot of what happened or is currently happening in a certain area, metric, or product.

- **Diagnostic analytics:** At the same newspaper, let's imagine that you have presented the results and now they want to know *why it happened.* In other words, you are asked to determine what caused the decrease in the number of subscribers over the past 2 months. In this case, you will be running a diagnostic analysis, since you will need to use the available data to understand the reasons for this decrease.

This likely means you will need to use more data than what was previously gathered since you will need to analyze all the factors that could contribute to this issue. If the newspaper has an "unsubscribe button" that enables the individual to select among several options the reasons for not receiving it anymore, this analysis will be much easier to carry out. However, if this is not the case, you will likely need to go even deeper to find the real reason for this. Maybe you discover that a new "rule" was applied so that emails that were deactivated no longer receive the emails and are automatically unsubscribed. Well, you would then have your answer.

It is important to reinforce that diagnostic analyses are not only carried out to identify the root cause of problems or to understand where the company is carrying out incorrect actions. It can also be used to show the reasons why positive change is happening. If the company notices there has been an increase in traffic to the website on the day that coincides with the release of a specific writer's new column, this could be relevant. It means that they could focus their marketing and front-page highlights to include more of this type of content when released to attract more individuals to it.

- **Predictive analytics:** You have answered the *what* and the *why*, but as you saw during the analysis, you also identified the potential of that specific writer. This sparks the interest of those who are listening to you and, because it could mean a possible opportunity, you are asked to run a predictive analysis. In this case, you will need to answer the question of *what will likely happen*, or what the potential outcomes the company will need to deal with are if this writer is given more space and visibility.

Once again, you are likely looking to analyze more data, since you will need to broaden your search even more. This type of analysis usually looks into what other companies of similar markets are doing and the direct impact on the public by identifying how many times a certain theme is mentioned. This could mean, for example, comparing how column writers of the same newspaper and of competitors performed with the audience when they were bumped up to the landing or top stories page or sharing parts of the content on social media.

By studying how the market and the readers reacted to these changes and what the effects they had on the other company were, it will be possible to create a likely scenario to be used as a baseline. Once this is done, the analysis will help identify the trend and establish a path for the company to make the best decisions. This could mean adopting different strategies on how to make this change, attract new and regular readers, and even find a way to possibly monetize the content.

Despite the three previous types of analytics being described in a process, it is important to know that this is not always necessarily the case. For example, the company can already see that there is a negative or positive result, and they want to understand why. In this case, they would jump directly to the diagnostic analysis. Similarly, it could also use predictive analysis to determine what would the achieved results be if a process continued to be carried out the same way or if there was no change in direction.

These analytics are not necessarily dependent on each other, just as the last type also isn't. As you might imagine, the last part of this process, considering the example that was given, is to make a decision. This is where the prescriptive analytics come in. Just as the doctor will likely prescribe you a treatment if you are feeling ill, determining the best course of action is exactly what the last type of analytics we will look at is going to do.

- **Prescriptive analytics:** If you already have all the previous analysis carried out and the information you will need, there is only one last step to take. You will now need to understand what the decisions that should be made are and the best paths to follow to ensure that a problem is solved or that success is maintained. For this, the prescriptive analysis needs to be performed and will answer the question of *what should be done next.*

  In this phase, the analyst will need to identify, based on the data, what it is that should be done and what the best way to obtain the best results is. This also means that when considering prescriptive analysis, it is "without doubt, the most complex type of analysis, involving algorithms, ML, statistical methods, and computational modeling procedures" (Stevens, 2023). The main reason for this assumption is the fact that the analyst will not only need to deal with a considerable amount of data, but they will also need to take into consideration all the possible outcomes and patterns that can happen if the decision is made.

This means studying and applying different scenarios to the matter in question by comparing each of them. In the case of our newspaper, the analyst might need to define what the outcome will be if the column is advertised on social media, if it is placed in a more visible location on the website, if readers are charged to access the content, and even what would happen if the frequency of releases was increased. All these issues would need to be studied based on different simulations and assumptions, that translate to a demanding, time-consuming, and often costly process.

While in the past explanations, you have seen one specific example that was used to illustrate how each of these data analysis types works and their purposes, this is just a part of the equation. There is no use in understanding what each of these is for if the analyst is unable to carry out the process correctly and efficiently to ensure the results are reliable and can be used. You must remember that companies use this information for *decision-making*, which, most of the time, can help determine the plan or path they will follow for the coming years.

This means that an incorrect analysis or one that is only partially true, because all the nuances were not taken into consideration, might bring catastrophic results to an organization. Even if it does not impact the strategy a company will apply at its core, it can affect marketing and targeted campaigns, make processes more inefficient, and even increase risks depending on where it is applied. For these reasons and others, the analyst must be able to present reliable and accurate results.

But what is this data analytics process, and what is it composed of? This is a really good question! This is exactly the second part of the equation that needs to be understood for a successful analysis to be made. In addition to this, it is possible to say that understanding this process and what it is composed of are the most essential parts of the analyst's job. This will be the exact starting point of your journey, as you are about to learn.

THE DATA ANALYTICS PROCESS

Much like you have seen in the previous section about data types, if you type in "data analytics process" in your search browser, you will find more than 1 billion results. However, contrary to having most results with a predominant answer, in this case, you are going to have a very diverse approach that can range from five to seven steps listed. But, I will tell you a secret: In most cases, where there are more than five steps, those that are "extra" can easily be incorporated into the five "standard" ones. It is all a matter of how the process is viewed and understood by the analyst.

This means that while there is no "maximum" number of steps that need to be carried out, there are five standard procedures that *must* be carried out in every data analysis process. In this section, you are going to learn what they are, their characteristics, and the reason they are so important. Finally, before you dive in, note that they have been numbered, and this is because they are usually carried out in this order to ensure the most accurate results.

1. **Problem/task identification:** The first part of the data analysis process is establishing what it is that you want to identify. In other words, what is the problem or task that you need an answer to? You must have this very clear in your mind since it is exactly what will guide your research. Some of the items that must be considered in the process include why you are analyzing this information, what the expected outcome or answer that you want to obtain is, and what the factors that influence this question and might affect it are. This is because, while it seems like a very objective approach, the answer you are looking for can be "hidden" between different processes, situations, and the correlation of data that was never explored.

Once you have the question and approach clear, you will be ready to move on to the next step.

2. **Data collection and storage:** While understanding the specific problem you are trying to answer is crucial to establishing the data you are going to gather, knowing the source of this data is as important. This is because you will need to base your analysis on reliable data that will give you the information necessary to answer what was asked. This data can be gathered from different sources, including those within the company (internal) or from public sources or third parties (external). When considering internal data, it will be essential that you have an open channel of communication with other departments, for example, so you can tell them exactly what the information you are looking for is. When considering external data, it must be provided from reliable and trustworthy sources. It is important to mention that this data can be both qualitative (written feedback and descriptive information) or quantitative (based on numbers).

3. **Data cleaning and preparation:** Regardless if you have the best data that can be found in the market, it will need to be adjusted. This happens due to many reasons, such as the format it is stored in, where it is extracted from, and the reasons for which it is used or gathered. This means that you will need to carry out a process to organize, clean, and structure the data according to your needs, so the analysis can be carried out. To organize the data, the analyst will usually place the data in some sort of spreadsheet in which it will be separated into rows and columns and carry out commands to reduce any irregularities that might interfere with the process.

4. **Data analysis and interpretation:** Now that you have gathered all the data, you will need to answer the question of *when to really start analyzing the data*. This means that you, as the data analyst, will use your preferred toolkit (SQL, Python, R, PowerBI, etc.) to carry out the analysis and identify

the factors that will help you answer the question. This will be carried out by performing calculations, identifying patterns and trends, and looking into the drivers of a specific behavior. In this process, other factors may come into light that might require you to gather more data to find the answer or solution, and this means that you will need to carry out steps 2 and 3 again. The analysis will be ready once you feel you have the best possible answer or solution to present to the person or group that requires the analysis.

5. **Data visualizations:** The final step of the process is to organize the data into visual models that will help the stakeholders see the result of the analysis. Usually, this is done by placing the data and the analysis results into charts, graphs, maps, and other visual representations that can be easily understood by all. When placing this information into visual aids, others will be able to understand what was done, analyze the usefulness of the information, and even suggest other approaches to the process. Sometimes, it is possible that your analysis is not understood or that there are disagreements, which means that you will likely need to go back, reorganize, review, and look into the matter from another angle. "Since you'll often present information to decision-makers, it's very important that the insights you present are 100% unambiguous. For this reason, data analysts commonly use reports, dashboards, and interactive visualizations to support their findings" (Hillier, 2023).

While the steps of this process are simple and logical to understand, you might have noticed they all have specific elements that should be carefully considered and learned in depth. This would be impossible to accomplish in such a small space—or even in just one chapter. For this reason, the overview you have just seen will not end here—not at all! It is just an appetizer for what you are about to see in the following chapters. In fact, if you go back to the table of contents, you will see that there is at least one chapter for each of these steps, and some even have more than one dedicated to them.

Therefore, if you are curious and excited to learn more about each of these parts of the process, read on! We will start by looking at the element that will determine what it is you are going to do and how you are going to do it. Can you remember what it is? If you said, "identifying the problem," you are correct! As you move on to the next chapter, prepare to learn about the core elements that make up data analysis and the best way to establish the question that will guide all the research you are about to carry out. Are you ready to find out?

CHAPTER 2:

UNDERSTANDING THE

COMPONENTS OF A DATA PROBLEM

As mentioned at the end of the previous chapter, as each chapter goes by, we will take a deeper look into the different components of the data analytics process. To do this, our first stop will be to better understand what originates the need to analyze data: the problem or question that needs to be answered. This is because the first step to solving any problem or answering any question is to identify the problem or the question or, in other words, identify what needs to be solved, if there are any constraints to the matter, and the conditions presented to do so.

However, just identifying the problem is not enough. The data analyst must be able to gather the raw data from somewhere so it can be treated and analyzed. For this reason, in this chapter, we will discuss problem identification and everything that can be related to this part of the process. After you are done reading, you will have a deep understanding of the fundamentals of raw data, variables, and functions, and how these help in defining the question and problem surrounding a dataset.

To start off, we are going to look into the main components of the data analytics process: raw data and datasets. As you read, you will see the importance of understanding what the available data you have to work with is and how this will impact defining and identifying the problem question. Furthermore, you will also understand one of the crucial issues a data analyst needs to comprehend: the difference between data and information. Are you ready to start?

DEALING WITH RAW DATA AND DATASETS

To understand the concept of raw data, the first thing is to identify what data is. Data can mean different things to different industries, but in data analytics (and technology in general), it can be identified as a piece of information that usually does not have any context. If you have, for example, a spreadsheet with different numbers on them that are not given any specification, they are each a different data point. The same can be said of individual words that are used without context. In fact, this is what data is: a piece of information that does not have any preliminary context or explanation. When we have these several data points together in one place, we can say we have *raw data*.

What Is Raw Data?

Raw data refers to a data point (or points) that has not yet been treated, or processed. If you take the example we have talked about before, we can imagine we have the following:

25	109	62	110	69
79	125	87	55	43
68	42	140	35	66
40	88	100	92	62
105	98	99	72	73

If you look at the above table, you will see that it is composed of 25 data points, correct? However, if I were to ask you what these data points represent, would you be able to tell me? Probably not, since they could mean anything, from the different number of people that enter a store on a given day to the measured temperatures of a city during autumn, or even the prices of products in a supermarket. This is what raw data is—a group of data points that do not have any cohesion or meaning and from which no conclusions can be made.

In this case, unless you format, process, and organize this data, it will be meaningless and have no use in solving any problems. Since this raw data has no attributes or characteristics, it is impossible to make any valuable inferences that might help in the analytical process. If you think about it, "the data could contain numerous human, machine, or instrumental errors, or it lacks validation. However, any change that serves to improve the quality of the data is known as processing, and the data is no longer raw" (Ot, 2023). It is only when you bring organization to this table and assign to it some significance that it will change from being "raw data" to being "information."

Data vs. Information

It is not rare to see people use the words "data" and "information" interchangeably, but the first thing you should know is that these are not the same thing. This distinction is especially important for the data analyst so they understand what it is that is being dealt with. In this case, when you have data, what you will usually be presented with are pieces of text or numbers or any form of representing "something" that does not have any meaning, purpose, or significance that can be immediately recognized.

On the other hand, when we have information, we are dealing with elements that have a specific meaning. This is the difference between having randomly used words and using them to build a sentence. In the first case, they would be considered data and, in the second, information. Here, it is possible to understand that when we have information, we are talking about a set of numbers, words, text, or any other elements that are organized and can be used to make certain conclusions.

If we had the following:

CAT ROOF IS GRAY THE ON THE

This would likely have no meaning for you since it is not organized, is apparently unrelated, and conveys no message. Therefore, the above are seven individual pieces of data. This means you could make no decisions based on this, which leads us to the conclusion that data does not depend on information. Conversely, let's say you had the following:

THE GRAY CAT IS ON THE ROOF

There is a meaning to the order of these words and, therefore, this is no longer data, but rather information. This will lead us to the conclusion that while data does not depend on information, information does depend on data since it was the previous seven individual data points that led to the information you can read. Hence, since you can read and understand what is being conveyed, you can make a decision.

But the next question on your mind is probably, *How can data be presented?* or, *How do I understand the different scales of how data is presented so I can transform them into actionable information?* Those are very good questions. It's very important to understand the formats that data can be presented in. Let's take a look at what these are and how they can be classified.

Data Scales

When we talk about data, it is imperative to understand that it can be divided into two separate groups: qualitative (any expression, usually in text) and quantitative (expressed in numerical values). These two types of data are further divided into two subcategories each: nominal and ordinal data for the qualitative type, and interval and ratio for the quantitative. Understanding the types of data you will be dealing with will help you determine how to structure and transform it into information that can be processed and analyzed to help you reach specific conclusions regarding the problem or question that needs to be addressed.

To do this, let's better understand each of these types of data with examples and uses:

- **Qualitative (categorical) data types:** are those usually composed of text such as the results of a customer satisfaction survey, in which the answers will be either *satisfied* or *dissatisfied*. In addition to surveys, these are usually extracted from documents, polls, and even comments in "recommendation" and "evaluation" fields on websites, such as the opinions travelers leave in the comment section of a hotel booking platform. These data types are classified as belonging to either the nominal or the ordinal kind, depending on their characteristics.

   o **Nominal data:** This type of data is made up of text, but it does not have any specific order or value that can be attributed to it. One example is if we were to analyze the hair color of students in a classroom. We could say that the results obtained are: blonde, brown, black, and red. In this case, there is none "better" than the others; thus, they cannot be sorted according to a specific order. "With nominal data, you can calculate frequencies, proportions, percentages, and central points" (Kumari, 2021).

   o **Ordinal data:** If nominal data cannot be ranked, this is not the case for ordinal data, which has as its main characteristic, the possibility to be ranked, organized, and placed into categories. For these data types, you will be able to identify a logical order in which they should be placed, allowing the data analyst to make comparisons between them, for example, as well as all the other tasks that can also be carried out with nominal data. An example of nominal data would be the client satisfaction survey previously mentioned, in which the customer can rate their experience by selecting between satisfied, neutral, and dissatisfied.

- **Quantitative (numerical) data types:** As you have already seen, these data types are expressed in numerals. This means that not only can you classify them, but you can also carry out calculations and other mathematical analyses with them to obtain the answer to a certain issue. If you look at the table provided when explaining raw data, that is an example of quantitative numerical types. Just like the qualitative data types, these can also be divided into two categories, ratio and interval data, which we will talk about now.

  o **Ratio data:** This type of data can be measured, ordered, and classified. However, its most important characteristic is that it does not accept negative numbers. Therefore, if you were to use a table with temperatures in Celsius, for example, that contained negative measurements, this would not be accepted. The values permitted for this data type start with 0 and, from there, it is possible to identify tendencies such as "central point (mean, median, mode), range (minimum, maximum), and spread (percentiles, interquartile range, and standard deviation)" (Kumari, 2021).

  o **Interval data:** When we talk about interval data, you might already imagine that the main difference between this data type and the ratio data type is that it accepts negative values. In this case, it would be perfectly acceptable to use Celsius temperature measurements within the data points, for example. The calculations that can be carried out with these data types are the same as those for the ratio data type and even some additional ones since negative numbers are accepted and thus, the range of operations is greater.

While this information will be useful for the data analyst to understand what will be possible to do, we still haven't identified how these can be ordered. We have mentioned data types, their characteristics, and the differences between data and information. Nevertheless, you might be wondering, *Where does the dataset come in? Is it a group of data or a group of information?* Well, there is no need to worry, as this is exactly what we will be talking about next, after all, the base of the work made by the data analyst is the dataset or datasets they use for reaching conclusions.

WHAT IS A DATASET?

A dataset is a collection of data that has an order or a meaning to it that is usually represented in the form of a table in which every column and row has a specific data type attributed to it. This means that when we have a group of raw data, it is not yet a dataset, the raw data will only become one once it has been ordered and processed so that all the data belongs to a specific matter. Therefore, the table we saw at the beginning of the chapter is not a dataset, while the below can be described as one:

Student name	Age	Birthdate
Sarah Griffin	15	02/14/1999
Conrad Gray	14	09/08/2000
Richard Simmons	16	01/25/1998
Summer Davies	17	03/30/1997

From the table below, it is possible to identify that we are talking about students, their ages, and the year in which they were born. As you can see, the dataset can contain numbers, letters, images, graphs, and other elements. Essentially speaking, these datasets "are normally labeled so you understand what the data represents; however, while dealing with datasets, you don't always know what the data stands for, and you don't necessarily need to realize what the data represents to accomplish the problem" (Byjus, n.d.).

This means that when considering datasets, there are different categories they can fit into numerical datasets, categorical datasets, multivariate datasets, and more. To identify the type of dataset you are dealing with, let's look at each of their characteristics to understand how to categorize them.

- **Numerical dataset:** As the name suggests, this dataset is composed of only numbers, there are no letters or other characters different from this. These datasets are prepared to be used for mathematical calculations and other analyses by the analyst. Examples of datasets with this information can include the number of students in a classroom, temperatures during a time of the year, the amount of time spent working, or the different lengths of movies you have watched.

- **Categorical dataset:** In this type of dataset, you will be dealing with words that establish a certain category of characteristic. These datasets can be divided into two categories: a dichotomous or a polytomous table (Byjus, n.d.). If these categories are composed of only two characteristics, such as boy/girl, yes/no, solved/not solved, and so on, they are of the first kind—dichotomous. On the other hand, if you have more than two category possibilities, it will be a polytomous table, such as hair color, eye color, nationality, and animal species.

- **Bivariate dataset:** As the name suggests, in this kind of dataset, the analyst will be looking into tables with two variables of different categories, such as the age and height of children in a class. By analyzing these variables, it is possible to establish a relationship between them.

- **Multivariate dataset:** If a bivariate dataset is composed of two variables, the multivariate is composed of more than two variables. In this situation, you will have a relationship between these, such as analyzing the age, study time, and grades of students in a classroom.

- **Correlation dataset:** Finally, we have the last type of dataset, which not only establishes a relationship between the variables but also indicates that there is a dependency between them. If you take, for example, the weight of a tub of ice-cream and the amount a person eats per day, they are correlated, since the weight of the tub will vary according to the amount an individual consumes of the product.

Now that you know the different types of data that can be collected and what is possible to do with them, it is time to see how they relate to determining the data problem. More specifically, we are going to see how each different data type and dataset can help the analyst determine what the question will be and the alternative approaches to each of these.

BREAKING DOWN THE COMPONENTS OF A DATA PROBLEM

The data analyst will use their skills to help identify, predict, or prescribe a solution to a problem. However, to do this, they need to be able to use data to do it. This means that the problem needs to have actionable data that can be transformed so conclusions can be made based on the analysis that can be carried out. If a business does not have this data within its databases, there are other places it can be looked for, but this we will look into deeper in the next chapter.

This means that there are certain problem "categories" that an analyst can deal with. You can, for example, be asked to find patterns in a certain behavior that will describe a tendency or identify unusual situations that are the result of a certain event. Based on the data, it is also possible to categorize information and identify predominant themes in a certain business aspect. Based on these analyses, the analyst can also discover connections between seemingly unconnected matters and make predictions about what will happen once a certain pattern is observed.

All these conclusions can be made based on data and help businesses determine the answer to a specific question or solution to a problem. This means that if there is no data to analyze, the conclusions will be based on other criteria rather than being data-driven. For this reason, it is important when establishing the problem statement and the goal, that you have adequate data to deal with. The available data will also help you filter and establish what it is that needs to be done.

This will make the analysis process faster and more efficient, saving the organization time and money to find out the answer they are looking for. For this reason, being specific about what you are going to ask and the goal you are trying to achieve is the essential point in the journey of data analysis. Incorrectly establishing these can lead to an incorrect analysis and conclusions; thus, a project failure. Let's take a look into the different aspects that should be considered when this phase is being carried out.

Problem Statement and Goal

The first question that should be asked by the data analysis is: What is the specific problem I am trying to solve or question I am trying to answer? The answer to this question will give you a general idea of what it is to solve. However, "general" is not good enough or specific enough for the problem to be adequately addressed. The question needs to be specific and targeted so it can be properly treated.

To ensure that you have the appropriate parameters to do this, one of the approaches to apply is to use SMART principles. SMART is an acronym used that defines the problem should be **S**pecific, **M**easurable, **A**chievable, **R**elevant, and **T**imely. When you apply these parameters to the problem statement and the goals of your analysis, it will be easier to work and obtain useful results.

Therefore, we can say that the SMART approach can be related to the problem statement with the following:

- **Specific:** What is the exact problem I am trying to solve? What is the impact this specific issue has on the business? What is the scope I am going to apply for this issue?

- **Measurable:** Can the problem or question I am addressing be measured? If so, what is the type of data I should use to ensure that this can be done? What is the method I am going to use to ensure that there is an objective and measurable answer to the matter?

- **Achievable:** Based on the data available, am I able to achieve the objective? What is the information I need to ensure that there is an actionable conclusion to what is being analyzed?

- **Relevant:** Why is the analysis I am carrying out relevant? What will it change, or what purpose does it have for the business I am working for? Does this problem or question need an answer or solution? How was this data collected, and is it a reliable source of information? Is there any bias in the data being used?

- **Timely:** Can this analysis be done with the existing historical data? How fast does it need to be answered? How much time do I have to solve this problem?

Apart from having a SMART approach to the problem, it is important to add the perspective of the four Ws to the creation process of the problem statement:

- **What** am I looking for?
- **Who** will benefit from this information?
- **When** (or what timeframe) did this take place?
- **Where** can this analysis be applied?

Despite the four Ws usually being associated with the "H" for *how*, we can say that it was efficiently replaced by the SMART goals, or how the problem statement should be addressed.

The next thing that will need to be done is to understand the variables and other data that will be fed into the program so the analysis can be carried out. These are usually known as the input, which will be studied and analyzed, and the output that will be generated. This process can be translated into the following statement:

INPUT → TRANSFORMATION → ANALYSIS → OUTPUT

This input will be composed of everything that will support the analysis process including the adopted parameters, the variables that will be taken into consideration, potential data constraints and limitations, and what each of them will be used for. You now have almost all the information you will need to start working—and you haven't even collected the data! But before this is done, there is one last step in the process that should be taken to ensure that you are on the right path: establishing a hypothesis.

Hypothesis

If you paid attention to your middle school science classes, you might remember what a hypothesis is. If you don't remember, there is no problem, we will do a small recap. A hypothesis is an educated guess of what the answer to your problem will be. This means that if you are asked to understand why clients are not purchasing the new company product, it is because they do not know it exists and, therefore, it is because of the lack of marketing. In this case, you are inferring that this is what the data will show you once it is analyzed.

Based on the hypothesis you have established, you will need to test (in other words, carry out the analysis) the data to ensure this is, in fact, what is happening, or if you need to look into other aspects of the matter, such as price and competitor alternatives to this product. According to Horsch (2021), this can be done by testing it with parametric or nonparametric tests. In this case, a parametric test is done based on a population description, or all the elements that compose a certain aspect of the problem.

This means you will be obtaining the "real" information of the whole group rather than an average, which would be based on a sample. In this case, we could say that, for example, when you are analyzing the ages of students in a class, you will look into the ages of all of them. In this case, it is safe to suppose that these individuals will have similar ages; therefore, it will be a normal distribution.

Now, if what you are going to run are nonparametric tests, this means that there is no normal distribution among the elements you are looking at. Using the same example as before, if we were going to look at the different grades these same students obtained in their final exams, it is possible to say there is no "standard" between them. This is because the grades can range from 0–100 and there is no specific distribution among these parameters within the students of the class.

Based on the determination, if you are going to work with a hypothesis that uses parametric and nonparametric data, it will be possible to understand how the data will behave. This will also help you determine the sample you are going to study and increase the results' reliability. In this case, it will be important to establish the correct analysis method to carry out the test and obtain optimal results. However, we are getting quite ahead of ourselves, since this matter will be addressed in Chapter 4.

In the meantime, let's take a moment and see if you have correctly understood the content of this chapter and if you can identify the problem and the solutions that should be used to solve them.

CASE STUDY: WHAT IS THE PROBLEM/QUESTION?

1. You work for a government agency that noticed there has been an increase in the number of homes being foreclosed. They want to understand why this is happening and what the factors that are driving this situation are. What would you do?

2. In the cosmetics company you work for, management has noticed there has been a significant increase in the number of sales of lipstick number 86, the new tone of red the company has released. They want to understand why this is happening. What would you do?

3. The dog shelter where you volunteer has observed that there is an incredible increase in the number of abandoned animals in August and December. They want to understand the reasons for this so they can come up with a campaign to prevent this from happening. What will you do?

Once you are finished thinking about these questions, it is time to move on and look into how to manage the data you are going to work with. From collecting to storing and cleaning the data, the next two chapters will teach you all the steps that need to be taken and guide you through the correct phases of the process. Are you ready to move on and continue this journey?

CHAPTER 3:
DATA MANAGEMENT TECHNIQUES FOR DATA COLLECTION AND STORAGE

Now that you have identified the characteristics of the data you will need to solve the problem or answer the business question, it is time to move on to the second part of the process: data collection and storage. It is not uncommon, in the beginning, to be overwhelmed with the amount of data that needs to be collected and the steps that will need to be carried out. Beginner analysts (and sometimes even the most experienced ones) usually find themselves "lost in a sea of data" or "drowning" with everything they will need to separate, store, and analyze.

For these reasons, in this chapter, we are going to look into the data management techniques that will help you efficiently and effectively collect and store the data that will be used. If you consider that data is the most important part of the process, you will see that "taking care" of it and being able to manage it will bring significant value to the process. The way this is carried out will also help you through the analysis, since badly managed data can bring hiccups to the process, leading to lost time and money.

DATA MANAGEMENT

When the broad term "data management" is used, it is applied in the context of collecting, organizing, storing, and safeguarding data so it can be analyzed and used by the organization for decision-making purposes. When you think about the reasons why a company maintains the "trace" of how many people visit their website and click on specific links, it is usually so they can analyze customer behavior and make decisions based on it. If this information was not going to be used, then it would not need to be monitored.

However, since this is not the case and the data that is generated is used for making decisions, solving problems, and looking for possible improvements, it must be well preserved so it can be reliable and effective for its purpose. If a company stores an incredible amount of data, for example, it needs to be safely and adequately stored so that it can be accessed and free from potential hacker attacks or system failures. When this objective is accomplished, it will provide the organization with reliable and secure data that can be easily visible, analyzed, organized, and scaled if needed to incorporate other areas.

Let's put it this way: If data is "gold" in our time, and it can define the success or failure of a business, this means that taking care of it so it can be used to the best of its advantage proves to be an essential process. Can you imagine what would happen if a business made a decision based on incorrect data because it was not stored or secured properly? Or, picture a company losing all the data it has gathered during the past years. Perhaps the systems are not updated and are not compatible with the data format that is being used. This could have serious implications for how the organization is run.

Essentially speaking, when we talk about data management, how you collect, organize, and store the data will determine how the process will be carried out. Some companies use different data storage systems, such as databases, data lakes, or data warehouses. This definition will be done according to their capacity, associated costs, and the type of data that will need to be stored.

However, you must be asking yourself, *What are the data sources I can use, and how can I store these and find the optimal approach?* This is a really good question. Let's start looking into the data management process by exploring the different options available for collecting data. As you move on to the next section of this chapter, we will start with the first step that will need to be taken: identifying the data sources and collection methods.

WHERE CAN DATA BE SOURCED AND COLLECTED?

As you might imagine, data can be collected from almost anywhere. This means that regardless if we are talking about data that is stored physically or electronically, there is a way to access and analyze it. These locations include documents, files, databases, websites, and any other place that stores information. When this is done, you can gather this data manually or by using automated methods, depending on the resources you have. For example, some time ago, people would input certain data manually into spreadsheets and other databases. Today, this information can also be extracted from programs and other sources by using certain commands in the language you are using to carry out the analysis.

TYPES OF DATA SOURCES

The first thing you should know is that there are two types of data: quantitative and qualitative. While the first refers to data that is based on numbers, the second uses other data formats, such as text, images, and graphs. Identifying the best way to extract and collect this data will be essential to the analysis process since conclusions will be made based on the quality of what you will extract. This data will come from either a primary or secondary source.

In the first case, the primary source will be those that come directly from where the data was collected. For example, if you survey your company's clients, these will be primary data. However, this data was not previously used and was obtained directly from the source, meaning that "the data gathered by primary data collection methods are specific to the research's motive and highly accurate" (Bhat, 2019). Other techniques that can be used include polls, interviews, focus groups, and time series analysis.

At the same time, we have the secondary sources, which are the data that has been used in the past and that was not necessarily created for the reason the analysis is being carried out. This can include magazines, libraries, the internet, company records, press releases, and others. However, one of the main issues of secondary sources is that they might not be as reliable or as conclusive as the primary source since they were not designed for that specific purpose or have been previously processed or interpreted by someone else (Bhat, 2019).

However, these primary and secondary sources can also be classified into three categories: first-, second-, and third-party data. Let's take a moment to understand what these are and how each of them impacts the analysis process, including the analysis, interpretation, and processing—which will also reflect on the reliability.

- **First-party data:** As the name might suggest, first-party data belongs to data that has been collected by you or your company. This means that we can have first-party data from a primary or secondary source, if we are talking about a poll and a CRM software, respectively. "Whatever its source, first-party data is usually structured and organized in a clear, defined way. Other sources of first-party data might include customer satisfaction surveys, focus groups, interviews, or direct observation" (Hillier, 2023).

- **Second-party data:** When speaking about this type of data, we are usually talking about the primary data that was collected by another company or person that is shared with us. Hence, this is considered first-party data to them, but second-party data to us. If you think about the statistics that a social media channel collects on a certain metric, for example, this will be second-party data, since it will be organized and structured by them, for their purposes and shared with you. One thing that must be considered when using secondary data is that it is not as reliable as first-party data, since you will likely not know how it was collected and other details.

- **Third-party data:** The last type of data that should be mentioned is third-party data. Just as second-party data is less reliable than first-party, third-party data is not as reliable as second-party. The place you will source the data from might or might not have a connection to your company, and this data can be rented or sold. In addition to this, it might be unstructured and need more processing than other datasets. Some of the examples of these sources are open repositories, which we will talk about soon, government data, and even specialized companies that collect data and preprocess it to sell to others.

Regardless of the data you will use, you must be aware of potential bias and variation in the information you will be provided with. This means that the analyst should be diligent when selecting the sources from which it will gather the data and how it will be interpreted. In addition to this, you will also need to establish the best method to collect this data so that you have "less trouble" formatting for it to be processed. It is safe to say that while structured data will usually be easier to manage, it is within some of the great big data sources that the most varied data will be obtained.

Since we have mentioned the different types of data, you must be asking yourself, *How can I collect this data in the most efficient way possible?* That is an excellent question. Although most of the methods will depend on how this data is stored, there are certain tools and software that can help you with the process. These are usually known as data management platforms, and choosing the one that best fits your needs will be key to ensuring that the process is as efficient and straightforward as possible. Shall we take a look at what some of these are and their main characteristics?

DATA COLLECTION TOOLS AND SOFTWARE

There are several ways to collect relevant data for your analysis, and how this will be done will depend (once again) on the business question or problem you want to solve. In this case, the method selected will depend directly on where you will obtain it from. If you want to hear from clients what their experiences are with a certain product, you might ask for a focus group, which means that the data will be gathered primarily by interviews. On the other hand, if you are going to gather this information from electronic sources based on statistics, reports, and other information, there is certain software that can make your job easier. Let's look into some examples you can use to make sure the best collection process is undertaken.

In the following table, 10 different collection tools have been listed based on internet searches and rankings found on several webpages. To ensure consistency of the information, they were listed in alphabetical order. As you will see, they will each have a pricing plan, purpose, and main features depending on what it is that you intend to collect. The information used to compile this list with the most popular data collection tools was obtained from Liza (2019), Valcheva (2017), Williams (2023), and Guinness (2023).

Tool	Pricing	Purpose	Main features
FastField	paid	forms	• simple and easy to use • manages large amounts of data
Fulcrum	paid	geolocation	• easy to share

		and maps	and export data • offers geotagging abilities
GoSpotCheck	paid	field data	• real-time analysis and mobile compatibility • field CRM
Jotform	free/paid	forms and surveys	• easy to integrate with other platforms and apps
KoboToolbox	free	forms	• provides most functionalities of paid apps
Magpi	paid	images, text, numbers	• interactive voice feature enabling users to input data with voice
Paperform	paid	text, image, files, numbers	• program automatically converts the data into the ideal format
QuickTapSurvey	paid	surveys	• real-time

			analysis and fast results delivery online and offline
Repsly Mobile	paid	CRM	<ul><li>used by sales teams in the field</li><li>for small/medium companies</li></ul>
Zonka Feedback	paid	forms and surveys	<ul><li>interface for customer interaction and real-time analysis</li></ul>

As you can see, the type of software you will use depends on several factors, such as the price, purpose, and who is going to use the tool. Some of them are designed to obtain input from clients and others from company members who will input the answers. The decision of which one to use will usually depend on the available budget and the client profile to establish the way they will best answer the questions.

However, even after the data has been collected, there is another issue the analyst must consider that will directly impact the security and integrity of the data: where it will be stored. While some companies decide to store them within their local infrastructure (servers), others have resorted to cloud storage to ensure more scalability and security. In the next section of this chapter, we will take a look at the different storage options available and guidelines to help you determine what the best option is for you and your company.

STORING HUGE AMOUNTS OF DATA

After you have collected the data, you must know where it is going to be stored. This means that it will be electronically kept so that its integrity and safety are preserved for the next steps of the process. Identifying the place where this data will be kept is essential because the bulk of what you are going to need to perform the analysis may be contained there—meaning that if this data is lost, breached, or tampered with, your analysis will no longer be valid or even possible. For these reasons, when considering a place to maintain what was collected, the analyst must consider all the pros and cons of each storage method.

Among many factors, this decision will be based on the business's resources, the amount of data, and even the sensibility it has. In addition to this, the analyst should consider if there are enough resources to scale up this data if needed and if it will be protected from malicious attacks, system failure, fraud, or even natural disasters. The first decision that will need to be made is whether this data will be stored in a data lake, lakehouse, or warehouse.

According to Microsoft Azure (n.d.)

> A data lake captures both relational and non-relational data from a variety of sources—business applications, mobile apps, IoT devices, social media, or streaming—without having to define the structure or schema of the data until it is read. Schema-on-read ensures that any type of data can be stored in its raw form. As a result, data lakes can hold a wide variety of data types, from structured to semi-structured to unstructured, at any scale (Data Lake vs. Data Warehouse section).

This means that the data lake will have much more flexibility than a data warehouse, which is naturally relational and has an established model according to the queries that will be performed. Therefore, while the data warehouse will only have a specific sort of data, the data lake will be able to store from raw to structured data, enabling it to be easily managed, transformed, and treated according to the analyst's needs. At the same time, data lakes are not perfect. They have several quality, structure, safety, and maintenance challenges that are not as common when data lakehouses are considered.

In this regard, we could quote Microsoft Azure (n.d), which establishes that

> A data lakehouse is an open standards-based storage solution that is multifaceted in nature. It can address the needs of data scientists and engineers who conduct deep data analysis and processing, as well as the needs of traditional data warehouse professionals who curate and publish data for business intelligence and reporting purposes. This ensures that everyone is working on the most up-to-date data, while also reducing redundancies (Data Lake vs. Data Lakehouse section).

Depending on the amount of data a company has, the processing that is carried out simultaneously, and the demand on its workload capacity, an organization will need to select one or the other. However, there is another item that comes into play in this decision: where the data will be stored. As you might imagine, data can be stored in different places that range from a pen drive to the cloud. What is the best option? Let's take a look at what each of them means for the business.

Types of Storage for Collected Data

When you consider the different types of storage for your data, here are the options:

- **Direct area storage (DAS):** In this type of data storage, you will be saving the data directly to the device. This can be a flash drive, hard disk drive, computer, or anything that is local and not connected to a network. This is the case of the solid-state drive (SSD) and other flash storage types, which are "technology that uses flash memory chips for writing and storing data. A solid-state system has no moving parts and, therefore, less latency, so fewer SSDs are needed" (IBM, n.d.). The main drawback of this system is that it is usually not sufficiently protected and that if escalation is necessary, you will need to change devices since there is a limited capacity for what it can store.

- **Network-based storage:** On the other hand, we have the data that is stored within a company's network or internal infrastructure (server), that will store this data. This usually means that more people can have access to it through the network and it is "less" risky than having it in a DAS system. It is usually composed of one of two options: network-attached storage, which is stored in a single device connected to the network, or storage area network, which as the name suggests, is a network of devices storing the data (IBM, n.d.). Each of these has its own set of characteristics, such as the number of users allowed, the speed for accessing and processing, scalability, and, of course, price.

- **Cloud storage:** As you will identify by its name, this type of storage is made on the cloud, usually by a third-party provider that will help grant the infrastructure, maintenance, and security for the data that it stores. This is a good option cost-wise for companies since they need to invest less in hardware and space to keep the servers on-site. "You use the internet to access your files and applications, which means that your team can access them anywhere—even at home or remotely" (blog-manager, 2021).

- **Hybrid cloud storage:** The last option that you can choose for storing the collected data is the hybrid format, in which you will have access to the data both in a local and in a public cloud. This is usually the option for companies that deal with both sensitive and nonsensitive data or those that want to divide the workload between both storage options.

As you might imagine, there are different costs associated with each of these options. As the analyst, you should discuss with the IT teams and management to decide the best place to store this data. Additionally, it will be important to see where it is originally stored if we are considering primary first-party data. The ability to easily manipulate the data with fast and reliable methods will be essential, especially considering the next part of the process, which we will look into in a little bit. In the meantime, let's tackle the data collection techniques you have just learned.

FINDING THE CORRECT SOURCE

In the examples that follow, we are going to look into the different sources that should be used to collect the relevant data for each of the problems seen in the previous chapter. Where can you find this information?

1. Government agency working to identify the reason for the increase in foreclosed homes

   - government databases on foreclosed homes in the region

   - government information on the number of people in homeless shelters in the region

   - unemployment numbers in the region

   - business indicators for the region

   - economic indicators for the region

   - bank reports regarding late payments

   - numbers from auction companies on homes in the region

2. A cosmetic company trying to understand the increase in the number of sales for lipstick number 86

   - Analyze social media posts to see mentions of the company.

   - Analyze social media posts for references to the lipstick.

- Carry out a poll with the buyers of the product on the website.

- Evaluate the numbers that refer to the number of units sold within a certain period.

- Check the place in which most units were sold; for example, the internet, physical stores, and marketplaces.

3. Dog shelters trying to identify why there is a greater number of animals abandoned in August and December

- Identify how many abandoned animals enter the shelter each month.

- Observe economic trends during these months for the region.

- Observe weather conditions in the region during these months.

- Obtain data on specialized businesses that deal with animals during these months, such as pet stores and veterinarians.

- Obtain data regarding the price of pet products during the year and its variation.

Now that you have identified the different sources you can obtain the data from, you will need to treat it before it is processed. This means carrying out the process of cleaning, removing errors, and preparing it to be processed. In the next chapter, we are going to look in more detail at how these steps are carried out, what should be considered, and some of the techniques that can be used to ensure an optimal analysis. Let's take a look at what they are and why they will be critical to ensuring a reliable data analysis.

CHAPTER 4:

REMOVING DUPLICATES, ERRORS AND INCOMPLETE DATA

It is always cheaper to do the job right the first time.
–Philip B. Crosby

When cooking, we usually clean the meat and cut off the extra fat for certain dishes before putting it into the pan or the oven. We also wash the vegetables before eating and we peel bananas. Similarly, we proofread a text before sending it or think about a structure before writing. These processes are carried out so that what needs to be done—cooking, eating, and sending a message—makes sense. There is a process and a right way to do it.

The same rationale applies to data. Once you have carried out the first steps, you need to prepare the data before analyzing it. This means ensuring that what will be processed by the computer or the program is adequately structured so there are no errors in it that could affect the final result. In this case, you will need to proceed with the data cleaning, which is nothing more than removing the duplicates, errors, and incomplete data from the dataset.

This is exactly what we are going to talk about in this chapter: the third step in the data analytics process—data cleaning. Here, you will learn how to carry out this process as well as tips and techniques on how to make sure your dataset is complete and error-free. If this can be done, you can be certain that fewer complications will be identified during the analysis process and that you will have more reliable results. Curious about how this can be done? Don't you worry! Read on and find out all about it!

DATA CLEANING: SCRUBBING DATASETS TO ACHIEVE GOOD DATA QUALITY

The process of data cleaning is also referred to as scrubbing, data wrangling, or data cleansing, so if you ever come across any of these terms, you can be sure that you are talking about the same thing. This means not only removing the data that has "strange" characters or even filling in blank spaces. It is also about identifying outliers, incomplete, incorrect, and "rogue" data. Taking your time to carry out this process will be essential to ensuring a reliable analysis that will be able to support correct business decisions, since you have eliminated most, if not all, the data that could cause errors.

"The importance of properly cleaning data can't be overstated. It's like creating a foundation for a building: do it right and you can build something strong and long-lasting. Do it wrong, and your building will soon collapse" (Hillier, 2023b). This is the same principle applied by professionals who deal with data: the concept of garbage in, garbage out. In other words, if you have bad-quality data and feed it to the computer, the results will not be good—garbage. However, if what you feed to the computer is good and clean data, you will likely receive a good analysis as a result.

It is no wonder, therefore, that data analysts (and even data scientists) can spend up to 80% of their time just on this specific task. This will help ensure that you have what is usually referred to as "quality data." Of course, this is considering that the collected data comes from a reliable source and that what was collected fits the purpose of what you will do. Usually, specialists refer to five characteristics that can be attributed to datasets that have optimal quality. Shall we see what they are?

Five Characteristics of Quality Data

When we talk about the five characteristics of quality data, these are usually the parameters that a dataset should have to ensure a reliable result. Based on the description by Sarfin (2022), let's take a look into what each of these means and how they might apply to the dataset you are working with. Before you start, please note that these are not in order of importance, but rather in alphabetical order for the sake of organization.

- **Accuracy:** To ascertain this characteristic, it is important to ask yourself, *Is this data that I am using correct and precisely approaching the subject I am dealing with?* This means that what you have collected reflects on a real-world situation and not just a hypothetical one. While sometimes, stating that the information has to be correct seems obvious, you will sometimes need to check for items to ensure this is the case. We could use bias, for example, which is consistently present in data, meaning it needs to be verified if all the population is reflected within the dataset, as well as all potential situations about the business case being studied.

- **Completeness:** Another question that you should always ask yourself is, *Is the data I am using complete?* This refers to not only if you have enough data to carry out an accurate analysis, but also if the dataset has no blank spaces or missing information. The data being complete is an essential trait of a good dataset, since if the data point is not there or even if more data points are missing, you might see a variation in the parameters analyzed. Let's say you are making a transfer to a bank account: If you are missing one of the account numbers, you will not be able to complete it.

- **Reliability:** This is one of the most—if not the most—crucial aspects of information that the data can present. To ensure that you have it correct, you should ask, *Can I trust this data that I am going to use?* Issues that should be considered include if there is no contradicting data, if it is correct, if it is trustworthy, and if it reflects reality. Think about what can happen if you misuse the data for an analysis; the results can lead to poor decision-making and determining wrong paths to follow. If you are going to guide the marketing department on a targeted campaign for a new product and the data is incorrect, for instance, pointing to customers between the ages of 30 and 40 instead of 20 and 30, this may lead to wasted money and time.

- **Relevance:** As you might imagine, the data you will analyze needs to be relevant. This means asking yourself, *Is this data information for what I want to solve or analyze?* If the answer is yes, then you can continue. If it is not, then it is likely you have wasted your time during the process; thus, costing the company money. Therefore, while this question must be asked when you are *collecting* the data you will use, you must also check again once you have the complete dataset. In simple terms: If you are not going to use it, you don't need it.

- **Timeliness:** The last characteristic that quality data has refers to *when* it was collected. While in some cases it is understandable that the data could have been gathered some time ago because the parameters do not change often and are mostly stable, there are other situations in which it is constantly being transformed. If we were going to measure the impact of an influencer mentioning your company's product, this could have immediate repercussions. Therefore, the sales data you collected before will not be as useful as the data you collect after, for example.

But how do we keep this data clean and ensure that it has the needed quality to make sure that we will make the right decision? While a good part of this process will be critical thinking on your part, which we will talk more about in Chapter 8, there are a few tasks you can carry out to help solve this problem. These are steps that most, if not all, data analysts carry out on their data before feeding it to the machine or the program. As you will see, yes, there are many steps and tasks that need to be performed. However, remember that this is an essential part of the process, which your results will depend on.

Key Data-Cleaning Tasks

As you will see in this section, the data-cleaning process is comprehensive and requires different steps. From removing all the existing formatting to organizing and finally validating the final result, some tasks need to be carried out more than once. At the same time, there are others, such as standardizing the language or the data types, that might not be needed. Each dataset has its own characteristics and specificities, and the magic begins when you can transform all these different inputs into one solid and structured source of information.

Here are the main tasks that should be considered during the transformation and preparation of the data you will use.

1. **Removing formatting:** Since the data you will gather may or may not have formatting, it is important that all the formatting is removed to make it easier to manipulate the data. Since you will also format in the end, it is unnecessary to have the data formatted now, although this step is optional.

2. **Removing unwanted data points:** Sometimes, the data we collect comes with columns or rows that we do not need or will not use. In this case, it is important to delete these. This will make the dataset easier to work with because there will be less information to manage and look into for the next step.

3. **Removing major errors, duplicates, and outliers:** This is one of the core tasks that will need to be done for the data cleaning. When you are looking at the data, it is important to look and check if any data stands out differently or if there are any errors in what you have gathered. This means, for example, letters where there should be numbers or duplicated information.

4. **Organize your data:** After you have "cleaned" the data, it is time to organize the data to ensure that it all makes sense. This step consists of four different parts, of which some are optional or might not need to be carried out.

    a. **Convert data types:** If you are dealing with survey results, for example, and want to count the answers, you might want to convert the "nos" to "0" and the "yeses" to "1." In this case, you will need to convert the data types to ensure they are within the expected format.

    b. **Standardize the information:** If you are going to use numbers, for example, and some of them have the decimal point and others do not, you might want to transform them all into the same format. The same is applied to letter capitalization and date formats.

    c. **Uniform language:** When you gather information from different sources, some of the data may be verbatim, such as having another term used that means the same thing. They could also be in different languages, measurement systems, and so on. You must make this uniform to ensure that all the variables are correctly accounted for.

    d. **Structure the dataset:** The last step of organizing the data is to structure it. In this case, you are going to name the columns and format them according to your needs. Despite this seeming like a "makeup" process, it will be important to see if anything is missing and understand what the data can bring you.

5. **Filter the information:** Some programs will give you the option to filter the information and see if there is any that needs to be adjusted. This step will help you see if there is any additional step you need to carry out. In this case, you will need to go back to step 3, review the data you have, and possibly clean it.

6. **Fill in major gaps:** You are almost done! This last step of the data manipulation process will enable you to see if there is any missing information within the dataset (on both information and values). This will enable you to see if there is a blank data point, for example, and if it can be removed or if the information should be searched for.

7. **Validating the data:** The data-cleaning process is complete! All that is left to do is to validate the dataset and ensure that everything is to start gathering insights from the data. You will need to check, overlook, and validate the data to ensure everything is in order and possibly carry out some tests.

Despite this being the standard process for data cleaning, some other techniques can be applied to ensure that your data is consistent and will bring relevant value to your analysis. These are tools that are commonly applied by data analysts and will depend on the software used. In the next two sections of this chapter, we are going to look into what these techniques are and what some of the tools are that you can use to help you with the data-cleaning process so it is not as manual as it seems. Are you ready?

DATA-CLEANING TOOLS AND TECHNIQUES FOR REMOVING ERRORS

Analysts usually have their preferred method for removing errors. Some prefer to use software that is available in the market, others would rather use programming commands in Python, and there are even those who prefer to carry out the process manually to ensure that nothing is missed. Here are five of the most commonly applied techniques that you can also use to carry out these tasks and ensure your data is optimal for processing:

- **Exploratory analysis:** When an exploratory analysis is carried out, the analyst will look into the dataset and, as the name suggests, look for different anomalies and possibilities with the dataset. This means you will visually inspect the data and identify if any issues need to be looked over. Anello (2023) mentions that this process usually "tends to be skipped, but it's the worst error because you'll lose a lot of time later to find the reason why the model gives errors or didn't perform as expected."

- **Binning method:** When you carry out the binning process, you are grouping the data into smaller sets, or bins. This is an effective way to clean the data since you will be able to see the information according to the relevant group. If you were analyzing data about temperature, for example, you might want to group them into months or seasons to check if there are any outliers or information that stands out and needs to be looked into closer.

- **Regression:** Some analysts who are familiar with coding or with advanced analysis tools, can carry out a regression analysis to visualize the data and predict the values in a dataset. This means, for example, if there is a value that you need and is blank, you can use regression to fill it in with a potential number that will not affect the final result of the analysis. The observation of this information can also be made when the information is plotted in a graph or a chart that will illustrate how this information is spread in the dataset.

- **Clustering:** The clustering method is similar to the binning method. However, in this case, you are going to separate the data into different centers and see what data points are the closest to them. While this might not be the best approach if you need to categorize the data into different sets, it is a useful approach if you are dealing with numbers, and you need to later find a meaning to them. In the clustering case, what will happen is that if there are errors, blanks, or outliers in the data, the process will immediately aggregate them, making it easier to be identified.

- **Data standardization:** While you have seen in the previous section that standardization is one of the steps of data cleaning, it can also be carried out as the first thing you do. This is because once you transform, structure, and organize all the data, you will be able to identify the missing or rogue values by filtering them. In addition to this, you will be able to visualize the dataset according to what you are expecting, making it easier to see if there is anything that needs to be changed or eliminated.

At the end of the day, the technique chosen by each analyst will depend on what they feel more comfortable with. However, some tools make this process easier and help expedite the task at hand. Selecting the right tool for you and your business is essential since it will determine how much time you will spend in the process, the final quality of the data, and even if more data is needed.

TOOLS FOR DATA CLEANING

Now that you know the main processes and techniques that will help you with your data-cleaning process, it is time to look into the tools that can be used for this purpose. In this list compiled with the tools listed by McFarland (2022), Reilly (2023), Ginsberg (2023), and Datacollector (2023), there are 10 options to choose from which go from the simplest tools, such as Excel, to those that will require programming, like Python. This list is, once again, in no particular order of efficiency or easiness to use, but rather in alphabetical order. Let's see what they are!

Tool	Price	Considerations
Akkio	paid	• ML platform that prepares the data through all the processing steps
Data Ladder	free/paid	• user-friendly and high accuracy for matching and cleaning processes • user-friendly
Excel	paid	• limited functions for predictions • better used with numbers
IBM InfoSphere DataStage	paid	• ideal for data management, cleaning, and warehousing processes
Melissa Clean Suite	paid	• can be used in ERP and CRM software enables data verification and real-time processing
OpenRefine	free	• easy process to convert data and maintain structure • friendly interface
Python	free	• basic programming knowledge required to manage the program
Tibco	paid	• good process to standardize the raw data collected

Tool	Price	Considerations
Akkio	paid	• ML platform that prepares the data through all the processing steps
Data Ladder	free/paid	• user-friendly and high accuracy for matching and cleaning processes • user-friendly
Excel	paid	• limited functions for predictions • better used with numbers
IBM InfoSphere DataStage	paid	• ideal for data management, cleaning, and warehousing processes
Melissa Clean Suite	paid	• can be used in ERP and CRM software enables data verification and real-time processing
OpenRefine	free	• easy process to convert data and maintain structure • friendly interface
Python	free	• basic programming knowledge required to manage the program
Trifacta	paid	• fast

Tool	Price	Considerations
Akkio	paid	• ML platform that prepares the data through all the processing steps
Data Ladder	free/paid	• user-friendly and high accuracy for matching and cleaning processes • user-friendly
Excel	paid	• limited functions for predictions • better used with numbers
IBM InfoSphere DataStage	paid	• ideal for data management, cleaning, and warehousing processes
Melissa Clean Suite	paid	• can be used in ERP and CRM software enables data verification and real-time processing
OpenRefine	free	• easy process to convert data and maintain structure • friendly interface
Python	free	• basic programming knowledge required to manage the program
		• uses ML to carry out the process

Tool	Price	Considerations
Akkio	paid	• ML platform that prepares the data through all the processing steps
Data Ladder	free/paid	• user-friendly and high accuracy for matching and cleaning processes • user-friendly
Excel	paid	• limited functions for predictions • better used with numbers
IBM InfoSphere DataStage	paid	• ideal for data management, cleaning, and warehousing processes
Melissa Clean Suite	paid	• can be used in ERP and CRM software enables data verification and real-time processing
OpenRefine	free	• easy process to convert data and maintain structure • friendly interface
Python	free	• basic programming knowledge required to manage the program
		• good for large amounts of data

Tool	Price	Considerations
Akkio	paid	• ML platform that prepares the data through all the processing steps
Data Ladder	free/paid	• user-friendly and high accuracy for matching and cleaning processes • user-friendly
Excel	paid	• limited functions for predictions • better used with numbers
IBM InfoSphere DataStage	paid	• ideal for data management, cleaning, and warehousing processes
Melissa Clean Suite	paid	• can be used in ERP and CRM software enables data verification and real-time processing
OpenRefine	free	• easy process to convert data and maintain structure • friendly interface
Python	free	• basic programming knowledge required to manage the program
WinPure	free/paid	• connects with different databases and sources

Tool	Price	Considerations
Akkio	paid	• ML platform that prepares the data through all the processing steps
Data Ladder	free/paid	• user-friendly and high accuracy for matching and cleaning processes • user-friendly
Excel	paid	• limited functions for predictions • better used with numbers
IBM InfoSphere DataStage	paid	• ideal for data management, cleaning, and warehousing processes
Melissa Clean Suite	paid	• can be used in ERP and CRM software enables data verification and real-time processing
OpenRefine	free	• easy process to convert data and maintain structure • friendly interface
Python	free	• basic programming knowledge required to manage the program
		• checks data quality and informs matches

As you have seen, many of these tools are free, so it is possible to carry out the process without thinking about potential extra costs. In addition to this, even if you have the most basic tool like Excel, it is possible to manage smaller datasets and clean data efficiently. Nevertheless, there is one last tool that can be used for this process and is more related to modern technology: blockchain. Read on to find out what it is and how it can help you clean messy data and prepare it for processing.

USING BLOCKCHAIN TO CLEAN UP MESSY DATA

If you remember the five characteristics of quality data (accurate, reliable, complete, timely, and relevant) it is possible to imagine that this might be an issue in some cases. This is because we can't always ascertain the quality of the data, depending on the source (especially considering third-party) data. However, there have been recent technological developments that will help increase the data's quality, integrity, and reliability: the application of blockchain technology.

While you might have heard about this technology related to cryptocurrency or even nonfungible tokens (NFTs), blockchain has proved to be an important asset in establishing the quality of the data that will be used. To understand the reason for this, we must first comprehend what blockchain is. In simple words, it is a form of technology that imitates a ledger system that cannot be modified or corrupted and offers an authentication system.

Now, if you take these characteristics into consideration, you will immediately identify why blockchain can prove to be such an important asset. It means that if certain data is compiled using blockchain technology, you will have data with quality, where if any changes are made, these will be registered and the old information will be kept and not overwritten. In addition to this, the technology accepts any type of digital information. All these features make data originating from sources with this characteristic an interesting place to obtain reliable information.

According to Gupta (2018), "Blockchain can help create data records which are irrefutable and authorized by key participants. As the data in this database is immutable, verifiable, traceable, and trusted, the data collected is of high standard and quality." This means that when you use data that is in the blockchain, you will have reliable, irrefutable, traceable, and overall, more trustworthy data to deal with. It is also an advantage that this data is public, which means that there are fewer costs involved when you need to "purchase" the data.

Despite this exciting news and possibility, there is still the need to make this technology more implemented and diffused within businesses. It might take some time, but for those who can find information using this technology, it will bring considerably more reliability to the process. Blockchain has the potential to change how we see and use data, therefore making our predictions and analysis more trustworthy.

While this does not happen, you will be happy to know that you are now ready to move on to the main part of the data analytics process: the analysis itself! As we move on to the next chapter of this book, we will get into the core of the activity and fourth step of the process. For the next four chapters of this book, we will explore the different ways this processing can take place, the tools you can use, and tips and techniques that will help improve and optimize your process. Therefore, get ready for the best part of the journey as we continue and explore how this can be done.

CHAPTER 5:
DATA ANALYSIS TOOLS,
TECHNIQUES, AND BEST PRACTICES

You have everything set and prepared. All the data is ready, the storage provided, and the necessary tools obtained. We now come to the core of the process, the one that will lead you to a conclusion and will be the purpose for all this preparation. It is the climax of the process: when the analysis process will be carried out and you start obtaining insights. As mentioned earlier, since this is the purpose for doing everything up to now, the analysis process will be divided into four chapters.

In this first one, you will be provided with the ultimate set of tools, techniques, and best practices that ensure any dataset is processed and analyzed correctly and accurately. This means understanding what the tools are that will help you carry out the analysis, and suggestions of software to do these if you don't know which one to use. In addition to this, we will look into the main tips obtained from professionals to ensure this is a seamless process that will bring you optimal results.

THE DATA PROFESSIONAL'S TOOLKIT: CRITICAL DATA ANALYSIS TECHNIQUES YOU NEED TO KNOW

The main idea behind data analysis is to identify what the correlation is between the variables, if any, and see if what this relationship "says" answers the business question that you first had. There are several ways to do this, which will usually depend on the data you have and what you are trying to identify. In this first section of the chapter, we are going to look at 10 of the most common analysis methods and their definitions, how they work, the main expected outcome, and their applications. In addition to this, you will be given examples of how they can be applied in a real-world situation.

Since there is no "right" or "wrong" way to carry out the analysis, these will not be listed in any specific order. The decision of the best tool to apply will depend on the circumstances and even the tool you are using allows you to do. It's also contingent on the quantity of data points, variables, and instances that need to be looked into. For this reason, the techniques described in this section have been listed in alphabetical order.

Cluster Analysis

When you carry out the cluster analysis, what you are looking for is the commonality between the different points in the dataset. This is a rather simple process that happens when central nodes are identified and then similar data "gravitate" toward these nodes according to their similarity. The main objective, in this case, is to help separate the data points into different groups. However, different from the factor analysis we will soon see, these data points are not divided into the categories in which they belong, but rather according to the similarity between them.

If you work for a company and want to identify the different segments that your clients belong to, you can carry out a cluster analysis, for example. In this case, you could separate them according to the products they buy or how much they spend on the brand. Based on this, it will be possible to create a more targeted market strategy to communicate with these clients. The different groups will be determined according to the category that is the most important to the business, making the analysis process more effective and personalizable.

However, despite putting the data points together, there is an important point that should be considered in this matter: "While cluster analysis may reveal structures within your data, it won't explain why those structures exist. With that in mind, cluster analysis is a useful starting point for understanding your data and informing further analysis" (Stevens, 2023).

Cohort Analysis

The next analysis type we are going to look at is the cohort analysis. In this case, what is going to happen is that the data will be separated into groups with similar characteristics. What will be done, once this division is made, is that the analyst will identify and compare how these different groups work within a certain period. This means that if you are "using this methodology, it's possible to gain a wealth of insight into consumer needs or a firm understanding of a broader target group" (Calzon, 2023).

One example of how this technique can be applied is if you are looking into the demographics of those who buy in certain stores. Suppose that you work for a retail company that uses fidelity cards to engage with their customers and grant discounts with purchases. It is possible to group these customers into cohorts according to their "status" as a client, such as gold, silver, and bronze clients. By identifying how each of these customer groups behaves with their shopping habits, it is possible to create targeted products and campaigns to make them purchase more.

The same strategy can be applied, for example, to new clients. If you have entered a website and read the message, "Sign up as a registered user, and you will get a discount on your first purchase," this is exactly the type of analysis that will be carried out. "Once you've attracted a group of new customers (a cohort), you'll want to track whether they actually buy anything and, if they do, whether or not (and how frequently) they make a repeat purchase" (Stevens, 2023).

Content or Text Analysis

As you already know, data analysis is not only made of numbers but can also be carried out with text. However, although this analysis technique is usually interchangeably used with sentiment analysis, they are not the same thing (we will explore sentiment analysis in a little bit). Context or text analysis are umbrella terms that are used for all the different types of analysis that can be done with text, and one of them is sentiment analysis.

However, when we talk about content or text analysis, it is more than just the sentiment. We could be talking, for example, about the quantity of words that can be found within a body of text or even how frequent it is within an interview process. For this reason, the text analysis can be applied to documents that range from those with legal characteristics to those related to medical fields. Based on this analysis, it will be possible to understand the relationship between the words and the context of the documents.

It is important to keep in mind that there are two types of content analysis: conceptual and relational analysis. In conceptual analysis, the number of times a word is mentioned within a text is analyzed, making it more focused on explicit data or hard facts. On the other hand, in relational analysis, you will be looking into how these different words are related among themselves and find the answers to certain solutions. Finally, you must remember that for this technique to be efficient, there needs to be a clear business question you want to answer or a problem you want to solve (Calzon, 2023).

Dispersion Analysis

When we talk about a dispersion analysis, this means that the analyst will be looking into how much variation there is within the dataset and comparing it to the standard deviation among the points. Other associated methods used with the dispersion analysis method are the identification of the mean, median, and other techniques that can be used to identify the data range. Based on the comparison that is made between the range and the data point, it will be possible to establish the dispersion of the set.

One of the main places that this type of analysis is applied is in the stock and investment market to analyze the risk that a certain financial product will have. "By looking at the dispersion of returns on a certain investment, investors can gauge its risk. Say you're looking at a stock that has high dispersion. In other words, its range of possible outcomes (returns) is far apart" (Smith, 2022).

By doing this analysis, it is possible to see if you need to look for more data to complete what you already have or even to see if this range between the different data points means something that should be considered within the analysis. In addition to this, you will be able to identify other factors that will give you insights into what is happening. While this is not necessarily the full scope of the analysis, it is a good starting point for looking into what kind of information the data can provide.

Factor Analysis

Factor analysis is one of the best ways to reduce a large number of factors and transform them into just a few variables that are easier to manage. Some people usually refer to this type of analysis as "dimension reduction," which makes it easier to understand what it does. Factor analysis is usually applied when there are too many variables to analyze, and the process of grouping them makes it easier to see what the factors are that impact the problem you are looking into. "In other words, instead of having 100 different variables, you can use factor analysis to group some of those variables into factors, thus reducing the total number of variables" (Smith, 2022).

One example of how this can be applied is if you pass a survey among the students' parents in a school to identify their satisfaction with the overall service of the school. When you do this, you will likely have hundreds of different answers; therefore, you might want to group the students into grades to better identify if the problem is within a group in a certain grade. Depending on how the survey is structured, it is also possible to identify other groups for it to be divided into, such as students who have siblings in the school, those who eat in the cafeteria, and based on their location, their distance from the school.

The main advantage of this technique is that it enables the analyst to work with huge amounts of diverse data and group them into different "categories," which might make the analysis easier. In addition to this, by applying factor analysis, it is possible to establish some connections that might have been missed in case it was not done. On the other hand, when you apply dimensionality reduction, it is also possible that you "miss" certain relationships between the data points when you start grouping them, which might lead you to not identifying important factors that could impact the analysis.

Monte Carlo Simulations

If you like dealing with statistics and probabilities, you might perfectly adapt to the Monte Carlo simulation, since it is a technique that uses these in its application. This is because when we are referring to this technique, we are talking about an analysis method that considers all the possible outcomes of a situation. Made by a computer, when using this simulation method, you will obtain all the outcomes of a specific situation and be given the probability of each occurring.

One of the ways that a Monte Carlo simulation could be applied to a real-life aspect is if you were trying to determine the outcomes that increasing the price of a certain product would have in the market. Based on the different analyses of customer behavior and purchase patterns, you would obtain the probability of this product selling less, more, or staying the same. For this reason, one of the most common applications of this method is when a company is looking to understand the risks of a certain action they will take.

Although this is a great tool, it is also one that will take longer according to the variety of outcomes that can be predicted. The analysis needs to be run several times by adapting each scenario through changing the variables and identifying how each of these changes will impact the constant being analyzed. Nevertheless, it is an essential tool to guide business decisions and help determine what should be done next.

Regression Analysis

Regardless of the data analysis method you are going to carry out, knowing what a regression analysis is and how to carry out one is essential for all data analysts. This is because it is the most commonly applied method to identify the relationship between different variables within the dataset. In this case, you are going to select the "situation" you want to analyze and see its different impacts and if they are dependent or independent variables.

We could say that, for example, if we were analyzing the number of customers who visited a shopping mall and trying to understand the drivers that brought more people to the place, a regression analysis could be applied. This means that, for example, if the weather is warm, it is more likely to have people visiting compared to when it is cold. The same can be said according to the season of the year and if any festivities are approaching that require gift exchanges.

While this analysis is extremely important to know, you should keep in mind that the only thing it will do is show you the different relationships between what you are looking at and the different variables that affect it. This means that while a positive correlation can suggest that one variable is directly related to the other, making definitive conclusions based on it is not always possible (Stevens, 2023). Nevertheless, applying this analysis will help you establish what the other factors you must look into are for the process to be complete.

Sentiment Analysis

The name of this analysis technique may already tell you what it does. As you know, sentiment analysis is a specific field of text analysis. However, in this case, it is aimed specifically at understanding what the "feeling" is that can be obtained from the textual data. This technique uses an ML technique called natural language processing (NLP) to identify the emotion that the speaker intended to convey.

If you worked for a hotel or a restaurant, for example, this is an interesting way to identify how the customers feel about your establishment. You could, for example, collect all the data regarding client opinions from a certain website, such as Google Maps, and carry out an analysis to identify what the most common opinions mentioned are or maybe even their thoughts about a certain dish. Because we are generally looking into the opinions of others, this technique can also be called "opinion mining," which will identify if the general "tone" is positive, negative, or neutral.

You should keep in mind that although sentiment analysis is a subcategory of text analysis, there are other different ways to carry out this process. According to Stevens (2023), some of these include emotion detection, fine-grained, and aspect-based sentiment analysis, each with a different way of identifying the content's emotion. When you apply this type of analysis, it will make it easier to improve customer service and identify things that the business is doing correctly or incorrectly based on the opinions of those who use it.

Time Series Analysis

The last type of data analysis we are going to talk about is the one known as time series analysis. As you may imagine, this tool is used to identify the different patterns that can be seen during different periods. This is a particularly useful tool to make predictions of what might happen in the future by analyzing the historical data.

Suppose you work for a manufacturing company, and you are asked to identify what are the periods with the most demand so that production can be increased. In this case, you would carry out the time series analysis to identify the patterns and the trends of when there is the most demand for the product. This will help management understand, for example, when the best time for employees to go on vacation is or even carry out maintenance tasks on the machines.

This analysis method will show the pattern and help you understand what times of the year, for example, you will have the best results. However, it will not give you a reason why this is happening. Therefore, if this variable ceases to exist, then your analysis may be at fault because you do not know the reasons why this changed.

Now that you know the main analysis methods, it is time to take a step forward and take a look into the main tools and software you can use to help you perform them. As we move on to the next section of this book, we will see what they are, their best uses, and their main features. You will see that while some of them are paid, others are free, so there is a wide range of options to choose from according to the resources you have at hand.

TOOLS AND SOFTWARE FOR EFFICIENT DATA ANALYSIS

The 10 tools you are about to see were selected based on my personal experience and the experience of colleagues. While some of these will require that you have some programming knowledge, such as for Python and R, other tools such as Oracle Analytics and Power BI are rather easy to use depending on the data that you are going to analyze. Here is the list you should consider and their main characteristics.

Tool	Price	Best Used For	Feature
Excel	license-based/available with Microsoft Office	dealing with data that is made of numbers, but can also be used with text	many options to write formulas and easily manage the data
Google Analytics	free	analyzing different datasets especially focused	easy to use and real-time reporting by

		on Google-integrated data	providing predictions
Jupyter Notebook	open-source/free	presenting the analysis work and basic analysis processes	has an independent language that might require coding
KNIME	open-source/free	mostly used for data analytics that involves ML	the user needs to have some programming knowledge
Oracle Analytics	paid	works best with Oracle databases and can be used will all types of data	can be used for all data analysis steps using ML and NLP
Power BI	free/paid	analyzing data in different circumstances and preparing visuals	easy interface to use to manage data, but with restricted options
Python	open-source/free	all the data analytics processes, from text to number processing	the user needs to have some programming knowledge
R	open-source/free	analysis related to math functions, such as statistical analysis	the user needs to have some programming knowledge

Tableau	paid	visualizing analysis and creating worksheets	does not perform the data preprocessing actions
Zoho Analytics	free/paid	different datasets that are contained in separate files	drag-and-drop feature as well as integration with other applications

Despite this being a short list of the tools you can use, there are several others available in the market you can choose from. Even if you refer to previous chapters, the tool you might have selected for the data-cleaning process, for example, can be used to carry out the analysis—it just might not be within the preferred ones. Before we move on to the next chapter, let's take a look at some tips and best practices to apply to your data analysis process and ensure that you obtain the best possible results.

DATA ANALYSIS PRO TIPS: BEST PRACTICES FOR DATA PROFESSIONALS

If you are looking for some of the most recommended actions to carry out when performing the analysis, look no further! In this final section of the chapter, we will look at the main best practices when analyzing data and how these are crucial to ensuring the success of what you have been doing. While there are several others, depending on the tool you will use, this can serve as a guide to help you avoid potential "mishaps" with the analysis.

1. **Select the best tool:** Deciding the tool that will be used for this process is crucial since it will be used for all your analyses. For this reason, before starting the analytical process, it is interesting to explore each of these and see if they are suitable for your purpose. Failing to select the right tool

might lead you to poor analysis and poor data insights, potentially leading to incorrect decision-making and poor results.

2. **Goals and key performance indicators (KPIs):** When you start an analysis process, you should be clear about the goal that you are trying to reach. However, not only do these need to be kept in mind, but the KPIs will also be monitored and observed through this process. Aligning the goals of the data analysis process and the company's or department's KPIs will be essential to obtain the process's most useful insights and see what can be improved or solved.

3. **Keep an open eye for bias in the results:** As you know, bias is one of the most critical elements that should be minded during data analysis. Therefore, ensure you go over the results you are obtaining and try to identify if anything is driving the data toward the direction it is going and also if more data is needed.

4. **Engage stakeholders:** When you are going to carry out the analysis process, you should work together with the different stakeholders to understand what they are expecting and keep them updated on the process. Sharing some preliminary insights with them may give you more ideas and help you expand the analytical process.

5. **You are only a single function in the algorithm:** Regardless of how good or efficient you are, it is almost impossible to work alone throughout this process. Therefore, as a connection to item 4, you should ensure that there is a team behind what you are going to do, with individuals from other departments or even a data analytics team that will help you collect the best possible data, clean the dataset, and even make conclusions.

6. **Even in analysis, there are still standards:** While the whole data analysis process might seem "free for creativity," this is not necessarily true. This means that you should ensure that

the compliance, privacy, and governance rules are followed to protect this data. You should keep in mind that the results of what you are doing will have an impact; therefore, you should be as clear as possible and even document the process as you carry it out.

7. **Explore different model applications:** When you have decided on the best tool for you, this might not immediately mean that what it will provide you with is the ideal solution to the problem. Especially when dealing with ML and programming algorithms, you should also look for other options that might give you different insights or techniques that can provide you with a different view of the same dataset.

8. **The world continuously evolves, and so should your models:** While the technique and model you are using might be good for the moment of the analysis, the dataset may keep growing and changing. This means that the analysis you did this month might not be valid in the following month, and there is no guarantee that the same model will continue to be used. Therefore, when you think about the different applications of models in your analytical process, remember that these can change, and you should always check if there are any new data or different approaches to the same problem.

9. **Save and backup results:** Would you like it if all the work you did got lost because of a system failure or lack of energy? Probably not. For this reason, it is always important to save and backup the results you are obtaining (and even from the previous steps) to ensure that you can access them if needed. Even if you are working on the cloud, you should check how often the backup is made and if it is possible to include the different results (first and intermediate) in it so that you can keep track of what you are doing.

10. **Keep organized:** The last thing you should seriously consider is to maintain your analysis process. This means, for example, taking note of the different analysis techniques and models

you have applied and the insights you have obtained. Depending on the type of answer you need, different exploration methods will be needed, and you might want to keep track of what you have done so that no time is wasted. Furthermore, by doing this, other members of the team will be able to follow what you have done in case they need to.

As we move on to the next chapter, we will take a glance into the different ML techniques that can be used for different analysis processes and some of the best methods to carry this out. However, as you might imagine, ML is a field of its own, with entire books written on it. For this reason, it would be impossible to write every detail of the process and what should be carried out if this is the path you choose to follow. Nevertheless, you will be given an overview of its main applications and uses and how it can positively impact your analytical development. Are you ready?

CHAPTER 6:

MACHINE LEARNING MODELS AND ALGORITHMS

With artificial intelligence (AI) being the topic of the moment, it is only natural if you have ever heard about ML and its related topics, such as algorithms and programming languages such as Python and R. However, there may be some confusion in the difference between the fields of *data analytics* and *data science,* since both of them use data to carry out analysis and predictions. If you have been reading up to now and imagining if there is a possibility of speeding up the data analysis process and expediting the results, then this is the solution you have been looking for!

In this chapter, we are going to discuss the topics of data mining and ML. As mentioned earlier, this chapter will not teach you how to carry out each of these processes with coding examples and algorithm uses, but rather give you an overview of the processes and how they can best serve your analysis process. Once you are done reading this chapter, you will have a thorough understanding of ML and data mining, enabling you to have discussions around ML models, algorithms, and predictive analytics.

ML ANALYTICS IN TODAY'S WORLD

When you are using a search browser, and it immediately gives you back suggestions once you start writing what you need, this is ML working. It uses the data it has compiled among all the users with the same profile as yours and the most common topics to suggest those that might be of interest to you. This is because the machine has *learned* what the patterns of these users are; hence, it can make these suggestions.

Similarly, if you have a video or music streaming service that you use, you will receive suggestions based on your profile and the products you usually watch or listen to. This is also a process of ML, in which, based on the definitions and the *learning* process of what you like, it gives you the most probable items you will also like—also comparing your profile to those of others with similar tastes. While these processes also involve the use of AI (since ML is a subset of AI), the essential point to note here is that these processes are based on the collection of data from these services, using it to make predictions and suggestions according to your preference.

Essentially speaking, we can say that ML is the process of having a computer gather data from various sources and use it to understand what the best outcomes for specific situations are. In this case, the machine is going to learn based on the several algorithms it has been trained with and, after this, will be able to learn on its own with any new data that is fed into it. This means that ML can solve complex problems and obtain insights by using an incredible amount of data (also called big data).

You might now be asking yourself, *Does this mean I can use ML in my data analysis process without any difficulty?* Well, not necessarily. While ML does help with the process and make it easier, it also requires you to have some programming skills. The most common programming language used for this is Python, which is one of the simplest to learn currently in the market.

In addition to this, there are also minor issues you will need to know, such as how to fine-tune the machine and how to test what you are doing. Nevertheless, while these are details that can be learned in specialized books, it is first essential to understand how data analysis can be applied to the analytical process. After all, if you don't really understand how ML can be applied to data analysis, then it is possible you won't be able to apply it. Therefore, let's start from the beginning: how data analysis and ML can be used together.

Data Analysis and ML

The first step to understanding how data analysis can be used in ML is to go back and revisit how it is used. For a quick recap, when we talk about data analysis, we are looking into past data to make predictions. This means obtaining data from different sources and then cleaning and organizing it to solve a business question or a problem.

However, at the same time, this is often confused with data science. The crucial difference between them is that while data analytics is focused on the past, in data science, the data is used in the ML process, so it can generate new information. This means that instead of making decisions in the present based on the data you have, you will be using ML to predict the future.

With this established, we need to take a look at the different processes that can be carried out by the data analyst. One of the main advantages of applying ML to analytical processes is the option to speed up the cleaning part. With just a few code commands, it is possible to clean an entire dataset at once, without the need to do the process manually.

Although there is software in the market that allows you to do this as well, applying Python code, for example, to the dataset is still faster. At the same time, you can use tools (some of which are mentioned in the previous chapter) that already have this function embedded— precisely because they have ML algorithms embedded with them. Therefore, it will be a matter especially of the budget you have, since most of these tools are paid.

Regardless if you are going to use software to carry out this process or Python, this does not mean that you should not carry out an exploratory analysis or structure the data. Even if we are going to use ML to analyze the data and make predictions, you will need to minimally structure the data, such as giving the columns names and looking into the spreadsheet to see the results of the cleaning process. Once the data is ready and prepared, there are several different ways you can apply ML algorithms for the analysis. Read on to find out what they are.

Common Applications of ML in Data Analytics

There are three common ways that ML can help enhance the data analytics process mentioned by Lawrence (2019): two of which we have already mentioned, and then a third one. The first is by facilitating the clustering process since there are specific algorithms that can be used for this, such as the K-means clustering. This can be used in fields such as social media and healthcare to understand the patterns and trends that are being shown by the data for user and client behavior.

We also mentioned text and sentiment processing, which can be used with NLP techniques in ML. Since many of the different applications that are "ready" to use in the market are more number-centric, this means that some of them might not perform appropriately with text. For this reason, using ML algorithms to process text is an interesting way to personalize the model and ensure that the relationships between the variables are adequately defined.

Finally, we must mention the elasticity that ML provides to the data analysis process. This is because it gives different ranges and applications that can be used without being limited to the specific software or tool you are using. This means that it will help you not only find the variables that impact the analysis but will also give you the reason why this is happening.

When you are using ML techniques for data analysis, you should remember that it is not all about coding. While this will be needed to give the machine instructions and tell it what you want it to do, you can also visualize the output depending on the library you download. To better understand the process of how a machine learns, let's take a look at what the different ML models are and the algorithms that can be used with them to make your work more efficient.

ML MODELS AND ALGORITHMS

When we use ML to manage data for the analysis process, there are four different types of models you can select from, and below these, several different algorithms can be applied to them. In this section, we are going to explore the differences between supervised, unsupervised, semi-supervised, and reinforcement ML and what some of the most used algorithms for these processes are. As you will see, the type of ML model you will apply will directly affect the outcome of the analysis; therefore, it is essential to have a better knowledge of them.

Supervised ML

Supervised ML is exactly what the name suggests: A human supervises the process to ensure that the outputs given by the machine will be correct. In this case, what happens is that there is a labeled dataset in which the developer feeds the machine with information that is known in both the input and the output. This means that the parameters are known and that during the training process, it is identified if the machine is making the correct associations.

For example, if you are going to teach a machine to identify the difference between two animals, such as a hyena and a wolf, you will give it information telling you what a hyena is and what a wolf is. Once the machine has learned to process the information, it should be able to identify all images of hyenas and wolves when it is given their images. As you will see, in this case, the answer for the process is already known, since we know what a hyena and a wolf look like; therefore, it is possible to evaluate the machine's performance.

When you use the supervised ML model, what you are usually looking to do is to classify the data that you have (such as the animal example previously given) or to solve a regression problem. The regression problems are those that have variable output or continuous data as a result of analyzing the relationship between the dependent and the independent variables. A few of the applications of supervised ML include the filters placed by email providers to identify spam and phishing messages, and carrying out predictive analysis based on trends such as prices, customer behavior, and recommendation systems.

To better understand how each of these algorithms works, here is a brief description of each.

Classification

The classification algorithms are used to, as the name suggests, break down information into different categories. "In ML and Statistics, Classification is the problem of identifying to which of a set of categories (subpopulations) a new observation belongs, based on a training set of data containing observations and whose category membership is known" (GeeksforGeeks, 2023). Therefore, if we have different fruits and teach the machine to classify them, we are using a supervised technique to classify them because the final output will be known.

In this case, the classification can be composed of two types: a *binary* classification, in which the input will be placed in one of two categories, or the *multiclass* classification, which will divide the input into different classes. The main objective of these will be to correctly identify to which of the classes each of the input data belongs and separate them according to the target class. To do this, there are several different algorithms for this purpose and, although the list is not exhaustive, we will only take a look into the five most common ones you should keep in mind. They are the following:

- **Decision tree algorithm:** used in the format of a "tree" that has a main item and the computer uses the different branches for the decision-making. It is similar to those images that we see when there is a decision-making process with arrows pointing to "yes" and "no" answers and the outcome of each decision, such as, if yes, then this, or if no, then that. This decision process is easy to explain and demonstrable, making it one of the best processes for classification and making predictions.

- **Random forest algorithm:** is the use of several decision tree algorithms together. Based on the output of each decision tree, the machine will decide on what the best answer is. In this case, if we were classifying animals, for example, we could have one tree that analyzed the number of paws, another if it has a tail, and so on. Based on all the decisions made from these trees, it will be possible to identify the final output.

- **Logistic regression algorithm:** When applying this algorithm, you will be telling the machine that it should identify the different patterns between classes and classify the input. This is an example of where both binary and multiclass classification can be used. It can be used for determining, for example, a client's credit score in a bank or even the outcome and prediction for customer-targeted marketing campaigns.

- **Support vector machine (SVM) algorithm:** This algorithm is ideal for those working with small, but complex datasets and need the machine to identify the relationship between the data points. While it can be used for both regression and classification, it is more commonly used with the latter, by applying both linear and nonlinear strategies. By using different vectors to separate the data, it will be possible to classify them according to their characteristics and understand how they relate to each other.

- **K-nearest neighbor (KNN):** In this algorithm, the machine will look into the data points to establish the closest ones to the "K" point that is being analyzed, or the target. This means that the value will be approximated based on what the machine is learning. For example, if you want to classify between two different types of birds, it will look at the beaks and put those with similar characteristics near to the "main" input.

These are some of the algorithms that can be used with this technique despite, as mentioned earlier, the fact that there are others you might want to consider looking into. These include the Naïve Bayes model and the linear discriminant analysis. Now that you have the basic idea of what the classification learning models can do, let's look into the different regression ML algorithms and what they consist of.

Regression

Regression analyses are those that are carried out to find the relationships between different variables. These variables can consist of one criterion and different independent and dependent variables that affect them or just one. It also means that you can have more than one variable to identify how these affect the data points. "Regression analysis is generally used when we deal with a dataset that has the target variable in the form of continuous data. Regression analysis explains the changes in criteria in relation to changes in select predictors" (Ghorakavi, 2023).

This type of supervised ML happens when the analyst has too many features that impact the problem or question they are trying to answer but cannot clearly see a relationship between them. In addition to this, they can help establish a reliable forecast based on the behavior of the data points so that it is easier to make predictions regarding certain outcomes. Just as in the classification algorithms, there is a vast list of algorithms to choose from, though not exhaustive. Nevertheless, we will take a look at the five most common algorithms applied for this purpose.

- **Simple linear regression algorithm:** This algorithm is used for simpler analysis that has one constant and one variable. In this case, you are looking to understand the relationship between them and establish how they are related. In this case, the relationship between them will be established by using a line to identify and illustrate the connection.

- **Multivariate regression algorithm:** If the simple linear regression is about one constant and one variable, when we use multivariate regression analysis, we apply more than one variable (either dependent or independent) within the analysis process. Also called polynomial regression, it will be used in a nonlinear form to establish how the different points connect and understand how the dependent and the independent variables are related to each other.

- **Decision tree regression algorithm:** We can also use the decision tree algorithm to perform the data analysis since it will be able to forecast different situations and analyze possible outcomes. The process of this algorithm is the same as what we have seen in the classification section, without modifications.

- **Random forest regression algorithm:** The random forest, like the decision tree, uses the same approach as would be used in the classification algorithms. In this case, we are talking about the algorithm analyzing the different outputs from each of the trees and using them to make a decision and prediction, establishing the relationship between the data points.

- **Lasso regression:** This regression analysis method is commonly used when the machine is allowed to select one of the available variables and how it will be identified. In this case, it will only select a subset of the variables to apply to the final model, make its prediction, and establish the relationships (Ghorakavi, 2023).

Other names of regression analysis algorithms that could be mentioned include ElasticNet, Stepwise, and Support Vector regressions, each being applied according to the data that is being used. In addition to this, you should consider what is the outcome you are trying to obtain and the best one that will be applied to your question or problem. However, as you have seen, supervised ML is not the only way to conduct the analysis process. For this reason, we are now going to look into its counterpart: unsupervised ML.

Unsupervised ML

Contrary to what happens in the supervised ML process, when you have unsupervised ML, the data is not previously labeled. Therefore, the developer will leave it up to the machine to make the associations and find the relationships between the data points. If you remember what we mentioned in the previous section, in supervised ML, you give the machine the inputs of wolves and the expected outcome is wolves. This is not what happens in this case.

When you have unsupervised ML, you will give the machine the relevant data points and, based on it, it will learn and create an output that might or might not be expected. If you think about it and also use images as an example, it is like feeling the machine has millions of pictures, and then you give it an input of what it is that you expect it to generate. Based on this information, it will bring you a result that does not necessarily match a "real" image, but rather something it has come up with.

When applying this technique to datasets, you will see that it will use its learning process to discover and identify relationships that were not immediately visible to the human eye or perception. This process is all carried out without the need for human intervention since the output is not labeled. It is based on its ability to analyze the data points and find similarities and differences among them that you can use to analyze incredibly large amounts of data and establish patterns.

Because of this ability, unsupervised ML techniques are ideal for dealing with big data when you don't really know what to expect—it will help you during the exploratory analysis and identify starting points. In this second section, we are going to take a look at the three different categories of unsupervised ML algorithms: association, clustering, and dimensionality reduction (Pykes, 2023). For each of these categories, you will be given three of the most popular algorithms so you can understand how they can be used and applied to your data analysis process.

Association

When we are talking about association ML algorithms, it is similar to what we have seen with the supervised ML models. In this case, what we are looking to do is identify relationships between the data points and see how they can be *associated* with each other. In a real-life example, this could be applied to the Amazon purchase algorithm, which informs the user that the people who bought a certain product also bought the other one with it. This is a clear example of association and how these algorithms are used.

The most popular unsupervised ML algorithms are the Apriori, Eclat, and FP-growth. However, once again, it should be mentioned that this is not an exhaustive list but of the most common ones. To better understand how each of these ML models can be applied to your data analysis, let's take a look into what they mean and what are their best uses.

- **Apriori algorithm:** This algorithm is applied when you want to identify transactions between the datasets. In the case of the Amazon recommendation system that was previously mentioned, this is likely the technique that is used to establish these relationships. In this case, it means that what the machine is doing is working based on an interesting measure to find what are the rules and combinations that occur within a specific dataset (Pykes, 2023). The application of this algorithm is interesting to identify what the most common purchases made together are and create campaigns for selling more products in a certain online store.

- **Eclat algorithm:** The name of this algorithm is short for "Equivalence Class Clustering and bottom-up Lattice Traversal," and it is commonly used to identify what the most frequent data points within your set are. Some examples of how this can be applied are the indication of the top-selling product on a website or the most popular movies in a streaming service (Korstanje, 2021b). The application of this algorithm is interesting if the company wants to identify its top-selling products and how they are associated with other products. By identifying customer behavior and patterns, it is possible to create targeted campaigns. Despite it being faster than the Apriori algorithm, it will bring the user fewer metrics to analyze.

- **FP-growth algorithm:** According to Korstanje (2021a), this algorithm is the "modern version" of the Apriori algorithm since it is "faster and more efficient while obtaining the same goal." Therefore, it is safe to say that it will be applied to similar situations as the previously mentioned model, but its processing time will be faster and possibly more efficient. The main reason for this is that it will organize the data in a tree structure that leads to a faster analysis when compared to analyzing the full set.

Essentially speaking, we are talking about recommendation systems that are based on the user's preferences. One of these three algorithms is likely being used. However, this does not mean that they are being used on their own or that there are no other processes involved. When the developer is creating an ML system, it can also use other techniques to previously treat the data, and clustering is one of them.

Clustering

Using clustering algorithms for the unsupervised ML process is a common practice because these are fast and efficient algorithms to identify groups of data with similar properties. Although this might seem like a difficult task, it is common to see these types of "groupings" in the different tasks we carry out daily. Some of them might include the way our refrigerator is organized or even how we organize our bookshelves. Generally speaking, we are bringing the most common elements together so they are easier to identify.

When you consider the clustering algorithms in an ML process, several different ones can be applied, although the list is not exhaustive. In this section, we will take a look into three different clustering techniques that can be useful for your data analysis process. These are only some examples to show the efficiency of this algorithm, but if you are interested in the process, I encourage you to look deeper into how it works.

- **K-means clustering algorithm:** This algorithm is applied when you want to break the data points into different subgroups related to a certain point. This means that the data points will be divided into separate clusters, each with a centroid. In this case, the data points that belong to each group are similar to each other, but very different from the others that you are analyzing. By applying this technique, you can define the number of groups you want to break the data into, and the process is repeatedly run until there is no change in the final output. The main reason why clustering is considered unsupervised learning is that "since we don't have the ground truth to compare the output of the clustering algorithm to the true labels to evaluate its performance" (Dabbura, 2018).

- **Anomaly detection:** The name of this algorithm already suggests what it does and how it can be used: finding rogue data points within our set. This is an interesting application of clustering since when you start to group the different data points, you might eventually identify that certain points do not fit into any group. In this case, you are looking at the anomaly, and it will be interesting to understand what is happening. An example of how this algorithm could be used in real life is to use a statistical analysis and assumptions made by the machine to identify potential fraud in transactions or peaks of activity in a store. When you apply this technique, you will be able to make forecasts based on previous data and understand where the difference in activity occurs among the clients.

- **Hierarchical clustering:** Lastly, we have hierarchical clustering, which will be used to rank the data points according to their values. For example, if you want to classify the "category" for all the clients in your store, you might use this process to identify what they are. In this case, the clients with the most purchases over a period can receive a larger discount, while clients with fewer purchases will receive a lower discount. Another example of its application is in insurance companies, where the clients can be ranked based on how much they use their insurance, which will help determine if they need an increase in their premium or not.

As mentioned earlier, these are only some of the clustering techniques that can be used. Others include exclusive clustering, probabilistic clustering, and overlapping clustering, all with their specific uses and applications when you are analyzing data. As usual, you will need to understand what each of these does, the amount of data you have, and the objective of your analysis to identify the best one that applies to your situation.

Dimensionality Reduction

The last category of unsupervised ML you will learn about is dimensionality reduction. As you might imagine by its name, this is the process of using unsupervised ML techniques to reduce the variation between the datasets and make the information easier to work with. This means that this is an excellent option to use if you are going to carry out an exploratory analysis of the dataset, and you want to organize it before applying other algorithms.

Because this technique and its algorithms help the developer to better understand the dataset, it is one of the best tools to apply for preprocessing steps. This is because "these algorithms seek to transform data from high-dimensional spaces to low-dimensional spaces without compromising meaningful properties in the original data" (Pykes, 2023). This means your dataset will be simplified and easier to process.

To give you an example of how this works, and the two and three-dimensional data, I want to imagine the following: You have a flat square and a cube. If you were to distribute different points within them, would it be easier to "read" their information that is contained in the square or the cube? Likely in the square, since it has only two dimensions and you don't need to consider all the different settings if you look at it as a cube. This is exactly what dimensionality reduction does: It enables the data to be seen in a square rather than a cube.

Here are the most popular algorithms that can be used to carry out this process:

- **Principal component analysis (PCA):** When you are applying a PCA analysis, you are reducing the dimensionality of the dataset according to the main criterion that you want to identify. For example, if you work in ecommerce and want to identify what product is the most attractive to customers, you will apply this analysis to find out what it is and then apply other methods to understand how and what influences it. Since there are different reasons why a product can be more attractive to some and not to others (based on a combination of characteristics), you will identify what the most common one is and then look into the dependent variables according to it.

- **Independent component analysis (ICA):** While the ICA is similar to PCA, there are some differences that must be taken into consideration. While for the PCA analysis, you focus on one main component, in the ICA, you are analyzing different independent components that will be analyzed at the same time. One of the negative drawbacks of this technique is that "while we expect independent sources that are mixed within linear combinations, the ICA would find a space where even not-independent sources are maximally independent" (Dieckmann, 2023).

- **Single value decomposition (SVD):** This algorithm has an extremely mathematical-oriented approach since it uses matrices and vectors to carry out the analysis. This means that the code you will need to write for it and the process are considerably complex if you are just starting. Nevertheless, this is a great option if you are looking to store images and analyze, for example, how different pieces of your brand's clothing are used by people. When you do this, you can offer them other options on how to use them and use it as a marketing incentive by showing its versatility.

As you have seen, these algorithms are extremely useful options to help you during the exploratory phase of your analysis. This has been a small, but comprehensive section that tells you about the intricacies of unsupervised learning and if you feel it could be the right approach for you, it might be the best solution to start learning Python or R, which you know are the best options for these cases. Nonetheless, we still have two more ML models to learn about, and the next one will surprise you with its versatility and diverse applications within the data analytics market.

Semi-Supervised Learning

Semi-supervised ML techniques are those that use a hybrid technique between the supervised and the unsupervised ML models. In these cases, the developer will use both ML approaches to understand how the data should be analyzed and reach conclusions. It will have a few labeled data points and many that are unlabeled, and the machine will need to establish what the best place is for them to be allocated to. It will be trained with identifiable (labeled) data, but it will need to learn and make conclusions of its own for the data that is unlabeled.

However, although the machine will be free to make its associations and bring different outputs, they are also expected to be within a certain known parameter. Usually, what will happen is that after the original labeled and unlabeled datasets are given to the machine, they will generate a new dataset that can be used for the analysis. This ML technique can be used for both regression and classification purposes, depending on the algorithms that will be used and the type of data that will be fed to the program.

This approach is commonly applied by banks when looking to identify fraud detection within their operations. The system is given certain parameters to study, such as client purchase behavior, and based on the new information it is given and different transactions, it will determine if there is a possibility of fraud or not. Therefore, if you ever receive a call from your bank trying to identify if you are the one making a specific purchase, this means that you are likely being flagged by a semi-supervised ML program!

Reinforcement Learning

Reinforcement learning is exactly what the name suggests: the ML algorithm is encouraged based on positive and negative reinforcements to identify if it is doing the right or wrong process. These two types of learning, which use positive or negative reinforcement techniques, will lead the computer to learn based on trial and error, looking to identify the best options in exchange for the best rewards. While it is impossible to determine exactly what the different incentives used for each machine program are, these can be based on points, for example, that will help the machine decide what it will do next.

In a real-life application, we could mention Google Translator, which asks you to rate the quality of the translation after it is done. We can even mention grammar and spell-check tools, when you can suggest that the provided information or suggestion is wrong, giving it feedback on the action it suggested you take. In these cases, the presented result will be according to the input that was given, making this a sequential process of cause and effect. The output will depend on the previous input, which is the output for the one before that, and so on.

Here are the main characteristics of positive and negative reinforcement learning according to Bajaj (2023):

- **Positive reinforcement learning:** When you apply positive reinforcement learning to a machine, this means that you are telling it that its behavior is correct and that it should continue to act this way to improve its performance. This means that it will continue with the same analysis for a long time, sustaining the change and enabling it to continue for a long time based on that specific goal. However, once the model becomes "tired," it might become overwhelmed with information, which might lead to incorrect information and system overload. In this case, the machine needs to be fine-tuned again and have its parameters adjusted. When applying this to the data analysis process, it means you will have a machine that can predict and forecast actions based on the success of previously implemented elements.

- **Negative reinforcement learning:** If you decide to implement negative reinforcement learning, it means that you are not focusing on what the machine is doing correctly, but rather on what it is *not* doing properly. When this happens, the machine will immediately be instructed to stop the incorrect behavior and look for better alternatives. However, on the negative side, this process only works with the minimum threshold, not looking for optimal solutions to the issues, but rather the simplest alternative that will make it correct. Similarly to the positive reinforcement technique, it can be used to input information on marketing strategies that went wrong so that it is identified, and it can be known what should not be done.

Now that you know the main elements of ML models, their algorithms, and methods to apply them, it is time to look into the smaller (but not less important) details that should be accounted for when using ML techniques. These include the processes such as building the model, training, testing, fine-tuning, and interpreting the results. All of these will be essential to bring you optimal performance and reliable answers to what you are looking to identify.

KEY CONSIDERATIONS IN BUILDING ML MODELS

In this last part of the chapter, the different aspects that should be considered when implementing ML are exactly what we will be looking into. These key considerations should also be taken into account when you decide to incorporate ML techniques since they require some more time apart from the learning process in the language you have chosen. Despite usually bringing more accurate results, it might not be the case of implementing immediately, but rather a process that you will slowly implement while you use the "ready" software for these purposes.

Let's take a look at what they are and the main elements that you should consider for each of them:

- **Model building:** Model building is a critical part of the process since it is in this stage that you will identify the best algorithm that will tend to your needs and bring you the best results. The algorithm should be chosen according to its relevance and to the dataset you are working with, numerical or text data, the type of prediction you want to obtain, and what the expected result is. Defining the best model for your process will determine what the rest of the data analysis will look like.

- **Model training:** Once you have chosen the model, it is time to train the machine, and this will be *the* most important part of using ML. If you do not train the model properly, it will bring you inaccurate and unreliable results, affecting your whole process. The model you'll use to train it is what will determine the outcomes of the fresh data and the analysis, and, consequently, the outcomes you'll attain. Usually, the model is trained with the same dataset you are going to "feed" the machine with by separating it into a ratio of 30% for the training and 70% for the testing, or even 20%:80%.

- **Model evaluation:** It is by evaluating the results of the output from the training that you will be able to identify if what the machine is doing is within the expected. You can use "written" outputs or even model visualizations to ensure what is being done. Analyzing how the model is performing and the outputs, based on the training data, can be done by determining the categories of true positives, false positives, true negatives, and false negatives. Based on this simple determination, you will be able to see what needs to be adjusted, which is exactly the next part of the process: parameter tuning.

- **Parameter tuning:** Based on the conclusion that you will make on the training process, it is likely that you will need to fine-tune the hyperparameters so that the model can perform better. This might mean increasing the number of trees in a random forest, the number of clusters in a K-means clustering, or even giving the machine more positive reinforcement. It is also possible that you might have to reevaluate the data you are using to ensure that the correct predictions are being made. Once the parameters are tuned, you will evaluate the model again with the testing data and interpret the results it brings you.

- **Interpretability:** During the ML process, we must not "fully" and blindly trust the output that it initially brings us. We need to be able to understand the decision the machine is making and why it is doing so. Therefore, interpreting the results and seeing how they can apply to your process will be essential and not just an extra, unnecessary step. It will help you identify if any other parameter needs to be evaluated, if more data is needed, and even help you establish connections with the situation you are looking into. Knowing and understanding how to interpret results will determine if the model is ready to be deployed or not.

- **Model deployment:** Deploying the model means that you will place it in a productive environment, or use it for the intention it was built for. This means that it will be integrated into a process, such as exposing it to real-time data collected from the internet. Once the model is deployed, you will need to continue to evaluate and monitor it to ensure it is maintaining efficiency and delivering reliable results.

As we move on to the next chapter, you are going to learn about real-time business intelligence (BI) analytics. This process is crucial for some companies, especially considering the speed with which information currently travels on the internet. The concept of BI will be discussed, and we will look into how this can be a game-changer for many companies. Finally, you will also explore the importance of being a data-driven business and using this to make better and more targeted decisions to increase performance. Are you ready to continue?

CHAPTER 7:
REAL-TIME BUSINESS
INTELLIGENCE ANALYTICS

As you know, when we are analyzing data, we are looking into past events and how they impact the present and the things these trends and patterns can do to optimize business performance in the future. If you consider these premises and the speed with which information currently travels, you will see that today, more importantly than ever, it is essential for companies to use real-time BI to evaluate their metrics. Think about the damage that a text or video post can inflict on your business—especially if they are made by someone "influential." Social media can be disastrous.

For this reason, it is of the utmost importance to learn and understand the benefits of using data in real time and making data-oriented decisions. These will help you understand, for example, who the target customer for your company is and the campaigns with the most success. For these reasons, in this chapter, we will discuss how to use data analytics to make data-driven decisions in business. You will be provided with BI tools and techniques for real-time analysis of raw business data.

To start off this discussion, we will look into how the data-driven culture in companies is making a difference for certain brands and how it can also impact yours. You will learn what it means to be data-driven and how you can increasingly benefit from it. Let's take a look into what this means and help you answer the following question: *Is my business data-driven? If not, what can I do to change this?*

THE DATA-DRIVEN CULTURE IN BUSINESS

Think about how organizations used to make decisions in the past. While many used polls, interviews, and customer-sensitivity analyses, most of the actions were determined based on what the managers thought would be best, "instinct," or their values. A long time has passed since this was the truth. Today, many companies are changing their perspective and instead of being driven by instinct or motivation, they are basing their decisions on the data analysis of their processes.

When this process is performed and business decisions are made based on this, it likely means that the company has a data-driven culture, using all the possible tools to collect information and use these to guide them. By incorporating this collection and its further analysis into its processes, the company can apply intelligence techniques to increase yields based on hard data, making the results and actions more trustworthy. In addition to this, they will be able to increase the speed with which actions are taken and solve any potential issues without delaying the matter.

However, just because a company collects and stores data, this does not really mean that they are data-oriented. According to Andersson (2016), when a company has a data-driven culture, it transforms the data into a main part of its strategy and decision-making. This means they are transforming the process from the beginning, when data is collected, to the end, the analysis, into crucial steps within the organization.

In this case, the company will do its best to ensure that everything that is related to data is structured, organized, and defined. This means, for example, that all of their systems will have data collection tools incorporated for analysis. This data will be accessible and collected in a way that it does not breach privacy or consent rules. There is governance to collect the data and use it, such as informing clients for what purpose it will be used and requesting consent to use it.

Finally, you must consider that this data is centralized and securely stored. There is an effort to collect internal and external data that is relevant to the business, and usually, there is a high budget for this matter. Andersson (2016) suggests that "many companies are establishing data reservoirs with a combination of internal and external data. However, it's of utmost importance that data flowing into the data reservoir is strictly controlled to reap the desired benefits of the investment."

How Does My Business Benefit From This?

Likely, from what you have read so far in this book, you can see how analyzing data will help you make better decisions and take more targeted action. However, by incorporating this mindset into your company culture, you will also be able to see more tangible results and measure KPIs with more efficiency. You will be able to understand the causes and effects of certain situations, and even define and refine strategies that have already been implemented.

In addition to this, when you make decisions based on data, you are decreasing the risk within the organization's operations and the impact that certain decisions will have on the teams. These can range from safety procedures to improving departments and identifying where processes can be optimized. You will be able to better understand the circumstances that help a specific department work better than others, or why some employees are more productive than others.

Overall, it is safe to say that when you implement data-driven decisions in company culture, you will see incredible results all around. By using the data you have collected to obtain insights and make forecasts, you will be able to plan better and take immediate action if necessary. For these reasons, more and more companies are choosing to bring the method into their process, and data analysts are in high demand.

How Do I Create a Data-Driven Culture?

If your business or the company you work for has not yet adopted a data-driven culture, there is no better way to demonstrate this should be the path to go than using... data! Yes! You have that right. When trying to show the company management that they will make better and more targeted decisions, you should use data to show this is changing organizations. You can look into the different tools the company has and what can be used, as well as what needs to be implemented.

Obviously, if the company does not have this approach to decision-making, it will take a reasonable amount of investments to ensure that it is prepared. This means investing in data gathering and analysis tools, hiring data analysts, preparing the infrastructure for data storage, and investing in governance rules to make it happen, to name a few examples. While some companies might already have this in place, others might need to start from scratch. Therefore, the first step that needs to be carried out is an analysis of the current situation.

Understanding what you already have that can be used and what should be implemented is the first step to making this happen. Once you have a list of all the available tools, you will need to identify the minimal structure that should be adopted to start incorporating data analysis into its processes. This phase is likely going to take more time and more investments, but in the end, you will see this will bring incredible benefits overall.

As the processes evolve and the data-driven culture becomes more rooted among all spheres of the company, they will start to evolve and become more robust. It is at this moment that the business will not only rely on collected data from the past but use real-time information to build what is known as BI. Let's see what BI is, how it involves data analytics, and how it will benefit your company.

HOW BI WORKS

BI is not only about data analysis. It is, in fact, a combination of several tools that can be used to help a company understand what is going on and take action. It comprises the full data analysis process and company best practices to ensure optimal decisions are made. When a company decides it will use the most prominent athlete at the moment for its marketing strategy, this means it could be using data to figure out if this athlete matches company values, that it will have a positive image in the eyes of targeted customers, and that the channels it uses will generate more data to understand this group.

When all these are put together, instead of just using the data to make a decision, you are using BI to create an allegiance between the athlete's image and the one you want your company to have. Therefore, it is safe to say that if data analysis can be used to develop BI, BI is a determining factor to ensure that a company becomes data-driven. When you apply BI, you are likely not trying to answer just one question or problem, but rather a series of them and looking for efficient solutions.

These answers will eventually lead to insights and predictions that will allow you (or the managers) to take action at the right moment—and it is exactly the right timing that must be considered today. When you apply real-time analytics and BI, we are talking about gathering, analyzing, and obtaining conclusions for the data almost immediately after it has been gathered. The concept is not as new as you might imagine.

If you use Google Analytics or campaign performance in social media channels, you will likely obtain real-time data analysis results. In this case, an *aggregator* will be incorporated into the process to help stream the data from different places and send it to a *broker*, which will enable you to process the data in real time. After this, the data is sent to an *analytics engine* that will process, blend, correct, and relate the data points, as well as analyze them. The final step will come from the *stream processor* that will execute the analytics and provide real-time visualization to the user and enable them to see how their processes are doing (Heavy.AI, n.d.).

To understand the importance of BI, I want you to think about the following. Suppose you are a restaurant chain and someone posts a video online claiming they found some sort of insect inside the food. As you might imagine, if this video goes viral, there will be significant impacts on the brand's image. However, if you analyze the metrics of such video in real time, you might be able to see what kinds of customers it has impacted the most and take immediate action before it escalates.

In addition to this, you will be given a forecast based on the user interactions and other data to identify the group you should focus on repairing your image with, if it had a significant impact on your business by analyzing customer attendance, and even forecast the effect this will have in a longer period.

Different service providers can perform this for your company (such as the previously mentioned Google Analytics), but this process can also be carried out with our structures by having the correct tools and applying the best techniques. To better understand the BI methods you could implement in your company, in the next section, you are going to see the main techniques, tools, and methodologies you must consider when implementing it. As you will see, many of the tools that were provided in previous chapters allow this, so it might be a good option to look into the possibilities of those that can incorporate all processes according to the demand.

BI ANALYTICS TECHNIQUES, TOOLS, AND METHODOLOGIES

BI techniques, tools, and methodologies refer to the best practices that can be implemented by a company or an individual to ensure that the process is carried out in the best way possible. In this case, they will determine the best outcome and the most reliable results. These include from the data mining techniques you use to how you are going to present the results. Based on how you illustrate what you have found, more or less insights will be made, and it will be easier to make a decision. In this section, we are going to look at each of these in more detail and show you their main features and applications to ensure that you have optimal results.

BI Techniques

BI techniques are those processes or actions that are carried out to obtain maximum value of the data you are using. However, in addition to this, it also comprises the tools that you are going to use to ensure the best result interpretation. Based on a study by Joshi and Dubbewar (2021), there are the nine main techniques that a BI analyst should consider when carrying out a BI process and their features:

- **Advanced analytics:** Ideally speaking, when you are going to carry out a BI analysis, you are going to incorporate advanced analysis into the process. This means that you are not only going to look into the predictions that the software will bring you but also work with brainstorming and acting on the best data that should be collected for the process and incorporating the appropriate visualization tools that will be created to visualize the results. This means that we are talking about the full analytical process and not only the "analysis" *per se*. In other words, when you are performing advanced analytics, you are taking care of all the processes we have read about so far in this book and that we will still learn more about.

- **Data mining:** In the article, Joshi and Dubbewar (2021) refer to "data mining" as the process we have been referring to as data analysis. These include the process of selecting, preprocessing, transforming, analyzing, and interpreting the data obtained. By now, it should be clear that this is an essential part of BI analysis, without which it cannot happen. Therefore, regardless of what you are going to do, data analysis will be the center of the process from which all the other actions will stem.

- **Dashboards:** If the analyst chooses a dashboard to present the BI insights of a certain process, then it is likely they want to make the data collected as clear, transparent, and understandable as possible. This means that they will use this visualization tool to identify all the possibilities and outcomes of a certain decision for an enhanced decision-making process. Because of the simplicity of creating and presenting one of these, it is likely that you have seen one during a presentation or that you will use one when time is of the essence.

- **Extract, transform, load (ETL):** This technique's name already says what it does: extract, transform, and load the data into a software program to obtain insights. They include obtaining data from internal and external sources and cleaning it before it is fed into your software of choice for the final analysis and visualization. In addition to this, during this process, the analyst will store and secure the data to ensure that it complies with company governance rules.

- **Online analytical processing (OLAP):** When this BI technique is applied, you are considering all the features that can be applied to online tools, such as the location, time, and product that is being consumed. Once the data is looked into with these different aspects, you will see it will have more than one dimension, which allows different insights to be obtained. Since we are talking about a processing method, it includes all the steps from the data mining to the reporting of the conclusions to management and the involved stakeholders.

- **Predictive analytics:** Predictive analytics are exactly what the name suggests: the action of using the data you have gathered to establish a forecast of what will happen if a certain action continues to be carried out or if it is stopped or modified. In most cases, these predictions will be made based on statistical inferences obtained from the data and is considered a part of the advanced analytics process.

- **Real-time BI:** The process of carrying out real-time BI will need the participation of both a human and a machine. This is because the human will not be able to make predictions based on the data without using a computer, and the computer will not be able to obtain insights or relevant conclusions based on the data it has been fed. This is done in real time by analyzing the data as it comes in and is made available to the system and the analyst.

- **Reporting:** When you are requested to carry out a task for the company you work for, you will likely be asked to provide a report. In the case of BI-related reports, you should mention the data you used and where it was obtained, the rationale behind the analysis you performed, the question you were trying to answer, and why this should be relevant for the company. For reporting, you can either provide the data in its processed state for management and stakeholders to decide what their insights are, or you can give them a structured report with all the conclusions. When this is done, you must ensure that you have incorporated all the necessary information, with a specific mention of how the results will be visualized.

- **Visualization:** The last and most important BI technique is the visualization of the results from the process. Because many individuals and decision-makers are not familiar with statistical graphs to make decisions, the way you present your data will be one of the most important aspects of the process. This part of the data analysis and BI process is so crucial that we are going to explore it more in Chapter 9.

Before we get there, it is time to look into the different tools that can be used in BI analysis. As you might imagine, with the increased popularity of data-driven decisions and using BI to make targeted decisions, there are several options to choose from. As you continue reading, you will see what some of them are and how they can make your process effortless and more efficient.

BI Tools

There are several different software programs in the market that are used for this purpose. Just as you have seen before, your choice should depend on the area in which you work, the quality of the data you have, and the metrics you want to observe. For this reason, I have separated 10 of the most commonly used applications for this purpose, their prices, and applications for a better overview. Here are the most popular and efficient BI tools available in the market and their main characteristics.

Program	Price	Features
Dundas BI	paid	• has a mobile application and can be customized for different purposes • analytics can be specified and built according to the business's needs
IBM Cognos Analytics	paid	• can be used for data analytics and data science • is scalable according to the business's needs and incorporates AI into the software
MicroStrategy	paid	• high-speed BI tool that can identify trends and patterns making the analysis process easier • provides insight and forecasts based on the data

Oracle BI	paid	• supported especially for users with Oracle databases and provide analytics, and real-time reporting with visualization tools
Power BI	free/paid	• can analyze medium datasets in the free version and gives immediate visualization for the analytical process
QlikSense	free/paid	• combines different datasets and makes the analysis process easier for decision-making • uses augmented intelligence and guided processes
SAS Business Intelligence	paid	• allows for predictive analysis based on the data and enables different devices to be connected to it, enhancing collaboration
Sisense	paid	• can be used with and without coding options • has AI embedded into the analytical process and accepts data from multiple databases
Tableau	paid	• one of the most complete tools that supports NLP, mobile devices, and several different tools, especially facilitating deployment

Zoho Analytics	paid	<ul><li>easy to use and with a friendly interface</li><li>gives the user the ability to share analysis results and provides API for connecting with other databases</li></ul>

Because of the incredible value these tools bring to a business, you will see that most of them are paid—and the price is not usually cheap. However, if you use Microsoft, IBM, and Oracle services, it is possible to obtain these at a discount. In addition to this, there are other products on the market you can choose to explore and see if they will be enough for your company's needs.

While these pieces of software help you make analyses faster, ensuring you obtain crucial information and BI insights, there are a few other methodologies you might want to consider carrying out, especially if you are using Python. In this case, it will give you the visualization tools needed by importing relevant libraries. In the final section of this chapter, we will take a look at three relevant methodologies you should consider studying and incorporating into your data analytics and BI processes.

Additional Methodologies to Study

Apart from the processes and tools that we have already read about, it is important to take some time and understand some of the additional methodologies that could be relevant to the BI development process. For this, we are going to take a look at three significant approaches that the analyst can choose to incorporate into their process and ensure that the results are more reliable. Let's take a look at what these are and how they can be used.

- **Operations research:** When you use operations research methodologies, this will help you better understand not only what you are doing but also *why* you are doing it. In this case, "operations research offers powerful tools for understanding and analyzing certain classes of problems. However, OR is by no means a 'one-size-fits-all' approach to solving intelligence problem sets" (Kaplan, 2011). This means that the analyst is going to study all the resources that can be applied and actions that can be taken for an analysis to take place. The analyst will then look into their relevance to determine the best one to be applied. When you understand how the operation will be carried out and the different options, this will help you make better and more informed business decisions.

- **Time series forecasting:** There is no difference in the concept of time series analysis that is applied as a methodology from what you have seen in Chapter 5. In this case, for a small recap, it refers to the statistical technique used to make predictions based on the statistics that are identified and the calculations that the software or the machine is making. It will identify patterns and trends that can be observed over time and, based on what dataset analysis shows through the graphs, charts, or other visualization tools that cover a certain period, the business will be able to make its decision. Essentially speaking, you will observe how a certain variable behaves within a specific period to see if this is something that repeats itself or if there are factors that are driving it (Halder, 2023).

- **Options trading:** If you are familiar with the stock market, you must be familiar with options trading. Essentially speaking, the buyer and the seller of a certain product have the option of buying or selling a product or financial instrument according to their price at the moment. In this case, if you are the buyer and the price is currently *higher* than what you initially opted for, you will then be able to call the option and pay less for it at that moment and sell at a higher price. On the other hand, if the price is *lower* than the initially agreed price, you have the option to put and not pay the higher price that you had agreed to. By practicing using options trading software, you will be able to develop a better understanding of when the analysis process should be stopped or continued based on the information and results you have obtained.

You now have all the necessary information to carry out not only a data analysis but also incorporate this into the BI process to improve the business's metrics. However, before we move on to the last part of the process, which is the interpretation and visualization of the results, I would like to talk about something that is a critical skill for an analyst. Can you guess what it is? If you said *critical thinking*, then you are correct!

For this matter, in the next chapter, we are going to talk about this essential skill data analysts should have and how developing a problem-solving mindset will help you throughout the process. If you are ready to continue this last part of the journey, then I will see you in the next chapter as we explore how you can improve and train these skills.

CHAPTER 8:

DEVELOPING A CRITICAL THINKING AND PROBLEM-SOLVING MINDSET

If there is one essential skill that a data analyst must have, it is the ability to think critically and solve problems. This is because when you are dealing with data analysis, you are usually, as you know, trying to answer a question or solve a problem; therefore, understanding the nuances and the details of the situations will be essential to know how you should proceed. Analyzing data is never black and white. There is no "essential truth" when we are talking about different factors and implications that can be found during the process.

It is not uncommon to see factors that we did not expect interfere with the final result, and those that were foreseen have minimal impact. While many analysis processes might bring the expected result, usually, you will be able to identify other details that were not previously seen after it is done. Being able to identify these and looking beyond the background that real-world problems bring is an essential characteristic that will make you a valuable and essential professional.

This is why, in this chapter, we will discuss how you can develop your problem-solving capabilities. You will be provided with tips, skill-building techniques, and exercises to develop a mindset that's able to think critically and creatively in the face of data-related problems. To focus on each of these matters, let's start by understanding what it means to have a mindset for problem-solving and understand its importance in more detail.

DEVELOPING A MINDSET FOR PROBLEM-SOLVING

Before we start understanding what it means to have a mindset for problem-solving, I want you to think about the following: How many problems do you solve every day? These include not only the serious and business problems that you might have to deal with, but also the small things, such as if it starts raining on your way to work, deciding what will be for dinner, and what you should do if you are unhappy at work. Come to think of it, we solve problems every day, almost all the time, and, sometimes, it is so automatic that we don't even think about it.

The beauty is that not everyone will solve the problems they are facing similarly. If you are on your way to work, and it starts raining, you will have to find a solution to arrive at the office as dry as possible. If you are hungry, you will need to decide between cooking, eating at a friend's, eating at a restaurant, or ordering takeout. If you are unhappy at work, you could look for a new job, speak to your manager, and even change professions. These are all solutions to things that are not usually seen as "problems" due to how small they are but are still problems nonetheless.

Therefore, it is safe to say that if you are already making these decisions on your own and not having anyone else do it for you, you are already working on your problem-solving skills. This is because problem-solving is a process, in which you are going to identify what the problem is, then see what the possible applicable solutions are, and once analyzed and decided, you can take action. In other words, it is what you do during most of your day in all types of situations.

On the positive side, problem-solving is a skill, and, as such, it can be developed; the more you practice, the better you become at it. The more complex the problems you are solving are, the more challenging they will become. The more elaborate they are, the more thought you will put into it and the better your decisions will be. In the end, you should ideally be more of a "problem-solver" than a "problem-controller." *What is the difference?* you might ask. Well, read on and find out.

What Is a Problem-Solving Mindset?

If you think about a person who is a problem-controller, as per the definition from Ale (2019), it is a person who has an approach that offers the least need to think about the issue, such as having a "yes" or "no" answer. Ale (2019) mentions that "it limits your decisions, actions, and attitude around you" when compared to the approach of a problem-solver, who "seeks problems out because they understand that in overcoming obstacles, they limit the number of obstacles facing them—they see problems as opportunities to grow rather than a painful experience." It is not a matter of identifying that there is a problem, but also how *you* are going to react to it.

One common approach that many problem-solvers have is to identify the *root cause* of the problem. In other words, getting to the bottom and identifying what the original problem is that led to the one you have today. By using techniques such as the 5W2H (what, where, when, why, and who; and how and how much) you will be able to understand the core of the matter. This also means asking questions and more questions until you get to the point where there is no answer, that you reach the truth that cannot be changed or modified and is the source of the issue.

However, it is important to consider that *not all* problems will require this approach, especially those that are not as big, urgent, or important. This is because if you *do* decide to implement this in every single problem you have, you will likely end up fixating on them and putting your brain in overdrive. There needs to be a balance between the "easy" solutions and those that require thought, and it is only you who will be able to decide what to do.

Swaminathan (2008) mentions that scientists have uncovered that the best way to approach problems and practice having a problem-solving mindset is composed of a few items:

1. Approaching the problem with an open mind

2. If you find no solution, leaving it alone for some time

3. The information which is stored in your brain regarding similar or the same matter

4. Your experience with a previous matter and how you dealt with it

These last two are important because it will be a case of "searching your mind" by using triggers and trying to understand what you did right and wrong the previous time and how to place a better solution. For this reason, if you are asked to analyze data with the same features and parameters, after doing it a few times, you might obtain new insights. This will happen especially if every time you look at the data, you do so with an open mind and after leaving it alone for some time.

When you fixate too much on a problem or a question, you will be hyper-focused on the matter, and it will not be so easy to do the first two. This is why many times, people have these "a-ha!" moments regarding the matter when they are doing something else. When they are taking a shower, cooking, or exercising—nothing that has actually any relation to the issue. Since your mind is relaxed, you can look at it from other angles.

In these cases, it is not about how good of a problem-solver you are, but how you are going to approach the matter in itself. This does not mean that all matters have time to be solved. Not at all. In some cases, you will need to bring an immediate solution to it and then go back, find the root cause, and start the thinking process. Since we are talking about data, you will likely have *some* reasonable time to make a decision, and this is exactly why it is so important to understand what it takes to be a problem-solver and how you can use this as your main trait.

Why Is This Relevant?

When you are a data analyst, 90% of the time, you will be dealing with problems, how to answer them, and using your critical thinking skills (Taylor, 2022). This means that you will need to think not only about the problem or question that you have been tasked to work on but also all the details and matters that might be related to it. No matter how good you are at programming, how many machine algorithms you can write, if you are unable to understand the nuances of a problem and the criteria that should be used to analyze them, whatever code you write will be useless.

If you think about it, several factors might interfere with how much a store sells every month, for example. For this case, you must consider several items such as if a special gifting season is arriving, if there are discounts applied, and even the payment options offered. However, you might still not be able to identify why most people buy at the beginning of the month rather than at the end. Have you considered when people receive their paychecks, which is usually as the month starts? As you can see, sometimes, the answer might not be as obvious; therefore, you should look at the situation from all angles.

Suppose that the company you work for does not have a data-driven approach. How would you deal with this? You would need to take in the cultural and financial barriers, for example, that might influence this decision. Therefore, you will need to find solutions to make this matter different, which you already know might be solved by presenting results based on data. Despite how much you invest in your technology team, in machinery, and in tools to optimize your structure, if you do not invest in data, and the team does not have a problem-solving approach, the issues you want solved won't be. This is the same as having a screwdriver without a screw: There is nothing to use it with and, therefore, it brings no value (Lee, 2023).

Despite what many might think, problem-solving is more than just making a nice chart with whatever data is available and showing different indicators. Does this bring any value or solution to the matter? Does it identify the root cause? Probably not. This is because the data analyst's job also includes "making a presentation to stakeholders showing one or two factors that greatly affected company sales while giving them recommendations on how to tackle the cause so that sales can improve" (Armandi, 2023). You will need to make a hypothesis that is the answer to the problem and work on it until you have the answer. However, problem-solving is a broader skill that is made up of several smaller skills, without which, it will not work properly. Let's see what they are.

PROBLEM-SOLVING SKILLS EVERY DATA PROFESSIONAL NEEDS

When you are a problem-solver or if you want to develop this skill to become a better data analyst, you will need to consider investing in other skills that will help you. This is because the act of problem-solving, in itself, involves looking at different points of view and understanding what is expected of you. To illustrate the need to develop these 10 skills in association with problem-solving, you will read an example that will be applied to all the items to show their importance.

The problem we will be referring to is the following:

On a certain highway, it has been identified that there have been many accidents around Exit 7C. The accidents especially happen when it is raining or during the night, and the authorities are trying to understand why and avoid a potential rise in the incidents. You, as the data analyst, have been asked to determine the reasons why this is happening and to identify potential solutions.

- **Active listening:** When you listen to the problem, you must not only be listening, but actively listening to understand the real matter instead of jumping to conclusions. Actively listening to others means that you will be empathic and understand where they are coming from. In the case above, you might deduce that the authorities are concerned with a potential increase in loss of life and that, therefore, this is an urgent matter.

- **Communication:** Communicating and asking more questions is the key to identifying unique points of view that might be used to your advantage. Restating the problem in other words and telling the person who requested what you understood is an important part of the process. Questions that could be asked above are the characteristics of the victims, for how long this has been going on, and if there has been any change recently in the region.

- **Creativity:** Using your creativity to understand the different matters that can be of importance to the situation is one good way to approach a problem. Sometimes, the individual who asks a question is so focused on their own ideas that they are unable to expand the matter. Therefore, you should be curious and try to understand the factors that are driving this to happen, especially using the 5W2H. The example above could lead you to finding different ways to approach the problem, such as looking into what is near the area of the accidents, such as a bar, and the characteristics of the drivers who suffered the accidents.

- **Critical thinking:** Sometimes, when we are asked to solve a problem, our unconscious bias might get in the way of the decision and solution we propose. However, it might be the case that the reality is not really what you expected. Therefore, being objective and looking at the facts will be a great way to help solve the issue. For the above example, you will need to think about the characteristics of the drivers, brands and models of cars, how the weather was on the days the accidents occurred, and even if there are external circumstances that might have contributed to the incidents.

- **Curiosity:** Being curious is an essential characteristic since it will help you find alternative solutions to the problem at hand. When you look into the situation with different and curious eyes, it is more likely that you will find the real matter that is causing the problem. You might want to know, for the previous example, why drivers use this exit, the driving habits of drivers within this age group, the tickets this particular group has received, and other matters that might influence your analysis.

- **Flexibility:** Being flexible is important because you need to understand that maybe the data you need is not available and that you might need to use alternate sources and solutions to help you throughout the analysis process. You must be willing to look into the matter from another view and all possible angles so that you can understand the best recommendation to be applied. In the case above, it is possible to say that you might not be able to gather all the characteristics of the driver, but you might be able to get data from the insurance company to understand the profile of the group, which should also help.

- **Initiative:** A good data analyst does not wait for instructions every step of the way to make their decision. In fact, they are proactive and take the initiative to understand the reasons why the problem is a problem, how it can affect the business, and the different approaches that could be taken to solve it. In the case of accidents, we could say that the analyst could suggest placing a "caution" sign before the exit to alert drivers while the analysis is being made.

- **Research:** You cannot solve a problem if you do not have all the necessary information to guide management's decisions. You must be aware of all the factors that implicate the matter and how a change in each of them can affect the results. When looking into the accident site, you could research the region and talk to neighboring areas to understand what their thoughts are, look into different businesses that have opened in the region, and all the other possible available data that you can find, such as police reports and court records.

- **Resilience:** Being able to go back and redo your analysis, in case the individual who requested does not agree with the results, is an important characteristic. It is possible that just because you have the data, it does not mean you have all the necessary information, such as that which is confidential. Therefore, you must be willing to go back and look at the data with other eyes. In the situation above, you suggested adding a "caution" sign, but this was immediately refused since, according to the decision-makers, the individuals would not pay attention to it. Therefore, you should go back and see what can be done to solve the problem as soon as possible.

- **Technical expertise:** Finally, to solve a problem, you must have technical expertise or know someone who can help you with the matter. This is because you might not have the technical tools or skills that will make your solution work. Therefore, it is important to have it or at least know someone who can help you and see if the proposals are valid and applicable. Let's see this last item in the next paragraph.

After you have analyzed the data, you learned that according to the reports and statements you read that the drivers claimed that it was not properly signalized; therefore, they had to take action immediately to not lose the exit. In addition to this, you also learned that many people were speeding, which was another issue that caused the accidents. Finally, while looking into the new businesses, you saw that a new veterinary hospital had opened right off the exit.

Therefore, you conclude that due to the lack of signs and the probable emergency that the pet owners were having, these accidents were happening. Most of the drivers were pet owners who frequented the clinic and were speeding at the time of the accident. Your solution to the department, based on the analysis of the data, is to use better signaling in the area and implement a fixed radar 2 miles before the exit to avoid speeding.

CASE STUDIES: WHAT IT TAKES TO BE A GREAT PROBLEM-SOLVER

Since in the previous section we have talked about using data to analyze the different skills that must be developed to enhance your problem-solving skills, below are three more questions for you to practice and think about what could be done to solve the problem. In this case, the answer will not be provided, just a few questions to consider, since the idea is to have each reader identify the best solutions to the problem. But, before we get to the questions, here are some tips.

- Check your bias!

- Look into the different databases you can use that are readily available.

- If the data is unavailable, what resources could you use?

- Apply the 5W2H questions until you have found the cause of the problem.

- Use the skills mentioned in the previous section to identify what situations you would look at.

Questions

1. You have lived in the neighborhood Purple Lilies for the past 10 years, and you have 2 small children. In the neighborhood, there is a playground where the children from the area go to play with an adult. For the past 9 years, this has been a safe and calm neighborhood to live in, ideal for young couples with small children and elderly people. However, for the past 8 months, an issue has been bothering not only you but also other parents: the increase in the number of homeless people in the region who sleep at the playground and ask for money.

   You have noticed an increase in the number of shops in the region as well as some governmental service stations. You talk about this matter with the homeowners association and ask them to take the appropriate measures. As chairperson of the association, you ask the data analyst to identify why this is happening. As the analyst, what are the questions you ask, the data you search for, and in what databases?

2. You are the owner of a traditional restaurant downtown in your home city. Since you have opened, the customers have been loyal and the reviews of your food incredible. You specialize in Italian food, and the quality of what you serve is something that has always amazed the customers. However, you have noticed, after a certain period of absence due to health reasons, that when you came back the regular customers did not come back as often and that many were surprised to hear you were back.

   While you were away, you discovered that the manager changed some of the staff, modified the menu, and no longer chatted with the diners. In addition to this, it seems like the restaurant is not even attracting new patrons, which is strange, since it was always the go-to option for families. Downtown is bustling, and the city is receiving more clients than ever. You hire a data analyst to understand what is going on with the business and how you can change this. As the data analyst, what would you do?

3. You are the owner of a successful clothing brand for women, with a target clientele aged 25–40. While you have expanded the store to include an online platform, you have noticed an increase in the demand for clothes that you currently do not have, such as mother–daughter styles and pregnancy items. You were thinking about investing more money into opening one of the two new clothing lines in your store, but you are unsure which one, since you do not want to invest in both. You hire a data analyst to help you decide what should be the focus of your new line and forecast what would generate the most sales. What do you do in this case?

We are finally arriving at the chapter which describes the last step of the data analysis process: visualization. As you will see in the next chapter, this is the part of the process which most analysts tend to get overwhelmed by, since they will need to communicate to management and the stakeholders the answers they have found and give their recommendations. Since you will be exposing yourself, your work, and your conclusions, it is only normal to feel this way. Read on to learn more about what this final step entails and get tips on how to improve your presentation.

CHAPTER 9:
DATA STORYTELLING AND
VISUALIZATION

No matter how good your analysis is: If those who requested it do not understand it, it will be of no use. Hence, it is important to use good storytelling and visualization to present the results of your analysis. They need to be clear and understandable, and those looking at them must be able to immediately recognize the patterns and the issues you have identified. If the stakeholders or management do not understand, it is likely they will not accept your solution to the problem or disagree with everything that you have done.

On the other hand, if you can present the results in an engaging way and with visuals that show your conclusions in an obvious manner, it is likely that your approach will be accepted and that your recommendations might be followed. After all, you did follow the data. For this reason, this chapter discusses the fifth and last step in the data analytics process: data visualization. You will learn how to create compelling and dynamic visuals that make it easy for others, especially management, to understand and gather insights.

THE POWER OF DATA STORYTELLING

Imagine you are studying a historical subject, let's say World War II. What would help you understand it better: looking only at charts and tables with the number of soldiers, battles, dates, and armory, or would you learn by being taught better about a certain topic with a context, a story? It is likely that, regardless of the matter you are learning about, you would rather have the numbers and the factual data embedded within a narrative so that you can better understand the situation.

This is exactly the same as presenting the results of your data analysis. To engage the audience and make sure that they understand what you are talking about, you are going to use a technique called storytelling, which is nothing but putting together the context and the visualization of the results with a narrative that attracts those listening to you. More specifically, you will be using *data storytelling*, which is the act of using data to tell a story and enhance it with the results of your study.

"It's a combination of science and art, where data visualization and storytelling come together to turn complex data into a meaningful and impactful story" (Visium, 2023). This means that you can use resources such as restating the problem you were looking for and telling the audience a narrative of the steps you took that led you to the conclusion. You will obviously not need to tell them the technical part, but rather engage them by using applications such as:

- Why was this data selected, or why is it relevant?
- What other questions were asked to identify the root cause?
- Were any underlying circumstances identified?
- Were there any challenges in the process related to the data?
- What was your initial hypothesis, and what did the data show?

You will obviously need to adapt these questions to the specific situation you are dealing with, but by creating an exciting narrative, you are more likely to find a receptive audience. According to Tableau (n.d.), telling a data story can use several different approaches, which are

- **Change over time:** using a timeline to establish the order of how events occurred and what is related to them.

- **Contrast:** using comparison to see how two or more situations are alike or different and how this impacts the business.

- **Drill down:** looking into the larger view of a certain matter and then magnifying each different circumstance until you reach the bottom line.

- **Factors:** explaining the situation by dividing it into different categories and all the features and variables that have an impact on the analyzed matter.

- **Intersections:** applying the different places in which the data's features overlap each other and one takes priority over the other, much like a consequence.

- **Outliers:** identifying the points that are different from the standard, what makes them stand out, and why.

- **Zoom out:** Contrary to the drill-down technique, you will start with the specifics and increase the view to the bigger picture step by step.

When incorporating any of these techniques, you should ensure you choose the one that best fits your story, the information, and the conclusion you are about to provide. However, no matter how good the story is, there is still the matter of needing to use visual aids to ensure that the message is understood. In my experience, one of the reasons that leads most people to lose interest in a presentation is using an Excel spreadsheet to show results instead of graphs, or using too much text to explain what could be done by an image. Due to this, you must consider the different visual aids that can be used, which can vary from a simple line graph to a pie or bar chart. Let's see some examples.

TYPES OF DATA VISUALIZATIONS

When presenting your data, it is important to consider that using more information in the simpler visualization format is the best way to go.

This means avoiding adding too much information or too many variables that can be confusing to the audience. Here are 15 alternatives you should consider for the best ways you can present your results, so they are visual and understandable:

- area charts
- bar graphs
- box plots
- bubble charts
- heatmaps
- histograms
- line charts
- maps
- network graphs
- pie charts
- radar charts
- scatterplots
- timetables
- treemaps
- Venn diagrams

While only 15 have been chosen to illustrate the options, it is safe to say that there are more than 50 different ways to show your data; some that include using code, and others that don't. It is also possible to present data with simple structures such as pivot tables, and more complex ones such as those that indicate proportions or show a distribution. In any case, much like the rest of the steps of the process, the visualization tool should be chosen based on the analyst's evaluation of the best way to illustrate the data in a simple and objective way.

At the same time, you can use specific software, some of which we have seen in previous chapters of this book, to help you identify the best option. While some of them will use a drag-and-drop feature, others will just change the visual aid's format as you select the type you want. To ensure that you have the best tools for this purpose, in the next section of this chapter, we are going to explore some of them and identify their characteristics.

TOOLS FOR CREATING INTERACTIVE AND DYNAMIC VISUALS

You already know that there are many options in the market that help you with your data analytics process. However, you will also be interested to know that some of these tools also enable you to create everything, including the visualization section of the process. If you are going to acquire the license to use one, it is always important to have in mind the features embedded in it according to the purpose of the analysis you will carry out and what the business does.

For example, if we are analyzing the data of a local store that does not ship and only has a physical presence, illustrating the data in a map might not be relevant. Therefore, looking into exactly what you will be needing might help you save some money. At the same time, as previously mentioned, if you have a Microsoft Office license, you might be able to upgrade it so it has Power BI, and then you will have all the tools you need at hand.

While the list of available options in the market is extensive, the list of the eight different programs named in this section was based on how frequently they are mentioned by various industry experts and their different capabilities. They have been placed in a comparison chart in which you will be able to see some of their main characteristics when compared to those that need to be kept in mind for a data visualization tool. They are the following:

	Data wrap per	Do mo	Klipf olio	Pow er BI	Sise nse	Qli k Sen se	Tabl eau	Zoho Anal ysis
AI and ML integratio n			X	X	X	X		X
Customiz able	X	X	X	X	X	X	X	X
Enable data discovery		X		X	X		X	
Embedda bility		X	X		X	X	X	X
Geotaggi ng and location	X	X	X	X	X	X	X	X
Interactiv ity	X	X		X	X		X	X
Managem ent easiness	X	X		X	X		X	X
Performa nce	X			X	X		X	X
Predictive analysis			X			X		

As you can see from the above table, each of these has a different characteristic. If you are looking for ML and AI integration, then you have to choose between the five options provided. If you are looking for tools that make predictions, there are others. Now, it's up to you! This is the last part you need to consider for your presentation, and you will be able to demonstrate the results you have obtained. In the meantime, before we reach the last chapter of the book, here are a few tips and best practices you should consider when preparing your visuals and presentations.

DATA VISUALIZATION AND STORYTELLING TIPS AND BEST PRACTICES

If after reading this chapter, you are still in doubt about the best way to use the data to tell a story, you shouldn't worry! In this final section, we are going to talk about some of the best practices to ensure that you can use the data the best way possible and tips you should use when creating the presentation. You will be given some characteristics of a good data story as well as the questions you should ask when the material is being prepared.

A good data story is not as hard to build as you might imagine. To start off, let's talk about the objective characteristics it should have and those that are potentially the most important. When preparing the presentation, you should ensure that the data collected, the results presented, and the conclusions made are all based on *accurate, ethical, relevant,* and *reliable* data. This should be the principle of it all, and it should be expressed and demonstrated. If the audience does not feel that the data you have is either of these, it is likely they will not believe what you have to say.

Next, you must look into the context of what is being said. If you are only stating problems and not bringing solutions, then your analysis was, in some ways, useless. This means you should use the data analysis process to make the audience feel *empowered, safe*, and *confident* that what you are suggesting is the right way to go. The best way to do this is to use *intuitive* visuals, enabling them to make these decisions on their own.

You should also consider if the actions you are proposing are *scalable* and can be replicated to other problems the company might be having. If the audience sees there is a possibility of getting even more benefits out of this analytical process, you will be on the road to success. This also means that the presentation must be *dynamic*, enabling them to identify connection points and other points of action that can be carried out based on the conclusions.

However, lastly, we should not forget about the *appearance* of what you are saying. This means selecting one color palette, for example, and sticking to it until the end so that the presentation is not a wild mix of colors. You should also remember that the more objective, the better, since it is likely the audience wants a conclusion. Finally, keep in mind that if it can be said, it does not need to be written. Visual aids should be self-explanatory, and you should not need to do much more than guide your audience to what they are seeing in the presentation or report.

What Should I Ask?

While preparing the data story, a good way to identify if what you are going to say meets the audience's needs and expectations is to ask yourself questions from their and your perspective. Putting yourself in their place and analyzing the process you have gone through will help you identify if any improvements should be made to the visual, the story, and the context in general.

For these reasons, you will now see 10 different questions that can be asked from the perspective of both management and the data analyst, which might help you narrow down what you are going to say and show. Shall we see them?

Requestor's Point of View

1. How important is this information to me?
2. What was the context of this presentation to my business?

3. Was the presented hypothesis accurate and well-studied? Does it make sense?

4. How will this help me solve my problem?

5. How can this information be used?

6. Who will use what is being seen here? Where can it be applied?

7. Is this the type of visualization I am used to seeing?

8. Are the actions proposed efficient and the least costly possible?

9. What will be the impact of these actions on my business?

10. In how much time can I expect to see results?

Analyst's Point of View

1. What do I want my audience to know or identify?

2. Does this narrative achieve the point I am trying to make?

3. How does this visualization help make my point?

4. Does the structure of the narrative make sense?

5. Does the narrative fit the data I am showing?

6. Is there a call to action at the end?

7. What do I want the audience to do?

8. Does the data support the actions I am recommending?

9. Will this information be shared?

10. Are there any open ends left?

You have finally finished the data analysis five-step process and are closer to becoming more knowledgeable in the area. As we reach the final chapter of this book, you are going to see that the future is full of opportunities if this is the path you want to trail. Whether you are just starting out, looking for a career change, or maybe just trying to improve your work tools, data will certainly be a part of your future. For this reason, we will wrap up with the opportunities that are emerging in the data analytics market and the things you can do related to the area.

CHAPTER 10:

PREPARING FOR THE NEXT

REVOLUTION IN DATA ANALYTICS

Now that you have been given all the necessary information regarding data analytics and its process, it is time to see what you can expect in the future. It is safe to say that data will continue to play a major role in businesses as they continue to learn and understand its importance. However, with the advent of AI and other emerging tools, it is likely that data, and its ethical uses, will soon take center stage in societal debates.

However, you might be wondering what some of these tendencies and potential work opportunities are in the area. Let me tell you: There are many! For this reason, in this last chapter, we will discuss the convergence of big data, the Internet of Things (IoT), AI, and edge computing in the field of data analytics and how these can fit in with a potential new career. You will be provided with the basic techniques on how to integrate these next-level digital pillars in efficient and accurate data analysis. Let's see what to expect of the future of technology, and data usage in particular, as we look forward to the new tendencies and opportunities data will bring us.

CAREER OPPORTUNITIES IN DATA ANALYTICS

As data becomes more democratic and available to others, it is likely to become a more frequently used tool by businesses. From being able to compile datasets with significant meaning that can help bring insights to being a sort of "compliance" officer regarding the data that will be used by the company, there are many different ways the use of data will help shape our future. "Analytics and BI are already omnipresent across all major business sectors. This demand for insights across all business units is challenging and will continue to challenge analytics leaders to keep up with the demand" (Amarnath, 2023).

Therefore, if you are looking to become a data analyst, there is no better time than now to start looking into the opportunities that are available in the market. Many of the products being released now are based on data, and more and more companies are making decisions based on the data generated and gathered by their clients. It is safe to say that understanding how NLP and text analysis can be done will be essential, especially in this time of social media, reviews, and comments on the internet.

If you desire to change professions or even make your business, the time is *now*. This is the moment where we are still working to understand how these alternatives can be of use to us and what the best approaches to make are. Different alternatives for generating, collecting, managing, analyzing, storing, and visualizing data are being developed, and you can be a part of this change. Regardless if you are using existing software for analysis or if you are going to design your own to generate the result, the use and collection of data will soon become pillars in our society.

Based on this collected data, decision-makers will be able to guide their businesses toward the best path and decide strategies—changing the dynamics of how their companies behaved before, compared to today. The more the world becomes digital and electronic information is gathered, the more the data is available. Those who can understand what this data means, how to use it, and the best ways to understand it will lead the path; they will be in front of others who are just still starting.

THE CONVERGENCE OF TWO WORLDS: HOW DIGITALIZATION IS IMPACTING THE DATA-DRIVEN WORLD

By the root of the word, you might already imagine what digitalization is. In simple words, it is the way that different companies and government agencies, to name a few, are structuring their activities around technology and the digital environment. If you think about a few decades ago, online shopping, scheduling government services, and several other activities did not exist. That is until the internet and, later, COVID-19 arrived and changed the way we saw the world.

Specifically speaking about the period after COVID-19, companies and other services saw the need to better understand their clients and provide online solutions to what they are searching for. When this happened, there was a big boom in how data was identified, used, and gathered. In addition to this, several governments started implementing data protection policies and other laws that had the main objective of protecting customer information.

Before this happened, there was no specific regulation for the matter. It is safe to say that digitalization is affecting the world and that the way our information is processed is no longer, and will likely never, be the same again. Businesses have started looking into how clients behave, their preferences, their opinions, and even what they would like to see based on the data they generate. As a simple example, think about the ads you see when you are on social media or navigating the internet. These are all generated based on the data, or cookies, that are stored in your computer after you enter a certain webpage.

If you allow these cookies to be used, this means that you are giving a company authorization to use your data. Most people don't even realize this, but they are allowing their data and information to be used for the purposes described in the pop-up that appears when you authorize the cookies. Interesting, right? Can you now see how it has become so "easy" to gather data and understand how each of these companies can understand your preferences?

This is the real impact of digitalization in our world. Our data, sometimes even without realizing it, is becoming a part of the "public domain." This helps companies to better understand what their clients want, where they can improve their customer service or products offered, and even forecast the possibilities for the future, including tailor-made products so the manufacturing is more effective. As people see the advantages of using data in their business, we see the digital transformation and the tendencies that are arising and will likely shape the future.

THE FOUR EMERGING PILLARS OF THE DIGITAL WORLD

As we turn our eyes to the future, it is important to understand the impact of emerging technologies that use data, how they might affect the way data is gathered, and how these will be used. In this final section of the book, we are going to briefly look into IoT trends, the much-mentioned AI, the uses of big data, and what edge computing is. You will understand better how these technologies will impact the profession of a data analyst and examples of how they might be used in the data-driven world. Join me in this last journey to understanding what to expect and how you can adapt yourself to these.

Internet of Things

If you haven't heard of IoT, you should know that the term refers to the connection of different devices to the internet. From the furniture in your house to your electronic devices and car. Yes, it does sound amazing! Can you imagine if your bed can understand how to adjust the temperature that suits you best according to the weather or how warm you like to be while sleeping? This is certainly a change that would modify our look into how "normal" devices work.

This is exactly what IoT is about and, if you think about all the information that can be gathered by these devices (or objects) according to a user's behavior, it is possible to see the importance that data will have. This will open the doors to different analysis possibilities and an incredible source of data for companies, governments, and other organizations. By using the vast amount of data points that will be made available and the structure that will be given to them, insights and forecasts will become better, timelier, and more reliable than ever.

If you imagine the amount of data there will be to analyze for all the devices, users, and locations, it is possible to not even visualize what they are. This is because we are talking about a concept that has been gaining popularity in the market and is expected to be predominant in the near future, being widely implemented into different everyday objects. Can you guess what it is? Yes! I am talking about big data and its incredible opportunities to enhance the quality of information we have today.

Big Data

Big data, or incredibly large quantities of data points that make up a dataset, is one of the most mentioned terms in data analytics today. Not only is it helping companies to reduce costs and make better and faster decisions, but it is also enabling them to develop new products that can attract new clients and retain the older ones. Consider the incredible volume of data that is gathered by streaming companies, social media channels, and businesses with large volumes of traffic on their webpages. All this data is not just data, but *big data* because of how much information is gathered.

This means that more and more, data analysts will be dealing with larger datasets. If before establishing a weather prediction there were a few digital sources to establish a pattern, today, we have years of data to help make this happen. As you understand the exponential growth of data available, you will see that this will make the analysis you will carry out both easier and more complex.

At the same time that more data will provide you with incredible possibilities to analyze and understand tendencies, it also means that there will be more datasets to clean and organize according to your needs. If you remember, this is likely where blockchain technology will come in and help this process, especially in creating more reliable data. It is safe to say that as big data grows, so will the opportunities and challenges of data analysis and analysts—and those who identify the best way to use it will have a head start.

Artificial Intelligence

Closely related to the concept of big data is AI, which you already know uses massive amounts of data to train the machine. Once more, data analysts are an important piece of the puzzle, not because they will be able to train machines but because they will also help identify if the outputs given by the machine are true. Regardless if you are using one of the four ML techniques, you will need to understand how data works and how to analyze it to ensure that the process is being correctly carried out.

Already, in 2018, Kibria et al. (2018) mentioned the impact and importance of data analytics in the ML process and the creation of AI software. Where ML and AI are concerned, it is possible to say that "the process of managing and leveraging a massive amount of data, designing algorithms for dynamic and efficient processing of sizable datasets and then exploiting the insights from the data analytics in networks can pose unique challenges" (Kibria et al., 2018). Therefore, those who work and understand how to process and analyze data will be at the center of the discussion.

Regardless if it is in assisting the data scientist to prepare the data to create an AI system or the developer creating an AI machine, the data is the critical point that converges between both. Understanding the steps that are needed to make this happen and how to explain results are essential to management decision-making and ensuring optimal outcomes. This links us to the last matter that should be closely observed: the one of edge computing.

Edge Computing

Edge computing is the process of collecting, processing, and analyzing the information made available by different hubs to ensure that there is an optimal collection of the data that can be used. By understanding what it is, the need for data analysts and the importance of data professionals in this market is clearer. In an area that has been called *edge analytics*, the data analyst who can understand the best applications to ethically source data from will see an increase in scalability and the speed at which data is delivered and gathered.

According to Kaur (2023), "it has similar capabilities as regular analytics, except for the various situations where the analysis is performed. The main difference is that its applications need to work on edge devices with more memory, processing power, or communication impediment." By obtaining data from IoT devices and other hubs, amazing possibilities for real-time analytics will appear, enabling timely and actionable insights and decision-making.

Along with this, the improvements and the infrastructure of internet communications with the arrival of 5G and other powerful technologies will certainly make this possible. It is no longer a matter of what or how, but of *when*. Therefore, being prepared for what is about to come will certainly be a game-changer for you.

Can you think of any applications for your profession or business? It is likely you can, and I can only imagine you are excited to start carrying it out. Data is the future, better yet, the present. The sooner you understand how you can use it to your benefit, the faster you will be able to shape yourself to what future models will be like.

As we move on to the conclusion, I want you to think about everything you have learned. It is even possible that you have already been dealing with a certain data analytics process when you are looking into the sales projections or analysis of the organization you work for—you just did not have a name for it. Well, now you do, you can implement the suggestions you have read in the past 10 chapters to make your process more efficient and reliable. Are you prepared to be a part of the future?

CONCLUSION

Congratulations! You now have all the information you will need to become a successful data analyst, whether you are looking for a new profession or to enhance your skills. Are you excited to begin this new journey in your life? I can bet you are, and I am excited for you and for what the future has in store.

Throughout this book, you have read about the five steps of the data analytics process and learned more about them in detail. These included the importance of establishing the question or problem you are looking to solve, gathering and processing the data, analyzing what you have, and finally putting the results into a story using visualization tools. All of these have been thoroughly described so that you know the exact steps you need to take to ensure that your analysis is reliable.

You have also seen and been presented with the different tools that can be used to carry out the processes. Remember that before choosing any of them, you should see if they fit into your needs and budget. While some tools may cost more than others, they will likely give you more options to manage the data. Many of the providers of the software that have been mentioned offer free demos and testing, so if you are still in doubt, try asking for one! It might help you clear any doubts.

Lastly, you should keep in mind that data is becoming more important by the day and that the future belongs to those who can use its power. And you shouldn't just stop with this book! Embrace continuous learning, stay updated with the latest trends and technologies, and never stop honing your analytical skills. Seize every opportunity to apply your expertise in solving real-world problems and making impactful data-driven decisions that reshape industries and drive success.

I wish you good luck in your new journey, and I hope that this book has helped you understand the next steps needed for you to thrive. You are certainly more than ready to start dabbling with techniques and manage your own data. If you are in doubt, start small—with small datasets and just "play" with the tools you have available. I am sure you will find success in no time. I hope you are successful on your journey, and remember: Focus on the data!

If you found this book helpful in your learning journey, please leave a review. With your feedback, you can help others who are looking for resources to enhance their data analytics knowledge and skills.

REFERENCES

Ale, M. (2019, May 30). *The mindset of a problem-solver*. The Startup. https://medium.com/swlh/the-mindset-of-a-problem-solver-1e3b3ae294e3

Amandi, N. (2023, May 19). *Problem-solving — What every data analyst must have*. Medium. https://amandinancy16.medium.com/problem-solving-what-every-data-analyst-must-have-a7e5dd1088da

Amarnath, R. (2023, January 11). *Five data analytics trends on tap for 2023*. Forbes. https://www.forbes.com/sites/forbestechcouncil/2023/01/11/five-data-analytics-trends-on-tap-for-2023/?sh=33ddef196cfd

Andersson, R. (2016, April 15). *4 characteristics of data-driven organizations—and how to get started*. IBM Sverige – THINK Bloggen. https://www.ibm.com/blogs/think/se-sv/2016/04/15/4-characteristics-of-data-driven-organizations-and-how-to-get-started/

Anello, E. (2023, August 3). *7 steps to mastering data cleaning and preprocessing techniques*. KDnuggets. https://www.kdnuggets.com/2023/08/7-steps-mastering-data-cleaning-preprocessing-techniques.html

Atha, H. (2019, April). *7 qualities your big data visualization tools absolutely must have and 10 tools that have them*. KDnuggets. https://www.kdnuggets.com/2019/04/7-qualities-big-data-visualization-tools.html

Bajaj, P. (2023, April 18). *Reinforcement learning.* GeeksforGeeks. https://www.geeksforgeeks.org/what-is-reinforcement-learning/

Bartley, K. (2020, March 27). *Big data statistics: How much data is there in the world?* Rivery. https://rivery.io/blog/big-data-statistics-how-much-data-is-there-in-the-world/

Bhat, A. (2019, June 27). *Data collection methods: Definition, examples and sources.* QuestionPro. https://www.questionpro.com/blog/data-collection-methods/

Byjus. (n.d.). *Datasets.* https://byjus.com/maths/data-sets/#Properties

blog-manager. (2021, September 28). *3 data storage methods for businesses: How to choose.* CT Link Systems. https://www.ctlink.com.ph/data-storage-methods-businesses/

Burnham, K. (2021, December 8). *Data analytics vs. data science: A breakdown.* Graduate Blog. https://graduate.northeastern.edu/resources/data-analytics-vs-data-science/

Calzon, B. (2023, May 3). *Your modern business guide to data analysis methods and techniques.* Datapine. https://www.datapine.com/blog/data-analysis-methods-and-techniques

Chapman, C. (2019). *A complete overview of the best data visualization tools.* Toptal Design Blog. https://www.toptal.com/designers/data-visualization/data-visualization-tools

Cote, C. (2021a, October 19). *4 types of data analytics to improve decision-making.* Harvard Business School Online. https://online.hbs.edu/blog/post/types-of-data-analysis

Cote, C. (2021b, December 2). *7 data collection methods in business analytics.* Harvard Business School. https://online.hbs.edu/blog/post/data-collection-methods

Crabtree, M. (2023, July). *What is machine learning? Definition, types, tools & more*. Data Camp. https://www.datacamp.com/blog/what-is-machine-learning

Dabbura, I. (2018, September 17). *K-means clustering: Algorithm, applications, evaluation methods, and drawbacks*. Medium. https://towardsdatascience.com/k-means-clustering-algorithm-applications-evaluation-methods-and-drawbacks-aa03e644b48a

Datacollector. (2023, August 4). *4 recommended data cleaning tools*. Medium. https://medium.com/@support_44319/4-recommended-data-cleaning-tools-80f2b3a2813e

Dieckmann, J. (2023, February 14). *Introduction to ICA: Independent component analysis*. Medium. https://towardsdatascience.com/introduction-to-ica-independent-component-analysis-b2c3c4720cd9

El Shatby, S. (2022, June 1). *The history of data: From ancient times to modern day*. 365 Data Science. https://365datascience.com/trending/history-of-data/

Erwin, R. W. (2015). Data literacy: Real-world learning through problem-solving with data sets. *American Secondary Education, 43*(2), 18–26.

Frankenfield, J. (2023, August 9). *Data analytics: What it is, how it's used, and 4 basic techniques*. Investopedia. https://www.investopedia.com/terms/d/data-analytics.asp

GeeksforGeeks. (2023, September 25). *Getting started with classification*. https://www.geeksforgeeks.org/getting-started-with-classification/

Ghorakavi, V. (2023, September 5). *Types of regression techniques in ML*. GeeksforGeeks. https://www.geeksforgeeks.org/types-of-regression-techniques/

Ginsberg, C. (2023, September 19). *Top 8 tools for data cleaning in 2023*. Classes near Me Blog.

https://www.nobledesktop.com/classes-near-me/blog/top-tools-for-data-cleaning

Guinness, H. (2023, August 3). *The 5 best data collection tools in 2023*. Zapier. https://zapier.com/blog/best-data-collection-apps/

Gupta, G. (2018, April 13). *Blockchain and data analytics*. LinkedIn. https://www.linkedin.com/pulse/blockchain-data-analytics-gaurav-gupta/

Haan, K. (2023a, September 18). *The best data analytics tools of 2023*. Forbes Advisor. https://www.forbes.com/advisor/business/software/best-data-analytics-tools/

Haan, K. (2023b, October 2). *The best data visualization tools of 2023*. Forbes Advisor. https://www.forbes.com/advisor/business/software/best-data-visualization-tools/

Halder, N. (2023, March 8). *What is time series forecasting in the context of business analytics?* Analyst's Corner. https://medium.com/analysts-corner/what-is-time-series-forecasting-in-context-of-business-analytics-c143b1885d3a

Heavy.AI. (n.d.). *Real time analytics*. https://www.heavy.ai/technical-glossary/real-time-analytics

Herrity, J. (2023, August 1). *Problem-solving skills: Definitions and examples*. Indeed.com. https://www.indeed.com/career-advice/resumes-cover-letters/problem-solving-skills

Hill, J. (2023, June 5). *Data vs information: What's the difference?* Bloomfire. https://bloomfire.com/blog/data-vs-information/

Hillier, W. (2023a, May 31). *A step-by-step guide to the data analysis process*. CareerFoundry. https://careerfoundry.com/en/blog/data-analytics/the-data-analysis-process-step-by-step/

Hillier, W. (2023b, September 14). *What is data cleaning and why does it matter?* CareerFoundry.

https://careerfoundry.com/en/blog/data-analytics/what-is-data-cleaning/

Horsch, A. (2021, May 24). *Hypothesis testing for data scientists.* Medium. https://towardsdatascience.com/hypothesis-testing-for-data-scientists-everything-you-need-to-know-8c36ddde4cd2

IBM. (n.d.). *What is data storage?* https://www.ibm.com/topics/data-storage

Joshi, M., & Dubbewar, A. (2021). Review on business intelligence, its tools and techniques, and advantages and disadvantages. *International Journal of Engineering Research & Technology (IJERT), 10*(12). https://doi.org/10.17577/IJERTV10IS120167

Kaplan, E. H. (2011). *Operations research and intelligence analysis.* National Academies Press.

Kappagantula, S. (2023, September 12). *Top 10 data analytics tools you need to know in 2023.* Edureka. https://www.edureka.co/blog/top-10-data-analytics-tools/

Kaur, J. (2023, June 13). *Edge computing data analytics | The complete guide.* Xenon Stack. https://www.xenonstack.com/blog/edge-computing-data-analytics

Kautsar, E. M. (2021, March 30). *Six problem types of data analyst.* Medium. https://emkautsar.medium.com/six-problem-types-of-data-analyst-f54e39f6e68c

Kelley, K. (2023, August 4). *What is data analysis? Process, methods, and types explained.* Simplilearn. https://www.simplilearn.com/data-analysis-methods-process-types-article

Kibria, M. G., Nguyen, K., Villardi, G. P., Zhao, O., Ishizu, K., & Kojima, F. (2018). Big data analytics, machine learning, and artificial intelligence in next-generation wireless networks. *IEEE Access, 6,* 32328–32338. https://doi.org/10.1109/access.2018.2837692

Korstanje, J. (2021a, September 28). *The FP growth algorithm.* Medium. https://towardsdatascience.com/the-fp-growth-algorithm-1ffa20e839b8

Korstanje, J. (2021b, September 29). *The ECLAT algorithm.* Medium. https://towardsdatascience.com/the-eclat-algorithm-8ae3276d2d17

Kumari, R. (2021, May 12). *4 types of data in statistics.* Analytics Steps. https://www.analyticssteps.com/blogs/4-types-data-statistics

Lawrence, A. (2019, July 24). *Data analytics and machine learning: Let's talk basics.* Answer Rocket. https://www.answerrocket.com/data-analytics-machine-learning/

Lee, I. (2023, March 10). *Data scientists: Problem solvers first, algorithm wizards second.* Medium. https://towardsdatascience.com/data-scientists-problem-solvers-first-algorithm-wizards-second-93daa031d131

Lewis, A. (2023, August 24). *Problem solving: The mark of an independent employee.* Target Jobs. https://targetjobs.co.uk/careers-advice/skills-for-getting-a-job/problem-solving-mark-independent-employee

Lib Quotes. (n.d.). *Philip B. Crosby quote.* https://libquotes.com/philip-b-crosby/quote/lbi9d5w

Liza, U. (2019, July). *How to use data collection tools for market research.* QuestionPro. https://www.questionpro.com/blog/data-collection-tools/

Lobel, G. (n.d.). *7 analytics best practices that guarantee success.* Toucan. https://www.toucantoco.com/en/blog/10-analytics-best-practices-that-guarantee-success

Mangalgiaishwarya2. (2023, April 6). *Six steps of data analysis process.* GeeksforGeeks. https://www.geeksforgeeks.org/six-steps-of-data-analysis-process/

Marr, B. (2021, July 2). *Comparing data visualization software: Here are the 7 best tools*. Bernard Marr. https://bernardmarr.com/comparing-data-visualization-software-here-are-the-7-best-tools/

Maryville University. (2021, August 2). *Data science vs. data analytics: What's the difference?* https://online.maryville.edu/blog/data-science-vs-data-analytics/

McFarland, A. (2022, April 27). *10 best data cleaning tools*. Unite. https://www.unite.ai/10-best-data-cleaning-tools/

Menon, K. (2023, October 26). *An introduction to the types of machine learning*. Simplilearn. https://www.simplilearn.com/tutorials/machine-learning-tutorial/types-of-machine-learning

Microsoft Azure. (n.d.). *What is a data lake?* Microsoft. https://azure.microsoft.com/en-us/resources/cloud-computing-dictionary/what-is-a-data-lake/

Monno, L. (2020, October 4). *Best practices in data analytics*. Medium. https://towardsdatascience.com/best-practices-in-data-analytics-cfcb2baebcb3

Nupurjain3. (2023, October 4). *Sources of data collection | Primary and secondary sources*. GeeksforGeeks. https://www.geeksforgeeks.org/sources-of-data-collection-primary-and-secondary-sources/

O'Toole, T. (2020, March 2). *What's the best approach to data analytics?* Harvard Business Review. https://hbr.org/2020/03/whats-the-best-approach-to-data-analytics

Ot, A. (2023, February 9). *What is raw data? Definition, examples, & processing steps*. Datamation. https://www.datamation.com/big-data/raw-data/

Pitsillides, Y. (2019, July 10). *The skills you'll need to be a great data analyst*. Jarmany. https://www.jarmany.com/what-we-think/blog/the-skills-youll-need-to-be-a-great-data-analyst/

Pykes, K. (2023, March). *Introduction to unsupervised learning*. Data Camp. https://www.datacamp.com/blog/introduction-to-unsupervised-learning

Reilly, J. (2023, April 5). *7 best data cleaning tools for analysts in 2023*. Akkio. https://www.akkio.com/post/data-cleansing-tools

Repustate Inc. (2022, December 15). *Top 10 data cleaning techniques for better results*. https://www.repustate.com/blog/data-cleaning-techniques/

Ribecca, S. (2019). *List view*. The Data Visualization Catalogue. https://datavizcatalogue.com/home_list.html

Roberts, C. (2019, November 3). *How blockchain technology helps to improve data quality and security*. Medium. https://chrisrob978.medium.com/how-blockchain-technology-helps-to-improve-data-quality-and-security-d4701aa16241

Robin. (2022, October 21). *What to consider when choosing a data visualization tool*. Executive Levels. https://www.executivelevels.com/what-to-consider-when-choosing-a-data-visualization-tool/

Sarfin, R. L. (2022, November 2). *5 characteristics of data quality*. Precisely. https://www.precisely.com/blog/data-quality/5-characteristics-of-data-quality

Smith, B. (2022, December 7). *12 useful data analysis methods to use on your next project*. Springboard Blog. https://www.springboard.com/blog/data-analytics/data-analysis-methods-and-techniques/

Stackpole, B. (2020, September 22). *10 best practices for analytics success (including 3 you can't ignore)*. MIT Sloan. https://mitsloan.mit.edu/ideas-made-to-matter/10-best-practices-analytics-success-including-3-you-cant-ignore

Stevens, E. (2023, May 11). *What are the different types of data analysis?* CareerFoundry. https://careerfoundry.com/en/blog/data-analytics/different-types-of-data-analysis/

Stitch. (n.d.). *Top 24 tools for data analysis and how to decide between them.* https://www.stitchdata.com/resources/data-analysis-tools/

Swaminathan, N. (2008, January 25). *What are we thinking when we (try to) solve problems?* Scientific American. https://www.scientificamerican.com/article/what-are-we-thinking-when/

Tableau. (n.d.). *Best practices for telling great stories.* https://help.tableau.com/current/pro/desktop/en-us/story_best_practices.htm

Tableau. (2022). *Data cleaning: The benefits and steps to creating and using clean data.* https://www.tableau.com/learn/articles/what-is-data-cleaning

Taylor, T. (2022, December 7). *What are the key skills every data analyst needs?* CareerFoundry. https://careerfoundry.com/en/blog/data-analytics/what-are-the-key-skills-every-data-analyst-needs/

The Upwork Team(2022, November 4). *The best data cleaning techniques for preparing your data.* Upwork. https://www.upwork.com/resources/data-cleaning-techniques

Valcheva, S. (2017, August 30). *7 best data collection tools & software: For accurate analysis.* Intellspot. https://www.intellspot.com/data-collection-tools/

Visium. (2023, May 24). *Data storytelling: The power of narrative in data analysis.* LinkedIn. https://www.linkedin.com/pulse/data-storytelling-power-narrative-analysis-visium-sa/

Warudkar, H. (2021, June 9). *What is machine learning and machine learning techniques: A complete guide.* Express Analytics. https://www.expressanalytics.com/blog/machine-learning-techniques-guide/

Williams, K. (2023, January 2). *12 best data collection tools of 2023.* SurveySparrow. https://surveysparrow.com/blog/best-data-collection-tools/

FUNDAMENTALS OF ARTIFICIAL INTELLIGENCE & LARGE LANGUAGE MODELS

Master Prompt Engineering and Monetize the Power of Language Processing

---

Russell Dawson

INTRODUCTION

Since the introduction of ChatGPT, in 2022, the world has undergone a significant technological transformation. This has resulted in artificial intelligence (AI) and large language models (LLMs) becoming popular and a constant in our lives. In 2025, AI is not just a technological advancement—it is a force reshaping our daily lives, businesses, and society at an unprecedented pace.

According to the "Stanford AI Index Report (2024)," over 80% of Fortune 500 companies now integrate AI into their operations, while 97% of mobile users already interact with AI-powered applications daily (*The State of AI*, 2024). The global AI market, valued at approximately $380 billion in 2022, is projected to reach $1.3 trillion by 2029 (*51 Artificial Intelligence Statistics*, 2024). These numbers reflect the technology's explosive growth and adoption across industries.

The effects of this revolution can be seen in almost every industry. In healthcare, AI algorithms now detect diseases with accuracy, rivaling human specialists. Financial institutions use AI to process millions of transactions while detecting fraud in real time. Education systems employ adaptive learning platforms that can personalize the content for each student. Even creative industries have embraced AI, with tools that assist in content creation, design, and music composition.

At the same time, this impact extends beyond large corporations. Small businesses and entrepreneurs are increasingly leveraging AI tools for customer service, marketing optimization, and operational efficiency. Studies show that companies implementing AI solutions report an average 25% increase in operational efficiency and a 20% reduction in operational costs (Matleena S & Brian, 2024). Still, according to the report, the impact of AI in business is set to increase, with 20% of the tech budget being allocated to AI and 58% of the companies looking to increase their investments in the technology.

If these statistics and technical terms seem overwhelming, don't worry. You are not alone. Many people find AI and LLMs intimidating at first glance. That is precisely why this book was written: to help demystify these technologies through clear and practical explanations you can understand, as well as to show how AI can help you with real-world examples. Whether you are a business professional, student, or simply curious about AI, this guide will help you understand how to harness these powerful tools.

By reading this book, you will

- have a clear understanding of AI fundamentals and how LLMs work

- obtain the practical knowledge to evaluate and implement AI solutions

- gather insights on AI's potential impact on diverse fields

- harness the skills to stay competitive in an AI-driven world

- gain confidence in discussing and working with AI technologies

Think about it this way: The AI revolution is not slowing down, quite the contrary—it's accelerating. Companies are looking to invest more in AI, and researchers are increasing their efforts to make it more powerful. Things are constantly changing, and you will miss out on the latest developments. At the same time, by understanding these technologies now, you're not just learning for the future but also preparing to be an active participant in shaping it.

As you get ready to start this discovery adventure into the world of AI and LLMs, rest assured that by the end of the book, you will have all the foundational knowledge to build upon. The future is AI-powered, and this book is your guide to understanding and thriving in it. If you are ready to see the world as many do today, get your computer to explore as we go and find a comfortable place to sit. You are about to start a learning experience that will forever change how you see the world and interact with technology. Shall we begin?

CHAPTER 1:
INTRODUCTION TO AI

Whenever your smartphone recognizes your face, your junk mail is separated from what really matters, or you receive that perfect recommendation for a movie night, that is AI at work. These everyday experiences and most of our interactions with technology today are powered by these intelligent systems. As you read this, AI systems are diagnosing diseases, driving cars, trading stocks, and even creating art and music. But what exactly makes these systems *intelligent?* What characteristics make machines able to work similar to how a human does?

In this chapter, we will decode the fundamental concepts of AI, moving beyond the buzzwords and jargon to understand how it actually works. For example, did you know that there is more than one type of AI? As you read, you will explore its different types, from simple rule-based programs to sophisticated neural networks, and examine how machine learning (ML) and deep learning (DL) revolutionized what computers can do. As you explore this technology and its applications, you will gain a broader understanding of how AI already plays a major role in our lives, from healthcare to transportation and entertainment, and learn to distinguish between AI fact and fiction.

Whether you are a business professional looking to implement AI solutions or simply curious about this incredible technology, you will find the information you need to build the foundation to understand why AI is considered the next Industrial Revolution.

WHAT IS AI?

AI represents humans' attempt to make machines think like them. In other words, it is the idea of recreating the human thought process in machines so that they can function as a human would. AI is a branch of computer science that is focused on building smart machines that carry out the most varied tasks, such as recognizing speech, making decisions, and understanding patterns. While these abilities were usually understood to be exclusive to the human mind, AI came to change this.

The concept of AI emerged in Ancient Greece when philosophers discussed the ability of objects that could think. Much closer to the present, in the 1950s, computer scientist Alan Turing proposed the Turing Test to determine if a machine could exhibit intelligent behavior that could not be distinguished from a human. This sparked a scientific revolution that continues today. While early AI systems were simple rule-based programs, that would function according to a set of preestablished parameters, modern AI has evolved into sophisticated systems that can learn from new experiences and adapt to new situations.

The main idea behind AI development is not just to replicate human intelligence but also to enhance and extend our capabilities. Today's AI systems excel at processing vast amounts of data, recognizing complex patterns, and making fast decisions, areas in which humans still have limitations. One example of this application is in medicine, since while a human radiologist might analyze dozens of medical images per day, an AI system can process thousands, thus supporting (not replacing) medical professionals in their diagnostic work.

But what sets AI apart from other computer systems? That is a good question. The main difference between a simple computer program and an AI application is the latter's ability to learn and improve from experience. While conventional software follows fixed rules, AI systems can adjust their behavior based on new data and outcomes. This adaptability makes AI particularly valuable for tasks where rules are difficult to explicitly define or where conditions frequently change.

This is the incredible magic of modern AI: It achieves these capabilities through multiple approaches ranging from basic statistical analysis to complex neural networks that mimic the human brain's structure, which you will learn more about further along in the chapter. These systems process information through layers of interconnected nodes, each contributing to the final output, regardless of the task.

But let's not get ahead of ourselves. The first thing you should understand is AI's fundamental nature, which helps explain its transformative impact across industries. AI is not just a tool for automation; it's a technology that augments human intelligence, enabling us to solve previously unsolvable problems and discover new possibilities. To start off, let's understand the different types of AI and how they are used today.

TYPES OF AI

Understanding the differences between AI systems can be confusing at times. To make it easier, you should think about these systems based on two general classifications: capability- and functionality-based AI. Let's see what each of them are and how they differ.

Capability-Based AI

These refer to what the AI system can *do*. It is divided into three subcategories: narrow or weak AI (artificial narrow intelligence [ANI]), general or strong AI (artificial general intelligence [AGI]), and artificial superintelligence (ASI). Here is a breakdown with a description and examples of each:

- **ANI:** Excels at specific tasks while lacking a broader understanding. This is the case when you unlock your phone with face recognition. When this happens, the system can perfectly recognize your features but knows nothing about your identity or preferences. Similarly, when you play chess against a computer, it might make masterful moves but cannot transfer that strategic thinking to another game or engage in conversation about its choices. These systems, despite their limitations, power much of the technology we use today. Think about how spam filters protect your email inbox—they are remarkably effective at identifying unwanted messages but cannot understand their content or context.

- **AGI:** AI systems might seem versatile, but they are actually combining multiple narrow AI systems. On the other hand, with AGI, you would be able to have a conversation with the computer about philosophy or ask it to help you solve complex mathematical equations. They are so versatile that they can compose music and design buildings, all while understanding their interconnection. In this case, AGI would match human-level intelligence across all cognitive domains, learning and adapting like a human mind. At the same time, systems such as these do not yet exist but are currently in development. Think of C-3PO from *Star Wars*: a machine that can truly understand context, independently learn new skills, and engage in genuine humanlike reasoning.

- **ASI:** This technology represents intelligence that would surpass human capabilities in every conceivable way. This means it could be a system that could solve climate change while simultaneously discovering new physics principles and revolutionizing healthcare—all in a couple of days or hours. While this might sound like a science fiction movie, it represents the ultimate potential and risks of AI development. Systems such as these would process information faster than the entire human population combined while demonstrating creativity and insight beyond our comprehension.

Functionality-Based AI

These refer to how AI systems process information and make decisions. They are categorized on their ability to handle data, learn, and interact with their environment. They are broken down into the following four categories:

- **Reactive AI:** Think about a traffic light system that adjusts the signal timing based on current traffic flow. It does not remember past traffic patterns or learn over time; it simply reacts to present conditions. This is reactive AI and the most popular example is IBM's Deep Blue chess computer, the first of its kind. This computer operated similarly, analyzing each board position fresh without referring to past games or learning from experience. While they might seem like limited technology, these systems are highly skilled performers who perfectly execute their tasks but cannot explain their methods or adapt to new situations.

- **Limited memory AI:** An easily identifiable example of this type of AI may be lying in the palm of your hand. This is because your phone's navigation app is one of the most relatable examples of the technology. It does not just react to current traffic conditions but learns from historical data patterns and your previous routes to suggest better paths. Modern self-driving cars can take this further, combining real-time sensor data with learned experience about how other vehicles behave, weather conditions affecting driving, and how to navigate complex intersections. These systems demonstrate how AI can use past experiences to make better present decisions.

- **Theory of mind AI:** These systems are purely theoretical, but it would be similar to having a healthcare robot that can monitor vital signs and recognize when the patient feels anxious. When this happens, it would be able to adjust its communication style accordingly and build rapport over time. This type of technology still hasn't been achieved, but some social robots being worked on by developers are taking steps in this direction. To make them fully functional, the system would need to understand that humans have thoughts and emotions that influence their behavior, capabilities crucial for meaningful human–AI interaction.

- **Self-aware AI:** The most advanced theoretical type of AI would be a system that is self-conscious and has awareness comparable to humans. This would be like the AI from the movie *Her*, a system that thinks, feels, and understands its own existence, forming genuine emotional connections. Technology such as this is still only in the speculation field and helps raise questions and debates on the nature of consciousness in humans itself.

Understanding these AIs allows you to identify the type of technology you are dealing with. While most applications today use narrow, reactive, or limited memory AI, the field continues to rapidly evolve. This evolution is largely driven by advances in ML and DL, powerful approaches that enable AI systems to improve through experience. In the next section, we will explore how these learning technologies work and why they have become the force behind the most impressive achievements in the industry.

MACHINE LEARNING AND DEEP LEARNING

To understand modern AI's capabilities, it is essential to explore two key technologies that power most of these applications: ML and DL. These approaches have revolutionized how computers learn and solve problems, moving beyond traditional programming systems that can improve through experience.

Machine Learning: Teaching Computers to Learn

Suppose you want to teach a child to recognize cats. Instead of listing every feature of the animal, such as whiskers, pointy ears, and fur, you would show them many pictures of cats until they can learn to identify one on their own. ML works similarly. Rather than programming explicit rules, the computer is fed large amounts of data and lets them discover patterns.

Let's use the email spam filter again as an example. Traditional programming would require manually writing rules that would identify the messages as spam. ML instead analyzes millions of emails marked as spam or not spam, learning to identify patterns that humans might not even notice. Over time, this system improves as it sees more examples, just as a person would get better at spotting spam with experience.

This approach transformed many applications we use today. Netflix, for example, recommends shows based on viewing patterns, virtual assistants understand different accents by learning from millions of samples, and fraud detection systems protect our credit cards by learning what suspicious transactions look like. In Chapter 3, you will learn more about how these learning processes take place and their different types. In the meantime, read on to discover what DL is and how it takes ML to the next level.

Deep Learning: Inspired by the Human Brain

DL takes ML further by mimicking how our brains process information. Just as our brains use neuron networks to understand complex patterns, DL uses artificial neural networks with multiple layers to solve increasingly sophisticated problems. This layered approach enabled breakthroughs in areas that were previously challenging for computers. Language translation, for example, now captures subtle context and meaning, medical imaging systems detect diseases with remarkable accuracy, and autonomous vehicles can interpret complex road situations in real time.

Consider how you recognize a friend's face. Your brain does not consciously think *oval face, brown eyes,* or *curved nose.* It simultaneously processes all these features through neuron layers. DL systems work similarly, breaking down complex tasks into layers of similar patterns. When identifying objects in photos, early layers might detect basic edges and shapes, middle layers combine these into features like eyes or wheels, and deep layers assemble these features into complete objects like faces or cars.

While these are the basic concepts of ML and DL, you will learn more about how this learning process takes place further into the book, gaining insight into how they learn and improve. In them, you will explore the training process, different learning approaches, and how these systems handle new situations. For now, let's look into areas in which AI is currently making a significant impact, affecting different industries and aspects of our lives.

WHERE IS AI USED TODAY?

So far, you have seen how AI is being used in email spam filters, streaming services, voice assistants, and even self-driving cars. However, AI has evolved well beyond these applications. While the previously seen examples have become everyday conveniences, their influence stretches much further, quietly transforming industries in ways that many people are unaware of. From agriculture to law enforcement, AI is enhancing decision-making, improving efficiency, and unlocking new possibilities. Read on to discover what they are.

- **Agriculture:** AI is being used in agriculture with precision farming techniques that improve yields while reducing waste. Smart drones and sensors collect real-time data on soil health, weather conditions, and crop growth. Advanced AI algorithms analyze this data to recommend optimal planting, fertilization, and irrigation schedules. Additionally, these systems are used to monitor livestock health by tracking behavior patterns and detecting early illness signs.

- **Fashion:** By analyzing vast datasets of consumer preferences, social media activity, and cultural shifts, AI is being used to forecast future trends that can impact the industry. Companies are also using the technology to create custom clothing designs tailored to individual body measurements, preferences, and sustainability criteria. AI-driven virtual try-ons are enhancing online shopping experiences by helping customers visualize how garments and makeup will look before purchasing.

- **Art conservation and restoration:** AI has become an essential tool in aiding in the preservation of cultural heritage by analyzing artwork and detecting deterioration that may not be visible to the human eye. ML models can predict material degradation over time and suggest conservation strategies. In some cases, the technology has been used to digitally restore damaged or incomplete art pieces, offering a glimpse into lost masterpieces.

- **Wildlife conservation:** Organizations and governments are currently deploying AI in wildlife reserves to prevent poaching. Cameras and sensors equipped with AI algorithms can detect human presence in restricted areas and alert park rangers in real time. These systems can also be used to track and study animal populations, helping researchers monitor endangered species and their habitats.

- **Journalism:** AI technology is being used to assist journalists by generating news summaries and even writing basic articles such as sports scores, financial reports, and weather updates. This allows the journalist to focus on in-depth investigative reporting and complex stories. At the same time, despite AI's growing role, human editorial oversight remains essential to ensure accuracy and ethical reporting.

- **Architecture:** Have you ever imagined living in a house that was designed by AI? Today, this is possible! AI is enabling generative design, where algorithms create thousands of design options based on specific parameters such as space constraints, material usage, and environmental factors. By using it, architects can choose the best designs or refine them further. This approach helps speed up the design process and results in more efficient and sustainable structures.

- **Entertainment:** In this industry, AI is used to assist with scriptwriting by generating plot ideas, dialogue, and character development suggestions. While these tools can help writers overcome creative blocks, the final script always requires a human touch to ensure depth, originality, and emotional connection. It is also being used to create background scenarios and help filmmakers create more realistic special effects.

- **Legal:** This sector is using AI to automate tedious tasks such as contract review and conducting due diligence during mergers and acquisitions. When correctly employed, it can quickly identify potential risks, flag unusual clauses, and ensure compliance with regulations. At the same time, as with many of the other industries, it is essential to have lawyers or paralegals review the work to interpret complex legal nuances and make judgment calls.

- **Logistics:** AI technology is fueling transportation platforms to help optimize delivery routes by analyzing traffic patterns, weather conditions, and road closures. This helps reduce delivery times and lowers fuel consumption and operational costs. To take it even further, AI can predict vehicle maintenance needs, preventing costly breakdowns and delays.

- **Mental health:** While AI can be used as a virtual therapist to provide support for people with anxiety, depression, and stress 24/7, this is a use that needs caution. Access to mental health resources and guidance on cognitive behavioral therapy exercises are a few of its benefits. At the same time, while helpful, they are designed to complement, not replace, human therapists.

- **Mining:** To ensure that mining activities are safer and operations are enhanced, AI is employed in the industry to predict equipment failures before they occur and monitor working conditions for potential hazards. By analyzing data from sensors embedded in the machinery, AI helps reduce downtime and prevent accidents.

- **Retail:** If you have ever noticed the increase or decrease of a product's price on a website, you are experiencing AI use first-hand. Retailers are using the technology to implement dynamic pricing models that adjust product prices in real time based on factors such as demand, competition, and customer behavior. This ensures optimal pricing strategies that maximize sales and profit margins.

- **Forensics:** AI is being used in forensic science to reconstruct crime scenes using data from evidence collected on-site. ML models can simulate scenarios and provide insights that help investigators piece together what happened. Finally, the use of technology allows investigations to be faster and more accurate.

- **Marine biology:** Underwater drones are being used to map the ocean floor with greater precision than ever before. These systems also collect data on marine life, underwater ecosystems, and geological features, aiding in environmental research and conservation efforts.

- **Education:** This is another area that is being greatly transformed by AI. In education, AI is transforming teaching by creating personalized learning experiences tailored to each student's pace, strengths, and weaknesses. Intelligent tutoring systems can adapt content based on real-time performance, helping students grasp difficult concepts more effectively.

The examples you have seen show the vast and surprising ways AI is being used today. From protecting wildlife to revolutionizing fashion and forensics, it may seem that AI's potential is limitless. However, it is essential to remember that while AI can automate and enhance many tasks, it still requires human oversight. Ethical considerations, critical thinking, and empathy are elements that only human beings can provide. As you continue to learn about AI, it is crucial to identify the right balance between AI-driven automation and human intervention.

And where do tools like ChatGPT come in? This is an excellent question that you will start to explore in the next chapter. In it, you will learn more about LLMs, the technology behind the most popular models used today. Get ready to see how these models work, what makes them different from other AI types, and how they are trained to generate humanlike language.

CHAPTER 2:
UNDERSTANDING LARGE
LANGUAGE MODELS

When ChatGPT burst onto the scene in 2022, it sparked a global conversation about AI and its capabilities. The tool uses a technology known as LLMs, which are sophisticated AI systems that can understand and generate humanlike text. These models transformed how we interact with computers, making it possible to have natural conversations with machines, generate creative content, and solve complex problems using simple dialogue.

In this chapter, you will learn more about LLMs and explore why they represent such a significant leap forward in AI technology. You will learn what makes these systems different from traditional AI, understand its key components, and discover how they are reshaping industries in the market. With the information you are about to see, you will have the essential knowledge to understand and later use and engage in the LLM revolution.

WHAT ARE LLMS?

Imagine you have an assistant at work who has read most of the text available on the internet and can talk about almost any subject. This is what an LLM is: an AI system trained on massive amounts of data that can understand and generate humanlike language. The "large" in

LLMs refers to the amount of data they are trained on and their complexity. Modern LLM models such as GPT-4 have processed more text than any human could read in multiple lifetimes. This extensive training allows them to understand context, recognize patterns, and generate responses across multiple topics and tasks.

To make it easier, think of an LLM as a superpowered prediction engine for language. When you type in "The weather today is," the model predicts what words might naturally come next. This is a similar feature to what you have on your phone and are typing a text; based on your writing style, habits, and common words, it determines what the next word you will type will be. The difference is that LLMs have a much greater capacity and operate at a much more sophisticated level. This ability comes from analyzing billions of examples of human writing, including books, articles, websites, conversations, and several other sources available on the internet. Some of these sources include

- books and academic papers
- websites and news articles
- social media conversations
- code repositories
- online forums and discussions
- educational materials
- legal documents
- technical documentation

All these are part of the training process that helps LLMs understand different writing styles, topics, and contexts. For example, when you ask an LLM to explain quantum physics, it can adjust its language depending on whether you are a child or a physics student. Similarly, it will cover the topic based on the angle you are looking for and the instructions you give it, which are known as *prompts*. The machine will analyze this information and, based on the feedback it receives and the follow-up questions you ask, will determine the best approach or answer to give you.

Let's use an example of how children learn once again to understand this process. As a child, you did not start to learn how to speak by learning and memorizing grammar rules. You likely learned by listening to others speak, reading books, and gradually picking up patterns. You paid attention to the order in which others spoke their works and mimicked it or were corrected until you got it right. LLMs learn similarly but at a massive scale. They analyze patterns in text: which words often appear together, how sentences are structured, and how ideas connect across paragraphs. When this learning takes place, it allows the machine to

- convert complex technical documents into simple explanations
- answer questions about specific topics
- write creative content
- help with coding
- translate between languages
- summarize long documents
- engage in natural conversations

While LLMs have all these capabilities, one thing that is essential to understand is that these LLMs don't actually "think" like humans do. They are simply a sophisticated pattern recognition system that can generate appropriate responses based on their training. They don't have real-world experience or consciousness; they are simply processing patterns in text data in a sophisticated way. No matter how powerful they are, LLMs are still an example of ANI that you have seen in the previous chapter, as they have an incredible capacity to work with language-related texts but cannot understand or reason like humans. LLMs are a result of the combination of reactive and limited memory machines, responding to current inputs while drawing on their training data. This helps explain their impressive capabilities and limitations.

On the other hand, what sets LLMs apart from other AI systems is their unique approach to processing and generating language. Unlike traditional AI programs that follow strict rules or make simple predictions, LLMs can engage with language in ways that seem remarkably humanlike. This differentiation is essential to have a deeper understanding of its potential and challenges, which we are about to explore next.

HOW ARE LLMS DIFFERENT FROM OTHER AIS?

While traditional AI systems are like highly skilled specialists trained for specific tasks, LLMs are more versatile, like conversation partners. In the first, it would be like a chess master player who can beat opponents but does not know how to explain how or why he did it. In the latter, it is like talking to a friend who can speak multiple languages and adapt to different topics or demonstrate creativity. The second clearly has an incredible advantage over the first.

In real-life applications, traditional AI could be represented in Apple's Face ID, which can only be used to unlock your phone, voice assistants that can only respond to specific commands, or autocorrect, which can only fix spelling mistakes. With LLMs, it would be telling the machine, *Hey, can you write an email to my boss asking about taking tomorrow off because I am feeling ill with the appropriate tone and formatting?* Once this has been entered, the machine would follow the instructions, creating a professional email with an explanation and the correct tone.

This flexibility comes from how LLMs process language. Unlike traditional AI systems that follow predefined rules or decision trees, LLMs understand context and can generate appropriate responses based on the situation. This means, for example, they can adjust the language from a text from casual, to technical or simple, based on the context. With the same application, you can write a professional business email and a playful children's story. These programs can also handle ambiguity and generate creative content, significant advances to the predefined templates other AIs have, giving them the ability to create stories or write poems.

Suppose you are planning on going on vacation. This is how each of these technologies might help you:

Traditional AI	LLMs
Book flights and hotels from a database.	Suggest destinations based on your interests and budget.
Predict weather patterns.	Create a personalized itinerary based on your preferences.
Show restaurant ratings and menus.	Recommend local cuisine and cultural experiences.
Can only convert specific phrases between languages.	Can help you communicate effectively by providing contextual translations.
Send templated messages with prerecorded requests.	Allows you to send and request special requests with personalized messages.

As you can see, LLMs have an incredible versatility that other systems do not have, allowing them to be a powerful ally in carrying out different tasks. At the same time, this versatility comes with its own complexity. To understand how LLMs achieve their capabilities, it is essential to have some comprehension of their key components. In the following section, we will explore the essential elements that make these language models work, from tokenization to attention mechanisms, breaking them down into simple and understandable terms.

UNDERSTANDING KEY COMPONENTS

LLMs are like sophisticated translation systems that can instantly process an incredible amount of information. They create a bridge between human intent and meaningful responses, transforming our simple prompts into coherent and contextual answers. It is like carrying out a search on your browser and receiving a cohesive response without having to read every single article available on the subject.

While these systems may seem magical, they operate through distinct components that work together like instruments in an orchestra. To have a better understanding of this process, read on to see how each of them relates to our everyday tasks, creating answers that seemed previously impossible. As you move through the section, you will see how tokenization, transformers, and attention systems function in collaboration to bring the results you see on the screen.

Tokenization: Breaking Down the Language

Tokenization is to break down the text into small, manageable pieces called tokens. These can be parts of words, full words, or each individual character. In a kitchen, it would be similar to all the ingredients that the chef needs to make a recipe. That will separate each of them and then put them together to make the dish. For example, look at the following phrase:

Example: Let's get ice cream!

Tokens: ["Let's"] ["get"] ["ice"] ["cream"] ["!"]

In this case, the computer would look at every individual word when separating the data. At the same time, some larger words would get broken down into small pieces, such as *overwhelming*, which would be ["over"] ["whelm"] ["ing"]. This process helps the model handle new or uncommon words that it would not usually find in the data it was fed by recognizing familiar parts.

Transformers: The System's Brain

Transformers are the chef who knows how to put all the ingredients together. In this case, they know exactly what work needs to go in each place based on their *experience* and the *knowledge* they have gained over the years. If you read, for example, *The ball flew through the air and smashed the...* you would immediately think *window* because you understand context. Transformers do this by maintaining connections between all words in a sentence.

If you compare this to traditional AI, it would be like a person reading a text with a tiny flashlight, only being able to see a small part at the time. Transformers see everything at once, like reading under a bright light. This allows them to connect related ideas even when far apart, understand context and references, and maintain consistency in long responses.

In this case, if you have ever used ChatGPT or a similar tool and you "continue" a conversation within the same chat, it still recalls what you wrote and can continue the same idea throughout. On the other hand, if you delete the conversation or start a new window, it will not be able to remember it, thus showing one of its vulnerabilities. Transformers are powerful tools, but they can only be used if they have the appropriate context and knowledge to make use of these tokens.

Attention Mechanisms: Focusing on What Matters

Finally, you have the attention mechanisms. To still use our kitchen analogy, it would be the chef knowing what techniques, time, and conditions under which to cook the recipe. In another example, it would be like how your brain works when reading a mystery novel. When you read the phrase "the butler did it," your mind will immediately connect to all the previous mentions of the butler. In LLMs, this attention helps focus on relevant information while generating all responses.

Think about the following example:

Example: John went to Paris because he loves French cuisine.

Attention mechanism: Connects the "he" with "John" and understands that "French cuisine" is related to "Paris."

This is where the magic of AI machines happens since if the cook does not know the correct techniques to apply, the food will be bad. Similarly, if the machine is not appropriately trained or the data is skewed, the answers will be unreliable, since it does not have the proper setup to work. This can lead to information inaccuracies or the inability to identify ambiguity or even false information.

Putting It All Together

When interacting with an LLM, the components you have seen will work in the following sequence:

1. Your input gets tokenized into pieces.
2. Transformers process these tokens, understanding relationships.
3. Attention mechanisms highlight relevant connections.
4. The model generates a response using this understanding.

This process is similar to how data analysts process information, as explained in *Fundamentals of Data Analytics in Today's World: A Comprehensive Guide for Beginners*. Just as they must break down complex datasets, understand relationships between variables, and focus on relevant patterns to draw meaningful conclusions, LLMs process language through structured steps. In our kitchen scenario, here is an overview of the process:

AI technical process	Real-life scenario
Tokenization	Breaking the order into ingredients
Transformers	Understanding how ingredients work together
Attention	Focusing on the right techniques and timing
Output	Creating the final dish

These components enable LLMs to handle complex tasks that were impossible for earlier AI systems. The impact of this technology has been revolutionary across industries and applications, which you will explore in the next section. In it, you will see the transformative power these systems have brought to the market for both good and bad.

THE IMPACT OF LLMS TODAY

In the previous chapter, you saw how AI is generally changing many of the markets in the world. However, this impact is even more significant when considering LLMs, since it has transformed different aspects of our daily lives, influencing how we work, learn, and interact with technology. From assisting in complex research to automating content creation, LLMs are driving a new era of efficiency and creativity. In this final section, you will explore some examples of industries you have seen before, but taking it a step further because they are also using LLMs.

- **Education:** This is one of the sectors that is experiencing the most significant changes due to LLMs. By providing instant and on-demand learning support, LLMs are making education more accessible and personalized than before. Virtual tutors powered by these models help students understand difficult topics, draft essays, and solve math problems. According to *AI in Education Market* (2024), it is estimated that education is the largest revenue share of this market, with 70.3% in 2024, estimated to reach a compound annual growth rate of more than $32 billion by 2030. Today, platforms such as the Khan Academy have integrated LLMs to offer personalized learning according to each student's pace and proficiency.

- **Content creation:** As the precursor among the earliest beneficiaries of LLM technology, content creation has seen a significant change in the industry. Writers, marketers, and designers now use these tools to generate blog posts, social media content, product descriptions, and even video descriptions in a fraction of the time it would take to do manually. Two examples of popular tools are Jasper AI and Copy.ai, which are powered by advanced LLMs that have helped people produce marketing content more efficiently, freeing up creative teams to focus on strategy. According to Khan (2024), 59% of marketers see the potential for AI in content creation, while only 26% agree to use it. At the same time, 71% of these professionals claim that LLMs will help eliminate busy work, allowing them to focus on more strategic tasks.

- **Customer service:** LLMs have substantially impacted customer service, especially when referring to AI-powered chatbots. Several companies have implemented the technology to offer 24/7 assistance, including virtual agents and helpdesk solutions to address customer queries. Doing so has allowed customer demands to be addressed at any time of the day, offering instant responses and reducing wait times. Companies like Zendesk and HubSpot have integrated LLMs into their support systems, enabling 24/7 customer assistance and improving user satisfaction. Implementing these systems has boosted operational efficiency by 25%, with 69% of customers preferring chatbots for communication with their service providers (A. Khan, 2024).

- **Healthcare:** From assisting doctors with medical research to helping patients understand complex diagnoses, LLMs have proven to be an incredible asset for healthcare. These systems can analyze large volumes of medical literature and offer suggestions for treatment plans based on medical best practices. With the implementation of LLMs in the medical industry, professionals have access to an integrated system with information that analyzes different drug combination possibilities. Tools like IBM's Watson and DeepMind's AlphaFold use LLMs to assist researchers in drug discovery and genetic analysis. While AI is not expected to be 100% accurate for these cases, LLM's responses to medical queries achieved a correct diagnostic 71.7% of the time, an incredible achievement for these machines (Kavanagh, 2023).

- **Legal:** LLMs are being leveraged in the legal industry to streamline labor-intensive tasks such as legal research, contract analysis, and document drafting. Using these tools enables companies to quickly swift through massive datasets to find relevant case law and statutes, saving lawyers countless hours. Companies like Casetext and Luminance currently use LLMs to assist legal teams in reviewing contracts and conducting due diligence more efficiently. The application of these tools can reduce up to 40% of the time spent by paralegals and lawyers in research while reducing errors by up to 90% (*Revolutionising the Legal World*, 2022).

- **Retail:** Retailers are currently deploying LLMs to create personalized shopping experiences, from AI-driven product recommendations to automated customer interactions. In this case, the tools analyze product reviews for sentiment analysis and compare them to customer purchases, offering a seamless shopping experience based on preferences. Ecommerce giants such as Amazon and Shopify use this strategy to analyze customer preference and offer tailored product suggestions, increasing sales and boosting profits. Customers are already getting used to this, especially with 70% expecting personalization in their shopping experiences, with 56% of them claiming a personalized experience motivates them to become repeat buyers *(12 Hyper Personalization Statistics*, 2024).

- **Game development:** Lastly, in the gaming industry, LLMs are being used to create content such as dialogue, quests, and even entire storylines. This reduces the workload for developers and enhances the player experience by offering dynamic and personalized narratives. In this case, the most popularly applied LLM is GPT, with OpenAI's model being integrated into experimental game engines to create interactive environments that will give the player a more immersive experience. A recent survey has identified that 49% of developers claim their companies are already using AI to enhance their video games, a number that is set to escalate, with 90% of these companies looking to implement the technology to decrease costs (Merchant, 2024).

While these examples illustrate the potential LLM technology has across industries, their rapid adoption has also brought challenges. On the positive side, these tools enhance productivity, enable personalization at scale, and reduce operational costs. On the negative, it includes job displacement, data privacy concerns, and ethical dilemmas related to AI misuse. In Chapter 9, we will discuss this use and how to implement best and ethical practices when using these applications.

In the meantime, let's look somewhat deeper into the LLM process by understanding how they learn, giving you a better overview of its potential challenges and opportunities. In the next chapter, you will learn about the LLM training process, from pretraining on massive datasets to fine-tuning for specific applications. Understanding these concepts will allow you to have a deeper insight into their capabilities and limitations as a preparation to start using them as a tool to make income.

CHAPTER 3:
HOW AI AND LLMS LEARN

Have you ever wondered how LLM tools can discuss the origins of the universe in one moment and write a song in the next? Or how these systems can recognize cats in photos or detect fraudulent transactions? These are good questions that help you understand how these tools work, so take the information they provide with a grain of salt. In this chapter, you will look under the hood of AI and LLM systems to explore the incredible manner in which they learn. From the massive datasets they train on to the fine-tuning that makes them useful for specific tasks, this is not a simple process.

In fact, as you will see, this training process includes parameters and data sources, both of which are a strength and a weakness for LLMs. Understanding how these systems learn is crucial for their best use, especially recognizing potential pitfalls. You will explore why AI sometimes makes mistakes, shows biases, or generates false information, giving you the necessary knowledge to responsibly and efficiently use these tools in your work and daily life.

TRAINING PROCESS

Teaching an AI system is much like training for a specific task or becoming extremely proficient in a subject. However, this process takes place for different tasks and subjects simultaneously, in which it will learn from millions of examples rather than just a few.

Regardless of the type of model you are working with, or what you want it to do, it must undergo rigorous training and testing processes to ensure that its capabilities are enhanced and its limitations decreased.

Think about learning something at university. You go to different classes to master the profession that you want to carry out in the future. If you are a law student, you will have classes on different types of legislation, processes, and even courtroom behavior. However, as you train, you will become highly specialized in one matter or another. In the case of AI and LLMs, it is like learning the process for all areas in all places and building this cohesive knowledge to act as a legal aid anywhere in the world.

The learning process can be carried out through different approaches, either individually or together. Here is what you should know about each of them:

- **Supervised learning:** To understand supervised learning, consider a medical student learning from an experienced doctor. During the training, they will receive information that is validated, similar to what happens to AI systems. In this case, the program receives clear instructions and labeled examples. It will work in real life when you rate a movie on Netflix or mark an email in your inbox as spam. The system will receive direct feedback stating what it is supposed to do with that information. With millions of these interactions, the AI learns to recognize patterns and make better predictions. In healthcare, this might involve showing AI thousands of labeled medical images to help distinguish between different conditions.

- **Unsupervised learning:** When the unsupervised learning process is carried out, it is like opening a box of building blocks that you have to sort through color, size, and type without any previous information about what is in the box. When you shop online, for example, the AI might notice that people who often buy running shoes often purchase sports socks too, even though no one explicitly taught it this connection. To use a similar example in healthcare, it would be similar to analyzing millions of patient records to discover previously known relationships between symptoms, helping doctors identify new disease patterns.

- **Semisupervised learning:** To understand semisupervised learning, think about a medical resident who carries out procedures by themselves but has an attending to guide them through the process occasionally. This is the main foundation of this learning system, which can be found in modern voice assistants such as Siri or Alexa. In this case, they come pretrained on basic language, but learn your specific speech patterns and preferences through an initial voice recognition test and later through continued interaction; they start with a foundation but improve through regular use and feedback.

- **Reinforcement learning:** Think about reinforcement learning as the process that you would carry out with a pet. Similar to them, the AI system will learn through trial and error with clear rewards, such as earning a point in the system, or penalties, such as losing a point. In a practical example, consider ride-sharing apps optimizing routes: When drivers arrive quickly following a suggested route, the system receives positive feedback. If a route consistently causes delays, it learns to avoid it under similar conditions. In medical diagnosis, systems might receive positive feedback when their predictions match expert diagnoses and negative feedback when they miss important signs.

During the learning process, the AI system will constantly validate its knowledge by testing new examples they haven't seen before. When you provide feedback on product recommendations or adjust your home settings, you are helping these systems learn and improve. The entire process requires amazing computational resources and careful monitoring. This power is so amazing that modern AI systems can process more information in a day than a human would in several lifetimes.

Here, as you will explore further in the chapter, it is essential to be careful with the data you are presenting to the program. Just as we wouldn't want medical students to learn outdated treatments or develop biases, AI systems must be trained with diverse and accurate data that constantly undergo quality checks. This validation process is crucial to ensure the system truly learns rather than memorizes patterns.

What makes this different from learning is the scale and speed: While we might learn from hundreds of examples throughout the years, AI systems can process millions of examples in hours. This leads to an enhanced improvement in their capabilities in real time, as long as they receive quality feedback and data. Every time you interact with an AI system, you are contributing to this massive learning process.

This basic training process will then get refined and specialized for specific tasks, transforming broad knowledge into focused expertise. The next time you see a surprisingly accurate product recommendation, for example, or a voice assistant perfectly understanding your accent, remember that these are the result of the tiny lessons these machines are learning at a scale that would be impossible for any human to process. Yet, they must be carefully guided to avoid learning wrong lessons or developing biases, which is where pretraining and fine-tuning come in, as you are about to see next.

PRETRAINING AND FINE-TUNING

Developing an LLM is a two-step process that involves pretraining and fine-tuning. To understand these, picture a person who is just learning how to write. Pretraining would be leaving them in a library, which has different types of books including novels, encyclopedias, technical manuals, and even cookbooks. In this case, they will learn grammar, vocabulary, sentence structures, and even general knowledge.

Fine-tuning, on the other hand, is like giving this person a specific style guide and asking them to write a marketing piece, a blog post, or even a joke tailored to a specific audience. At the same time, this process is not as complex as it seems. When they are broken down into parts, as you will see next, the process becomes clearly understandable and brings insights into what these systems can do.

Pretraining

Pretraining is the foundation of all LLMs. This includes exposing the model to incredible amounts of data from books, websites, articles, and other places. The goal, in this case, is to help the model learn how language works. As the model and the algorithm understand each source it is given, they can see how words are formed, sentences are structured, and how meaning can change depending on the context.

If you have ever been to another country that speaks a language other than yours or have tried learning a new language, understanding this process is easier. Suppose you want to learn Spanish. You might start by listening to Spanish radio, reading Spanish newspapers, and watching TV shows in Spanish. Even if you don't understand a word right away, you can start picking up patterns and common words. Additionally, you will be able to recognize common phrases, sentence structure, and word use. Over time and with dedication, it is likely you will start to pick up a general understanding of the language and context.

For an LLM, the process is similar, but on a greater scale. The model processes billions of sentences and learns based on probability. This means it learns to understand what word is likely to come next, given the previous words. For example, if you type in, "The dog is eating a..." the machine is more likely to predict "bone" than "banana." When the machine applies probability based on what it has analyzed, it will generate more humanlike text based on how many times the same information was identified within the sources.

The difference between humans and machines, in this case, is that during the pretraining phase, the program does not know or understand facts or information the way we do. It simply becomes very good at predicting language patterns. In the case of the previous example, a human would know that dogs are more likely to eat bones than bananas, but the machine simply "knows" this because of the instances in which this same word formation appears. As a result, while it can generate coherent text about almost any topic, its responses may still be general or lacking in depth when asked about specific or ambiguous subjects.

Fine-Tuning

Once the pretraining is complete, the model can generate text for general purposes. However, most real-world applications require models to perform specialized tasks, such as answering customer queries, generating creative content, or summarizing legal documents. This is the part where the fine-tuning comes in.

This process involves taking the pretrained model and training it further on a narrower dataset tailored to a specific domain or task. For example, a company that develops virtual assistants for financial advisors might fine-tune a general LLM using data from financial reports, investment strategies, and client communications. This process helps the model be more accurate and reliable in that specific field. The same can be said about a company that decides to use LLMs for their chatbots. They will need to fine-tune the program to what their company does, specifications, and details that will enable them to help customers.

To relate this situation to real life, imagine a student who has completed a general degree in communications. They now want to become a sports commentator. To specialize, they start studying the rules of different sports, watching games, and practicing play-by-play commentary. While they already understand language and communication thanks to their degree, they now need this focused training to excel in the desired role. Fine-tuning works similarly: It helps an already well-trained model become an expert in a certain topic.

It is also important to know that fine-tuning can be done for tasks requiring specific writing styles. If a social media company wants a chatbot that writes playful and informative replies, it can fine-tune an LLM on a dataset containing lighthearted conversations, memes, and casual language. On the other hand, a law firm might fine-tune its model on formal legal texts to ensure it generates professional and precise responses.

Putting It All Together

Both processes you have read about—pretraining and fine-tuning—are essential for creating versatile and effective LLMs. While the pretraining phase will provide a broader knowledge base, fine-tuning can be used to ensure it can be applied in certain contexts. Without the first, the model wouldn't have a general understanding of language, and without the latter, it would struggle to accurately perform specialized tasks.

At the same time, while these are powerful techniques, they come with their own set of challenges. Pretraining usually requires enormous computational resources and vast datasets, which can be costly and time-consuming. Additionally, the data in pretraining can often lead to biases present in real-world text, leading to the same result in its outputs. Similarly, fine-tuning presents the risk of *overfitting*, especially if the dataset being used to do it is too small or too narrow, leading it to become overly specialized and lose its generalization abilities. Moreover, fine-tuning requires careful curation of the dataset to avoid introducing errors.

In both cases, these processes must not be carried out by automation. Human oversight is critical at every step, from selecting the data to evaluating the model's performance or ensuring ethical use. As you will explore in Chapter 9, the responsible use of LLMs requires continuous monitoring to mitigate these risks, which can even be harmful outputs.

However, before you can understand these challenges and obstacles and why they appear, it is crucial to understand the specific components that make up an LLM. While you have already read about tokens in the previous chapter, the following section will bring you a recap on the subject and include parameters and datasets. Understanding these will provide you with a clearer view of how these systems operate and why their outputs are produced in a specific way.

TOKENS, PARAMETERS, AND DATASETS

Many people often wonder what makes models such as ChatGPT, Llama, Gemini, or Microsoft Copilot so powerful. To give you this answer, we must break down their main components into three parts: parameters, datasets, and tokens. These elements are essential for any LLM, and each directly influences how well the model performs. They are similar to the bricks in the house or the ingredients in a recipe: each plays a critical role and the final result will depend on how they are combined. To better understand the role each of them has in these programs, this is exactly what we will do: examine each individually to understand their part in the final outcome.

Tokens

As you have seen in the previous chapter, *tokenization* is the process of breaking down words or phrases into tokens, a piece of text that can be a word, part of a word, or a character. In practice, LLMs don't always split sentences into full words, they use tokenization to make them easier to process. Think of tokens as individual notes in a piece of music. Just as a musician reads each note and plays it in sequence to create a melody, an LLM processes each token to generate coherent sentences. In this case, the more efficiently it can handle tokes, the better it can understand and produce language.

Parameters

Now, let's talk about parameters. They are like the adjustable dials inside the model that help it decide. When an LLM is pretrained, it learns patterns from its training data, and these are stored as parameters. Generally speaking, they determine how the model connects one token to the next and how it predicts what word should follow based on the context. In LLMs, parameters serve as the tool it can use to recall and apply its acquired knowledge.

The more parameters a model has, the better it becomes at capturing subtle language patterns and generating accurate responses. GPT-3, to name a popular example, has *175 billion* parameters. That is an incredible number, and it's one of the reasons why it can generate such humanlike text. At the same time, models with fewer parameters may struggle with complex language tasks because they do not have the same "memory" depth or robust pattern recognition systems.

Datasets

Finally, we have the third component: datasets. A dataset is the collection of text that the LLM will be trained on. During the pretraining phase, it will be exposed to massive datasets containing all types of text you can imagine, most of which are available online. You will learn where they come from in the next section. In the meantime, you should know that the size and quality of this dataset are extremely important since the model can only learn from what it has been shown. A diverse and comprehensive dataset allows the LLM to handle a large range of language tasks.

A special emphasis must be given to the dataset quality. A large but poorly curated dataset can introduce biases or errors into the model, just as bad ingredients can ruin a dish. That is why human oversight is so important during pretraining and fine-tuning, ensuring that the data the model is being exposed to is balanced and relevant.

How These Elements Word Together

As you might imagine, these three elements must work together seamlessly to ensure that the model presents its best performance. During the pretraining phase, the model will be given an enormous dataset and learn to predict the next token based on the tokens it has already seen. This process adjusts the model's parameters millions of times, gradually improving its ability to understand and generate language.

In the fine-tuning phase, the process will become more focused. The LLM will be trained on a narrower dataset specific to a particular task or industry. Suppose a company wants to create a virtual assistant for a travel agency. They might fine-tune the LLM using a dataset filled with travel guides, booking information, and customer queries. This way, the model becomes highly skilled at answering travel-related questions.

For an even simpler breakdown, look at the following example:

- **Tokens:** The model processes customer questions like *Can you recommend a hotel in Paris?* by breaking them down into tokens.

- **Parameters:** It uses billions of parameters to understand the context of the question and generate an appropriate response.

- **Datasets:** Thanks to its fine-tuning on the corresponding data, the model knows that *hotel* refers to accommodation and *Paris* to the city in France, not a person with the same name.

While having numerous parameters and a vast dataset can enhance an LLM's capabilities, more isn't always necessarily better. Overloading a model with parameters can make it slower and more resource-intensive, while a dataset that is too large might introduce noise or irrelevant information. Striking the right balance is key, and that is why fine-tuning a carefully selected dataset is often necessary to tailor the model for specific applications.

As you can imagine, the data given to these models is what determines its performance. Without vast and diverse datasets, even the most sophisticated models would struggle to produce meaningful results. The questions that remain, then, are: *Where does all this data come from? How do developers gather all this text? Are there any challenges in the process?* Read on to discover the answer to these and much more, giving you a full understanding of how these datasets can build effective models and bring to the surface unique challenges regarding ownership, privacy, and ethics.

WHERE DOES THE DATA COME FROM?

You already know that training an LLM requires exposing it to enormous amounts of text data. *But where does all this data originate?* Generally speaking, data for the training process to take place is sourced from publicly available text, licensed content, and in some cases, proprietary datasets. While this abundance of data is what makes these models powerful, it also created significant ethical and legal concerns, especially regarding data ownership, privacy, and bias.

Publicly Available Data

A significant portion of the data used to train LLMs comes from publicly accessible sources such as websites, blogs, forums, and social media platforms. Models like GPT and Llama have been trained on vast datasets scraped from the internet, which might include everything from Wikipedia articles to online reviews and technical documentation. The advantage of using this type of data is that it provides a broad and diverse set of language samples, covering everything from formal writing to casual conversation.

However, relying on internet data comes with its own challenges. First, not all publicly available content is high quality. Some data may be poorly written, factually incorrect, or even harmful, such as hate speech or misleading information. Since LLMs learn from everything they are exposed to, poor-quality data can degrade the model's performance or introduce harmful biases. Additionally, there are also legal concerns surrounding whether web-scraped data can be used without explicit permission from content creators.

Licensed and Proprietary Data

To overcome the limitations of public data, companies often incorporate licensed or proprietary datasets into the training process. Licensed data refers to content that is legally obtained through agreements with publishers, academic institutions, or other organizations. For example, a company might license a collection of scientific journals or business reports to improve its model's understanding of specialized fields.

Proprietary data, on the other hand, is information collected directly by the organization developing the model. This could include internal documents, customer support transcripts, or other business-specific content. Using proprietary data allows companies to fine-tune models for industry-specific tasks, such as legal research or financial analysis. While this type of data offers significant advantages, it also raises ethical questions such as who owns the data and how it should be handled.

Data Collection Challenges

Despite the power that comes from having access to vast datasets, collecting and using data for LLMs is not without its challenges. Some of these include

- **Data privacy and ownership:** One of the most common and urgent issues in LLM training is ensuring that the data used respects privacy laws and intellectual property rights. Many jurisdictions, such as the European Union (such as the GDPR), have strict regulations around privacy.; The US has HIPAA. If a dataset includes personal information without consent, it can lead to legal and ethical repercussions. Additionally, using copyrighted material without permission raises concerns about intellectual property rights.

- **Bias:** Since LLMs learn from the data they are given, any bias present in the data can be absorbed by the model. If a dataset predominantly consists of English language content from certain regions, the model may become biased toward those linguistic or cultural norms. This can result in incorrect responses or a limited understanding of diverse perspectives.

- **Quality vs. quantity:** As mentioned earlier, while having large datasets is important, the quality of what it will add to the LLM matters just as much. Poor-quality data can lead to models that produce unreliable or nonsensical responses. Balancing a dataset's size and quality is a constant challenge developers have to deal with when developing effective LLMs.

- **Ethical data use:** Lastly, there is an ongoing debate about the ethical implications of training LLMs on content created by individuals who do not give consent for their work to be used in this way. While scraping public data can provide valuable resources, it can also be seen as exploiting the intellectual labor of countless writers, artists, and content creators.

Despite these challenges, and you will learn about more throughout the book, the datasets used to train LLMs have undoubtedly unlocked new possibilities in AI. These models started a revolution in how we interact with technology, making it easier to create content, solve problems, and automate complex tasks. However, as powerful as they are, the ethical and legal concerns surrounding data use cannot be ignored.

CHALLENGES: BIAS, HALLUCINATION, ETHICAL CONCERNS, AND OTHERS

Although LLMs are incredible programs with diverse purposes, this does not mean that they come without challenges. They still have several imperfections and limitations that, if the user is unknowledgeable, may lead to mistakes. Most of these challenges come from how they are developed and trained, which makes it essential to have some guidance on their ethical, responsible, and effective use. Here are, nine of the most common limitations for LLMs where human insight is crucial:

- **Bias:** Since LLMs are trained on datasets reflecting the content available on the internet and other sources, biases in these places can be conveyed during the learning process. This bias can manifest in different ways, including stereotypes based on gender, race, or socioeconomic status. Reducing bias requires a careful review of the information being used and carrying out periodic audits.

- **Hallucinations:** When an LLM produces information that seems plausible but is entirely fabricated, this is known as an AI hallucination. This happens because the words are predicated on patterns rather than knowledge or understanding, leading it to "invent" facts and statements when responding to a prompt. These can be particularly problematic in areas that require accuracy and reliability, once again pointing to the need for human oversight during use.

- **Outdated information:** Most LLMs have a cutoff date, which is the date up to when the data was collected. This means that, unless they have access to web searches, these models will have a limited vision of current events, cultural trends, and breakthroughs. For example, if the program has a cutoff date of August 2024, it will now know who the president of the US is if there is an election held afterward.

- **Lack of contextual understanding:** It may seem that the LLM you are working with has convincing knowledge, but do not be fooled by this impression! These models do not have any consciousness or genuine comprehension, meaning they fail to grasp emotional context, sarcasm, or even complex queries. As a result, it can lead to irrelevant or misleading responses, especially when considering a user looking for advice. When using LLMs for critical issues, do not forget to use a human consultant to help you with the matter.

- **Difficulty with specialized jargon:** Most of the LLM tools in existence today on the market can handle general tasks with efficiency. However, they might struggle with domain-specific knowledge, especially if they were not fine-tuned for this purpose. This means struggling in fields such as medicine, law, or even engineering, leading to potential hallucinations and misinformation.

- **Inconsistent performance across languages:** English is usually the primary language in which LLMs are trained, meaning their performance in other languages can vary. Even though many of these models are multilingual, they often demonstrate reduced fluency and accuracy in languages with fewer digital resources or that are not as common.

- **Resource-intensive development and operation:** Training LLMs requires incredible computational resources, including significant energy use. This raises environmental concerns, as the carbon footprint of generating this processing power and its subsequent. Additionally, the high costs associated with training and developing these LLMs can create a technological gap between larger and smaller companies, especially for those looking for innovative systems.

- **Sensitivity to prompt phrasing:** LLMs are very sensitive to how you write prompts. Even the smallest change in wording or typing mistakes can generate different responses, frustrating users who are looking for consistent results. This makes it essential to have some knowledge of prompt engineering, which you will learn more about in Chapter 5.

- **Limited ability to verify sources:** The lack of ability to verify output accuracy is one significant challenge faced by LLMs. While today several tools are using citing options and resources to show where the data came from, it is still very much needed to cross-reference the information in the output with other sources and explore other possibilities. Even with the citing features, there are still imperfections, so it is always best to be safe and double-check the information before using it.

Understanding and addressing these challenges is essential so that we can start building trust in AI systems. While LLMs have already made significant contributions to the fields you have seen, their limitations remind us they are tools, not replacements, for human judgment. Addressing issues like the ones you have seen in this section ensures the technology is developed and used responsibly.

Now that you have this comprehensive view of AI, LLMs, and how they work, it is time to move on and explore some of the most popular LLMs available in the market today. In the next chapter, you will explore and learn more about tools such as ChatGPT, Claude, Gemini, and Llama. As you read, you will start to identify the best tools to help you with tasks while gaining insight into how different LLMs can be applied to solve daily problems.

CHAPTER 4:
EXPLORING THE MOST POPULAR
LLMS

With so many options on the market, choosing the best LLM to work with can seem overwhelming. Millions of people use these tools daily, making it one of the fastest-growing industries in the present. Despite its millions of users, this rapid implementation is not just about numbers, it is a significant change in how we work. By the end of 2025, it is estimated that 50% of digital work is expected to be automated by companies using LLMs (Uspenskyi, 2024).

But how do I choose the best tool for me with so many options available? The first thing you should know is that it is a concentrated market: "In 2023, the world's top five LLM developers acquired around 88.22% of the market revenue" (Uspenskyi, 2024). As soon as OpenAI announced and released GPT-3, Big Tech rushed to start creating their own models. These include Google, Microsoft, Apple, and Meta, to name a few. Today, companies large and small are investing in creating and improving the technology, building models of their own, and increasing the supply of what we find in the market.

To help you understand how to make the best choice and find the most suitable one for your tasks, in this chapter, you will learn about six of the most popular platforms. These are general-purpose LLMs, each with its strengths and challenges and best applications. As you read, you will find that there is much more to the world of LLMs than GPT, and some may even surprise you! Read on if you are ready to learn more about these chatbots and see how they can be integrated into your daily life to make it a little easier.

CHATGPT

Do you remember the first time you heard about ChatGPT? Maybe it was at work, with a colleague showing you the incredible new release on the market or perhaps it was a friend who always stays ahead of tech trends. When the chatbot was released in November 2022, what started as mere intrigue for many quickly became a gold rush, forever changing how we deal with technology. Just a few days after its launch, it reached 1 million users, a number that reached an amazing 100 million by February 2023.

From there, the tool gained significant traction and continues to grow. Its versatility is usually considered one of its top advantages, since it can be used for brainstorming ideas, debugging code, and even asking questions on complex subjects. In its latest version, it can even look at images and engage in voice conversations, making it more like a digital assistant rather than a computer program.

ChatGPT is available in the free (and limited) and paid versions. In the free version, you can use prompts to conversate and use most of its features. However, it has a limit of queries you can carry out per period, there are speed limitations, and even some features are unavailable. On the other hand, you can also subscribe to the paid version, known as ChatGPT Plus, which costs $20 per month and brings an amazing toolkit to the table (*ChatGPT*, 2024). The paid tool thinks faster, has no limits, and includes Dall·E 3 to create images and analyze graphs.

The tool's greatest ability is to create relatable and everyday text, regardless of the audience to whom the information is directed. It can instantly adapt the language being used to the user's needs. It has also become the go-to tool for most users, meaning it gets trained and fine-tuned more often with use. Developers are using it to cut their time dedicated to coding, customer service teams are using it to respond to queries, and marketing teams leverage it for content creation.

Finally, the introduction of custom GPTs in the newest version to replace the plugins has been a game-changer. Companies are using the feature to create their own specialized version of GPT tailored to their needs, language, and style guide. Others, who are not as keen on doing so, simply use the standard GPTs available to all users to get answers on specific themes, obtain "expert" advice, and get a more fine-tuned response from the model.

At the same time, ChatGPT also has significant limitations. Although the tool currently can search the internet, it was trained only up to April 2024 and, unless you prompt the tool to use the search feature, it will automatically default to the training data. Another challenge is the high level of hallucinations the tool produces. In many cases, for the unadvised user, it can create misinformation by confidently speaking about elements it is unsure or incorrect about. Although the tool is usually right, it is essential to always double- and cross-check the information it produces.

The future is bright for ChatGPT, especially since with every update it becomes more capable, understanding, and helpful. Additionally, with paid features being constantly implemented into the free version, you can have a small taste of what to expect with the paid and more capable version. Still, it is essential to remember that no matter how perfect and humanlike the tool is, it is not meant to replace human expertise but rather assist and make our lives easier.

GEMINI

When ChatGPT was launched, Google was one of the first companies to start looking at how it could develop its own model. Initially, it launched Bard, which was often seen as a bad copy of ChatGPT with fewer features and more errors and hallucinations. However, in December 2023, the company rebranded and launched a new version now called Gemini. This change marked an important change in the company's strategy and AI capabilities.

One of the main differences of this chatbot is that it was built to be different from other tools, more specifically due to the fact it is multimodal, meaning it naturally understands and works with text, images, audio, video, and code. Differently from ChatGPT, which has Dall·E implemented as a separate feature (and what happens with many other tools), Gemini has all the features integrated as a whole. This means you can have a conversation with the program about a picture you just took, and the AI will understand what is in the image and relate it to information it finds across the web.

This, in fact, is yet another feature the program offers (and was one of the first to do so without cost), which is the integration with the internet and web searches. But what really sets the tool apart is its integration with Google's applications. These include Google Search, the Google Docs suite, and even Android. By using Gemini, you can use AI in the Google ecosystem, including extending to Gmail, Google Maps, and all the other tools the company offers.

The chatbot comes in three different versions, tailored to the user's needs. There is Gemini Ultra, the most advanced tool, which costs $19.99 per month. Then there is Gemini Pro, the tool that powers the free version, which is already incredible in itself. Finally, there is Gemini Nano, which is specifically designed to run directly on mobile devices. As you can see, there is a version of Gemini for everyone!

Its ability to connect to your Google account also allows Gemini to provide personalized assistance while maintaining privacy and security. This means you can go through your documents, photos, and every file stored in the cloud, and it will be able to answer questions without needing to look for more information. Features such as these prove to be useful when you are looking for an email you don't immediately recall or pictures you do not remember to have taken and need to find. This personal touch makes it feel less like a generic AI and more like an assistant that knows you and your workflow.

However, Gemini does not come without its own set of limitations. While integrating with Google apps is certainly an incredible feature, it can also feel limited if you do not use the company's products. Like other AI chatbots, it faces challenges such as hallucinations and requires fact double-checking, especially for critical information. Additionally, its multimodal capabilities, while impressive, still have a long way to go as it is not unusual to have it misinterpret complex visual or audio inputs.

On the other hand, for those already comfortable with using Google's ecosystem, Gemini is not just another tool, but an extension of the workplace. Looking ahead, the company's massive data advantage and integration with widely adopted tools means that the technology can evolve quickly and with precision. Today, the company works toward developing responsible AI with fewer biases and hallucinations, with promising results in studies published so far (*Gemini*, n.d.).

LLAMA

This chatbot is Meta's response to GPT, even if it wasn't the company's first priority back in 2022. At that time, Mark Zuckerberg was looking to invest in the metaverse and even changed the company's group name from Facebook, Inc. to Meta Platforms, Inc. due to its increasing investment in the technology (Thomas, 2021). However, when ChatGPT was launched, it led to one of the fastest changes in strategy the technology world has seen, as the company shifted billions in resources from virtual reality to AI. From this originated Llama (short for Large Language Model Meta AI).

One of the main distinguishing characteristics of the program is the philosophy that was used to build it: The model was released to the research community in early 2023 and by the middle of the same year, it had been launched as a full-scale open-source model. While companies such as Google and OpenAI kept the inner workings and code behind their powerful programs locked in secrecy, Meta went the other way and decided to give away the blueprint for one of the most sophisticated AI engines ever built.

The program's latest version, released in February 2024 and known as Llama 3, is available in three parameter sizes: 8B, 70B, and 400B (*Llama*, 2024). In its most powerful version, 400B, the tool showcases improvements in reasoning, mathematical concepts, coding, and word knowledge, leading to a significant improvement from the previous version. This, and the company's impressive reach with Instagram, Facebook, and WhatsApp has the market wondering what will come next.

What makes Llama 3 particularly interesting is the type of architecture that was used during development. According to the company, the new structure has led to a decrease in hallucinations, more nuanced responses, and better contextual understanding (*Introducing Meta Llama 3*, 2024). Some innovations in the model include a greater number of tokens used and a variety of learning and training strategies, allowing the model to specialize in different tasks. These new capabilities would be similar to having multiple experts on one problem and, instead of reading the full studies to understand the issue, they can do it at once.

At the same time, the company claims that the new Llama 3 model is not just about performance and increasing its capability. Meta has focused on making the model more efficient, requiring less computational power to run effectively, thus addressing critical elements such as energy use and the ability for other companies to implement the program. A smaller processing power means smaller organizations and researchers can work with the tool without needing massive computing resources, which essentially means making the technology available to all.

Nonetheless, even with its decreased computational power processing requirements, this does not mean that it is a cheap technology. To have the program work with the minimum parameters, hardware that is worth thousands of dollars is still needed. Additionally, without a controlled environment that systems like Gemini and GPT have, there is a greater risk of misuse or creation of harmful applications. To address the issue, Meta has included within its user and license agreements terms that include safety and ethical use requirements.

Finally, whether the company's decision to release Llama as an open-sourced software was a good decision still remains to be seen. On one hand, it allows the company to separate itself from competitors by empowering users and researchers to innovate and help them improve the model. On the other, it opens up the opportunity for ill-intentioned individuals and companies to take advantage of a superior technology for unlawful purposes. Whether this strategy will pay off is still unknown, but one thing is for sure: Meta changed the way we think about AI development and accessibility.

CLAUDE

When Anthropic, the creator of Claude, appeared with a new chatbot proposal to the market, the chatbot came with significant knowledge. The main reason for this is that it was founded by former OpenAI researchers who wanted to create more transparent and ethically aligned AI systems. To achieve this goal, the company took an approach of promoting honesty, allowing the tool to even admit when it doesn't know something.

One of the most interesting aspects of Claude is the fact that developers are not looking at what *to do* or features to add. Quite the contrary. They are exploring the elements and features that AI programs should or should not have. As it develops a system that is not shy of admitting it does not know or does not have the information, it brings a paradox and a different landscape to the AI industry. This approach comes from Anthropic's constitutional principles, which aim to create AI systems that are powerful, truthful, and aligned with human values (*Meet Claude*, 2024).

The tool's latest model, Claude 3.5, comes in three versions: Haiku, Sonnet, and Opus, each for different cases. Opus is the most capable version, with highly skilled reasoning, analysis, and problem-solving capabilities. At the same time, the tool also has free (Sonnet 3.5) and paid versions, (Haiku 3.5 and Opus 3.5); the latter costing $18 per month without VAT. What sets these models apart is their consistent approach to safety and transparency, allowing you to consider and reflect upon the implications of what the prompt is requesting.

While this might seem like the ideal tool, being so ethically inclined comes with its own challenges. The tool's constraints sometimes mean that it will fail to help you when other tools might. This excess of caution reflects on the chatbot's speed since answers can be considerably slower when compared to its competitors. Therefore, most of its applications are for where certainty is essential, such as in healthcare and legal industries, education, and research and analysis.

Conversely, one of its most distinctive features is its approach to cutoff dates, an element that other chatbots fail to acknowledge. Rather than pretending to know about recent events or making assumptions, the model clearly communicated its knowledge limitations and suggested verifying current information from reliable resources. This honesty is limiting, but it builds trust with users who need reliable information. Additionally, it can search the internet, but in the free version, this can consume a significant amount of tokens, leading to waiting times to have longer conversations.

Although Claude does not have the massive user base of ChatGPT, which allows the tool to be constantly trained or the integration and multimodal features of Gemini, it is a promising tool for those looking for reliable information. It has created a base of loyal users who prioritize reliability and ethics with their AI use. Its ability to handle complex documents, engage in discussions, and maintain consistent behavior made the tool indispensable in regulated industries and educational and research institutions.

MICROSOFT COPILOT

If you are a user of Microsoft 365, you have probably noticed that new updates have quietly been added to its applications. Microsoft

Copilot, previously known as Bing Chat, is one of the most audacious integrations of AI into everyday tools. If you imagine the number of people using Microsoft programs and the impact that using and implementing AI into them can have, you will understand why the tool is considered a game-changer in the market. In addition to this, Microsoft combines its AI capabilities with an impressive cloud environment in Azure and its several years of experience in the technology market.

To name a few examples:

- In Word, documents can be drafted, edited, and summarized.

- In Excel, data and formulas can be analyzed.

- In PowerPoint, presentations can be generated with a simple prompt.

- In Outlook, draft emails can be written in specific tones, and email threads can be summarized.

- In Teams, meeting summaries and action items can be automatically generated.

However, the tool's most important feature is the ability to understand context. Suppose you are working on a document, the chatbot will see the text and understand its purpose, analyze your previous work patterns, and the idea behind what you are creating. When this happens, the tool can offer suggestions that are more relevant to the content you are creating, rather than giving you a generic response that other AI models would.

Since the Microsoft suite is mostly dedicated to corporate and enterprise users, the company built the model considering special circumstances for privacy and security. To ensure this happens, Copilot operates within Azure, Microsoft's secure cloud infrastructure, ensuring the entered data does not leave the business's environment. This means they can enhance the application of the company's data protection protocols and prevent the information from leaving the corporate environment.

Although it has impressive capabilities within the Microsoft suite, its capacity extends beyond this primary use. Microsoft Copilot is also able to develop code, write cohesive text, and troubleshoot Windows problems. Its access to the internet enhances search and browsing experiences with AI-powered insights. The company's idea is to bring an all-in-one solution that will increase its use within other organizations.

This integration, at the same time, comes at a cost, especially for those looking to scale their operations and deploy the system throughout businesses. The subscription model is particularly expensive for these, with proposals being tailored to each need. Similarly, the experience of having AI embedded in all programs you are using might seem overwhelming—and even excessive—to some users. It is also important to mention that there is a learning curve in understanding how to effectively prompt Copilot for optimal results.

Microsoft's AI implementation across its multiple programs stands as an example of what the future might look like. In it, rather than being presented as a standalone solution, LLMs and AI chatbots are set to become virtual assistants embedded in most of the programs we use. While on one side it will enhance user experience and allow for a more productive workspace, it is essential to think about what it would mean for one company to manage all this information, especially with the increase in cyber threats.

GROK

In November 2023, Elon Musk revealed Grok to the world, an LLM created by his company xAI that had a mission different from other AI virtual assistants. It was designed to have a sarcastic, irreverent, and witty personality, setting the tone of how it would be used. The tool was first developed to be used with X (formerly Twitter) and is still limited to a "Fun Mode" (Research Graph, 2024).

xAI's idea was to develop a tool that maximizes curiosity and seeks truth, making it even more interesting as it has real-time access to X's database. Its approach is to be direct and even *engage* in controversial topics on social media, many including subjects other platforms would avoid. While it has a certain liberty to engage, provoke, and answer to these, xAI ensures it has built-in measures to prevent harmful comments.

This approach to AI development has led Grok to have a few, but loyal users. It is still a limited tool, restricted only to X's Premium subscribers for $16 a month, and there is no report of expanding the tool. It serves the purpose for which it was created: engaging an especially dedicated audience who are looking for more personality-driven and entertainment-focused AI tools that are not afraid to challenge conventions (*xAI: Understand the Universe,* 2025).

Grok is still quite different from other LLMs, but it shows an illustration of what could happen in the future. With its transparency, truthful, and personality-filled features, not to mention data analysis in real-time, it can be a game-changer in the market. This means that we might be looking at AI systems chosen not only by their capabilities but also by their communication style.

While xAI has not yet released any information to date on future implementations, increasing Grok's capabilities is within its plans. With the range of Musk's empires, it would be no surprise to soon see the LLM in other tools developed by the mogul's companies, leaving open the question of its impact on the AI industry. For some, this might be a new way to communicate on social media and for tasks that do not require professionalism or educational features. For others, it is a tool that might never be used, especially considering current adoption rates and limitations to X.

The key here is to see if this approach to AI assistants is sustainable in the future. Today, many people look for tools that can help them carry out multiple tasks, and if a tool is seen as limited, it might not reach the expected numbers. It certainly adds questions and flavors to what some consider "boring" and "mechanical" writing, but how far it will go remains a question.

As you continue to read, it is important to keep in mind that no AI tool is perfect and that many of them have different but significant limitations. Each is ideal for a set of tasks, representing a vision of how AI can increase our productivity and enhance our lives and work. But having access to these tools is just the beginning.

Now that you have understood how AI and LLMs learn and operate and the main competitors in the market, it is finally time to learn how to interact with them. You might wonder why some responses are different from others, and why some people have more success using these LLMs than others. The answer is actually simple: They have started to master the art of *prompt engineering*.

In the next chapter, you will learn the secrets of how to effectively communicate with these programs, learning to prompt the machine to give you exactly what you need. Just as you would learn any other language, in this case, you will be learning "AI language," allowing you to achieve the best results during your interaction. If you are ready to start taking some notes and testing prompts, read on. There is still much to learn, see, and do!

CHAPTER 5:
UNDERSTANDING PROMPT
ENGINEERING

Think about all the people you know. Certainly, one of them is the type who can always get what they want, especially because they can explain exactly what they want or need simply and concisely. Instead of asking "Can you help me with this document?" they will say, "I need help fact-checking this document. My deadline is in two hours." The first, as you might imagine, opens up several possibilities, while the second gives the individual exactly the person's needs and time to conclude it.

The same principle can be applied to AI programs and prompt engineering. How you speak to the machine will determine exactly what the output will be and if it will be useful or not. It is the difference between receiving a generic response and a more precise one. Today, prompt engineering is not just some new fancy word—it is the key that will give you access to using LLMs efficiently.

This chapter's objective is to give you the necessary tools to achieve this, obtaining insightful analysis that matches your needs. You will learn about the principles that make prompts effective and the structures that deliver results, see examples of how to put these into practice, and discover advanced techniques to enhance your experience. It does not matter for what purpose you are using the tool:

By understanding prompt engineering, you will start to get better results immediately! Are you ready to see how?

Author's note: As you have seen in the last chapter, there are several LLMs to consider, and each has its unique approach to prompts. The structures you will see in this chapter can be applied to most of these tools, with some fine-tuning needed. Due to the number of users and market reach, the structures and information you will see in this chapter will be based on results produced by ChatGPT.

WHAT IS PROMPT ENGINEERING?

Prompt engineering is the action of writing effective inputs for AI language models to generate optimal results. It involves designing, refining, and optimizing text prompts that will allow you to achieve optimal outputs and meaningful responses. Being able to generate these inputs is so significant that a whole new career has been developed for it, and specialists in the subjects are known as *prompt engineers*. However, prompt engineering is not only for specialists. With some knowledge, you can also learn this skill and become a specialist at extracting useful answers from LLMs.

As mentioned earlier, learning about prompt engineering is much like learning a new language. Only, instead of speaking to another human, you will be doing so to a machine that thinks and responds similarly to how humans do. At the same time, while powerful, they process information differently, with patterns, as you have also seen before. Therefore, it is essential to learn how to structure our requests to help the models better understand what our intentions and needs are so responses are useful.

You might be thinking, *If this is something professionals do, it might require some intensive studying and learning.* The answer to this statement is both "yes" and "no." To address the first, yes, you will need to understand the different techniques and strategies that can be used, including the formatting choices and what exactly you are going to ask. This might include providing context, setting constraints, offering examples, or even breaking tasks into smaller parts. You must learn not only *what* to ask but also *how* to ask.

While this might initially seem overwhelming, you do not have to worry! Unlike other spoken languages, once you understand the main concepts, you will be able to seamlessly implement them, especially since most of the prompts follow a similar structure. There is also a secret: Mastering "AI language" is similar to speaking to a child or giving direct instructions to someone who gets frequently confused. As you will see, it is about getting the best possible response, not just *any* response.

Why It Matters

Just by the previous explanation, you might be starting to get the big picture of why prompt engineering is so important. Today, with more AI and LLM-fueled applications being presented to us at work, school, and home, knowing how to use prompt engineering is not just a nice-to-have, but essential. To summarize its importance: Poor prompt engineering can lead to subpar and even misleading results, while well-crafted prompts can help decrease the time to carry out a task from hours to minutes.

Suppose you are a history teacher in a class full of students. You are explaining to them the events that led up to and succeeded World War I when a student asks, "But I don't understand World War I." This question is too broad, and you catch yourself thinking, *What about World War I don't they understand?* The same concept applies to AI. When you are writing a prompt, you must tell it the desired tone, structure, format, and intended audience so it can provide you with an accurate response.

A few other reasons to learn prompt engineering include

- Maximize efficiency and resource use, reducing the number of iterations needed to achieve outcomes.

- Prevent hallucinations and off-topic responses, ensuring more reliable and consistent results.

- Create a connection between human intention and machine capability, ensuring your needs are met instead of adapting to the tool's limitations.

- Stay up-to-date with the market, allowing you to implement AI use in your personal and professional lives.

When you learn how to ask, you will see that speaking to LLMs will become second nature to you. You will see that the outcomes you obtain are better and that you spend less time achieving goals with the program. You will become empowered to use AI's full potential and use these tools as partners that help you solve complex problems or automate tasks. *And how do I achieve this?* you might ask. Well, read on to find out!

EFFECTIVE PROMPTS: KEY PRINCIPLES

The essence of creating a prompt is to efficiently and clearly communicate your intent to the machine. When prompts are specific, well-structured, and easy to understand, LLMs are more likely to provide accurate and relevant results. To help you master the skill, you will now see a list of *dos* and *don'ts* to start practicing and have a greater understanding of what AI prompts should look like.

Dos

- **Be specific:** The more clear your prompts are, the more focused the answers will be. When the task is objective and detailed, the model can avoid producing broad or irrelevant information:

  - *Instead of:* "Explain marketing."

  - *Use:* "Explain three principles of digital marketing for small businesses."

- **Use simple language:** Although most LLMs are trained in different types of languages, avoid using complex or technical language unless necessary. This helps avoid confusion and improves output accuracy.

- *Instead of:* "Articulate the economic ramifications of fiscal policy alterations."

- *Use:* "Explain how changes in the government affect the economy."

- **Break down complex requests:** If what you need requires several steps, the best idea is to break them down into parts to improve coherence and avoid hallucinations. This always makes fact-checking easier and faster.

  - *Instead of:* "Write a report on climate change and renewable energy."

  - *Use:* "Write a brief summary on climate change. Then list five types of renewable energy with a short explanation for each."

- **Provide context:** Providing the LLM with background information helps the tool better understand what you need. Without context, the response may be too generic or off-topic.

  - *Instead of:* "How does blockchain work?"

  - *Use:* "How does a blockchain system verify transactions?"

- **Determine the audience:** Since the LLM can adapt the language and tone of the message, it is essential to tell it who the intended audience is. This allows you to adjust the content to different people and increase comprehension.

  - *Instead of:* "Explain the seasons."

  - *Use:* "Explain the seasons as you would to a seven-year-old."

- **Use examples:** Including an example of the output you wish to receive allows the model to understand what you are looking for. This is especially useful for formatting and tone adjustments.

- ○ *Instead of:* "Write an email to a client answering a complaint."

- ○ *Use:* "Write a polite email to a client to apologetically answer a complaint."

- **Ask for explanations:** Requesting detailed explanations and step-by-step responses helps the machine to understand better what you need and also allows you to have a better comprehension of the output.

  - ○ *Instead of:* "Explain why it rains."

  - ○ *Use:* "Explain why it rains step-by-step with a brief description of each process."

- **Ask for sources:** Since there is a possibility that the AI tool might hallucinate, depending on the topic you are researching, you should include the request for sources. This will speed up fact-checking time and allow you to establish credibility.

  - ○ *Instead of:* "Give me a list of things I must take when considering camping during the winter."

  - ○ *Use:* "Give me a list of things I must take when considering camping during the winter. Provide sources."

- **Test and refine:** Effective prompting will usually involve trial and error until you find the correct flow. If the first response you receive is not what you were expecting, refine the prompt to get better results.

  - ○ *Use:* "Include detailed examples," "Can you explain it in simpler terms?" "Provide more information," or, "Be more specific."

- **Provide feedback:** Although the tool will learn based on your interactions, if you do not provide feedback on the output it is providing you with, it will never identify where it is getting it wrong. Use thumbs-up, stars, or other feedback mechanisms available in these chats to let it know your level of satisfaction with the tool.

Don'ts

- **Be vague:** Vague prompts lead to board or irrelevant responses. When you provide clear instructions, it ensures that the AI understands exactly what you want.

  - *Instead of:* "Tell me something about history."

  - *Use:* "Summarize the causes of World War II."

- **Use ambiguity:** Ambiguous words can confuse the AI, resulting in inaccurate responses. Where possible, use words that have a clear meaning and ensure that the context does not allow for double interpretation.

  - *Instead of:* "Explain the principle."

  - *Use:* "Explain the principle of supply and demand in economics."

- **Input too much information:** Giving the LLM too many instructions might confuse it, especially if the tasks are not related. This can lead to disorganized or incomplete answers.

  - *Instead of:* "Describe the impact of the Industrial Revolution on society, technology, and politics."

  - *Use:* One prompt for each piece of information you want to talk about.

- **Use excessive jargon:** Specialized terms without explanation can confuse general-purpose models. Use simple terms and provide definitions and context when necessary to make the instructions clearer.

  - *Instead of:* "Describe the process of cytokinesis in the miotic division."

○ *Use:* "Using simple terms, describe the cell division process, particularly cytokinesis."

- **Assume the machine knows your intent:** Since AI programs do not understand feelings or comprehend what you are asking about, you must not assume that it knows the prompt's intent. If there is a specific answer or reason for what you are doing, explicitly state it so the model can understand.

  ○ *Instead of:* "Talk about the advantages and disadvantages of renewable energy."

  ○ *Use:* "I am preparing for a debate and would like to know five pros and five cons of renewable energy."

- **Ignore feedback:** If your request was not fulfilled, maybe you need to adjust or refine the prompt instead of repeating it verbatim. Learning from this feedback helps you refine results over time.

  ○ *Use:* Prompt adjustments and refinement, rephrasing the prompt, asking it a different way, review to see what information is missing.

- **Expect perfection:** While this might seem obvious, it is important to state that AI models are far from perfect. Yes, they can provide helpful information, but you should always review critical information to ensure accuracy, cohesion, and completeness.

  ○ *Use:* Human oversight and critical thinking to verify the provided output and check for sources if you are in doubt regarding the information.

By following these dos and don'ts, you will be able to start your experience with LLMs. As practice, I would suggest that you now put this book aside for a minute and open your preferred program. Try adding the prompts you have seen to the dialogue and explore the answers it will give you. You can start with generic questions and then create a more suitable alternative to the one you have just read.

Take some time to practice and see the differences that using these simple rules will make.

Once you are done, come back so you can start to explore different prompt structures to use for multiple purposes. Not only will you see templates that can be easily adjusted, but you will also see detailed examples of how different prompts can bring you very distinct results. What are you waiting for? Grab a computer and try some of these out!

PROMPT STRUCTURES AND EXAMPLES

In the previous section, you have read about the dos and don'ts of prompts. But did you know that there are certain structures you can follow to achieve the best results? This means not just typing in a question or a line of text to obtain the relevant output. These are structured prompts, each with a specific purpose that can be more effective in certain circumstances instead of others. Here are the main types of prompt structures and how you can use them in daily situations.

Prompt type	Use	Structure	Example
Directive prompts	• specific and focused outputs with minimal deviation • limited time and focus on efficiency	• clear command or instruction • specific parameters or constraints • desired format or output styles	*Write a professional email template following up with clients who haven't responded in 30 days. Use a friendly but professional tone and include a placeholder for customer name and previous interaction details.*

Conversational prompts	<ul><li>use a more natural and dialogue-based approach</li><li>engage the AI iteratively and collaboratively</li><li>obtain detailed responses</li></ul>	<ul><li>natural language phrasing</li><li>set context</li><li>use open-ended questions or situations</li></ul>	*I am preparing for a major client presentation next week. Can you help me think about how to structure it? The client is a retail company looking to improve their online presence. I want to ensure pain points are covered while showcasing solutions.*
Context-rich prompts	<ul><li>complex tasks that need a nuanced understanding</li><li>consider multiple factors</li><li>customization is important</li></ul>	<ul><li>detailed background information</li><li>requirements or constraints</li><li>target audience</li><li>desired outcome or objective</li><li>relevant examples</li></ul>	*Our software company is launching a new project. Target audience: small to medium-sized businesses (10–50 employees). Current market pain points: complex interfaces, poor mobile integration, and pricing transparency. Create a marketing strategy that will address the audience and their pain points in different channels.*
Role-based prompts	<ul><li>specialized expertise</li></ul>	<ul><li>clear role assignment</li></ul>	*You are an experienced financial analyst*

	• specific perspective • industry-specific jargon	• specific task or question • relevant context • level of expertise	*who will review our company's investments. Review our company's investment portfolio and provide recommendations for rebalancing, considering market conditions and our goal of moderate growth and risk mitigation.*
Zero-shot prompts	• no examples to give the machine • to be used with highly capable models	• straightforward tasks • effective results • quick activities	*Generate five names for a new eco-friendly cleaning product brand.*
Template prompts	• to obtain consistent structures for repeated tasks • uses placeholders you can fill in • standardizing outputs • maintaining consistency	• elements needed must be in between square brackets [] • clear instructions stating what you need • title, structure, problem, requirements, context,	*I need to build customer files with standardized information and order. The information must be complete with [insert information needed] and the output should be [describe].*

		and constraints	
Comparative prompts	• compare and contrast different information	• provide the elements you want to compare and the context in which the comparison will be used	*Compare these three marketing channels for my startup:* 1. *Social media advertising* 2. *Content marketing* 3. *Email campaigns*

These basic prompt structures will provide you with the necessary tools to start working with LLMs. At the same time, they will be useful tools to help you start with advanced prompting techniques, which can transform your interactions with AI from simple question-and-answer exchanges into incredible problem-solving partnerships. In the final section of this chapter, you will explore advanced techniques that separate casual users from those who can obtain the best results.

ADVANCED PROMPTING TECHNIQUES

If you are looking to use AI to leverage your business's capabilities or to start a side income activity, advanced prompting techniques can be the key to helping you unlock the best results. The techniques you will see in this last section will help you deal with complex challenges, generate creative content, and develop innovative solutions, even if this means starting a business from scratch. These are strategies that those with experience in AI commonly use to increase productivity and efficiency.

Iterative Refinement

One of the advantages of using LLMs is that you can carry out conversations with them, meaning that you can refine the result as it is given. In this case, you will need to undergo several rounds of prompting, asking questions, and guiding the machine until it reaches the desired output. This would be similar to making a sculpture, in which you would start with a rough shape and gradually refine it until you reach the desired result.

An example of iterative prompting would be

- *Initial prompt:* "Write a product description for an online translation service for ecommerce."

- *Refinement 1:* "Make the description more technical, including the areas in which it can help."

- *Refinement 2:* "Add to the description the number of languages that can be used."

- *Refinement 3:* "Include the options of machine-performed and human-performed translations and editing."

This technique will help you ensure that each iteration builds upon previous responses while adding new layers of detail and precision to the final output.

Chain-Of-Thought Prompts

Similar to the iterative prompting process, when you use the chain-of-thought prompts, you will ask the machine to carry out different activities by breaking the task into smaller steps. In this case, each output will be what feeds the next prompt, allowing you to maintain a chain of thought throughout the process. One example of these types of prompts is:

Prompt 1: Analyze these customer service responses and identify key themes.

[output]

Prompt 2: Using these themes, draft a potential solution approach.

[output]

Prompt 3: Based on these solutions, create an implementation timeline.

[output]

Prompt 4: Generate a presentation outline incorporating the analysis, solutions, and timeline.

While this structure is similar to what you have seen in the previous section on *conversational prompts*, it is different because you are breaking the steps as the outputs are being given. Additionally, you are *building* on them, which is a difference, especially in the results that will be generated.

Few-Shot Prompts

These prompts will allow you to first show the machine examples of the inputs you will give and the outputs you expect. After this has been done, you will be able to give it the main task, which should mimic the information you provided. This structure is especially effective for establishing patterns and ensuring consistent formatting. Here is an example:

Prompt 1:

Example 1:

Product: Wireless headphones.

Description: Premium noise-canceling headphones with a 30-hour battery life, perfect for professionals on the go.

Prompt 2:

Example 2:

Product: Smart water bottle.

Description: Tracks hydration levels and reminds you to drink water throughout the day.

Prompt 3: Now write a description for:

Product: Smart home security camera

By implementing this strategy, you can standardize product and service descriptions on webpages, ensuring your company adopts the same tone throughout the channel. These can also be used for social media posts, emails, and other business tasks that must be standardized or have a similar format.

Constraint-Based Prompts

In the real world, sometimes we need solutions but face constraints to make it happen just as we would like. In this case, you can use constraint-based prompts to help you find the best alternative among the options. To do this, you will need to tell the machine what the constraints are and what it is expected to do, as follows:

Prompt: "Generate a marketing campaign concept that uses not more than a $5,000 budget, must include social media and email, cannot use paid advertising, and must be measurable within 30 days."

By giving the machine the limitations you face for the task at hand, it will be able to obtain different points of view and opportunities to explore. At the same time, this does not mean that you need to be restricted to just one type of prompt. You can use these different structures and combine them to achieve the best outputs for your company. In this case, you could associate a role-based prompt with a constraint-based prompt to help you obtain more specific information, such as:

Prompt: You are an experienced marketing specialist used to working with companies with limited budgets. Generate a marketing campaign concept that uses not more than a $5000 budget, must include social media and email, cannot use paid advertising, and must be measurable within 30 days.

You can combine any type of structures you have seen so far or even create new ones of your own. As you continue to gain practice in prompting and speaking with LLMs, especially depending on the AI you choose, you will be able to find the strategy that best works for you. Remember: You can use together any of these you have seen, as long as they are clear, direct, and understandable.

Meta Prompts

Did you know that you can have the chatbot create the prompt for you? While many people do not know this, it is certainly a possibility that can be explored, especially in those times when the AI does not seem to be understanding you. In this case, you will use meta prompts, which are used to generate or improve other prompts, helping you to optimize the interaction with the machine. This can be done as follows:

Prompt: "Help me create an effective prompt for generating product descriptions. The prompt should ensure consistent tone and style, and inclusion of key features and benefits, appropriate length and format, and compelling call-to-action."

Once you input this information or any other that you need into the machine, you will see the magic happen. While you might need to adjust and refine the prompt the machine gives you, it is already halfway on the path to achieving optimal results. It is also a great opportunity for you to practice and see the best types of prompts you can create, refining your new skill for what is next to come.

As you continue to practice and master prompt engineering, you will enhance how you interact with AI systems. You should remember that the ability to write effective prompts is not just about the answer you will get, but also about how you can connect to the machine so that it understands you. The skills you have learned in this chapter will be essential for the next parts of this book, in which you will learn how to leverage these machines to your advantage.

The first stop is how you can use AI to increase productivity and business, allowing you to discover how these tools can help you streamline workflows, enhance decision-making, and drive business value. You will understand how to make yourself more productive by using technology to carry out basic tasks and for professional success. It is now time to move on from theory to practice that will drive tangible and real-world results. Are you ready?

CHAPTER 6:

USING AI FOR PRODUCTIVITY AND BUSINESS

It is undeniable that AI will continue to change the world in almost all aspects we can think of. As it reshapes how companies carry out their business, it is essential to understand how to effectively leverage AI tools regardless of the industry you are in. So far, we have covered the theoretical aspect of AI systems and LLMs, but now it is time to see how this can be put into practice, which is what this chapter is all about.

From tools that are built exclusively on top of LLM models to programs that can analyze data and create cohesive text, there is an AI for almost any task you want to carry out. You will see how these tools can be integrated into your workflow and automate routine tasks to be more productive. Additionally, you will learn how these models can enhance your decision-making processes using advanced user business analytics.

POPULAR TOOLS BUILT ON LLMS

Since ChatGPT was released, the number of AI models available to the public has significantly increased. These tools have transformed from simple automation aids into sophisticated assistants that can handle complex tasks and enhance productivity. From industry-specific applications to the more general models you have already seen, some of the popular tools you are about to read about might even surprise you!

- **Jasper:** Tools such as these have completely changed how marketing teams carry out their work. With it, you can create multiple campaigns across different channels, even if you are on a tight deadline. Another advantage of this LLM is that it can generate initial drafts and maintain a consistent voice as well as tone throughout different channels. The AI's ability to understand context and adapt tone according to theme and instructions has made the tool a must-have for content teams globally.

- **GitHub Copilot:** For software developers, GitHub Copilot has proven to be an invaluable asset, especially for programming tasks. With it, even junior developers can code as if they had an experienced professional helping them, offering suggestions, and helping address challenges. This has increased tech professionals' productivity and allowed them to even work with unfamiliar code. Its ability to troubleshoot based on the knowledge it was trained on allows millions of lines to be debugged and improved in seconds, speeding up the development process and improving code accuracy.

- **Notion AI:** This tool has become widely popular in business environments, especially due to its versatility. The AI assistant allows teams to collaborate and organize information, allowing daily workflows to be enhanced. Some of its features include the ability to draft documents, summarize meetings, and manage projects. While this is one of the most popular tools on the market, powered by ChatGPT and Claude, others are also gaining traction, due to their abilities to understand context and generate relevant content for teams that need to collaborate in person or remotely.

- **Grammarly:** One of the most popular tools on the market today is this AI-powered app that has become a must for those who work with written content. Especially in the Business version, the app goes beyond simple grammar checking and becomes a writing assistant to help maintain communication consistent and well-written. With its different features to adjust tone and other settings for text correction and adjustment, you can use it to proof and review text so that it is aligned with your brand voice and the highest professional standards.

- **Harvey AI:** Professionals in the legal industry are irreplaceable, but this does not mean there aren't AI tools that can help carry out some of their tasks. This LLM is one of the most used among these professionals, especially due to its wide range of abilities that include contract analysis to case law research. Although the information still must be fact-checked, and it is essential to use with human oversight, tools such as these allow the legal back office process to be faster and more streamlined, reducing costs associated with research and drafting times.

- **Elicit:** It would only be natural that if all other industries have tools that target their needs, the research community would have a few as well. In this case, Elicit is a platform that helps researchers fine-comb vast amounts of academic literature, synthesize findings, and identify relevant studies. This process is extremely efficient and has reduced the time needed for these processes, allowing researchers to focus more on analysis and interpretation.

Tools such as these continue to evolve at an amazing pace, with new features and capabilities being regularly added to increase their power. One of the most important aspects to consider is integration— by looking for tools that have APIs and native connections to popular business applications. This process leads to more robust workflows where AI assistance is available where and when needed.

These capabilities have also been seen in tools that we explored in previous chapters, such as Gemini for the Google suite and Microsoft

Copilot for Microsoft applications. As organizations adopt these tools, they are finding out that the real power is not just in each application's capability, but in how they can be combined to create efficient workflows. A marketing team, for example, might use Jasper for content creation, Grammarly for refinement, and Notion AI for organization and collaboration. Associating these tools will allow the content production pipeline to be more comprehensive and free of errors.

At the same time, it is important that when selecting these tools, companies look at the immediate and future needs. It is important to consider tools that are scalable at a reasonable cost and that will support the company. The best tools offer scalability, allowing teams to expand their usage as comfort and capabilities grow. Other factors that should also be considered include data security and the level of customization available to meet specific industry or organizational requirements.

As powerful as these specialized tools are for enhancing productivity, the power of AI lies in its ability to analyze complex data and support strategic decision-making. Although content creation and task automation tools streamline operations, an AI's analytical capability can change how your company understands its data, identifies patterns, and makes informed decisions. Read on to learn more about these practical applications in business intelligence and decision-making processes, transforming data into actionable insights that lead to strategic change.

AI FOR ANALYSIS AND DECISION-MAKING

Decision-making is one of the most complex and challenging tasks of engaging in business. When action is needed, you must look into different aspects of the same situation, and it is not uncommon to miss data simply because the relationships are not seen. When you use AI-powered tools, it is like gaining a super-powerful ally that will transform raw data into actionable insights. Using these systems can help uncover patterns and opportunities that might otherwise remain hidden, thus changing how business strategies and operations are carried out.

Think about your business and how you carry out your workflow. Now, take a moment to consider your market intelligence needs. Tools like Forrester AI and Crayon can serve as your digital market research team, working 24/7 to keep you informed. These systems enable you to track movements made by competitors and also alert you to emerging trends before they become obvious to the market. This means that you could spot a shift in consumer preferences or an emerging technology months before other companies, giving you the time to adapt your strategy and maintain your competitive edge.

Now, suppose that your needs are more financially related. There are AI tools for that too! By using apps such as Alphasense and Bloomberg AI, you can reduce the time spent on research while improving insight quality. These tools can, among other things, analyze earning calls, financial reports, and market indicators in real time, helping you make more informed investment decisions. Leveraging such tools allows you to have in one place a team of expert analysts tirelessly working to identify opportunities and risks in your financial health.

Another area that can also be significantly affected by AIs and LLMs is the supply chain. These operations can benefit from tools such as Blue Yonder and o9 solutions to manage and optimize your supply chain for the future. Implementing these into your workflow will allow the business to predict demand more accurately, optimize inventory, and receive warnings about potential disruptions. This means you can maintain optimal inventory levels while reducing costs and improving customer satisfaction, ensuring the products that are close to running out are always available.

Speaking about customers, businesses must understand their needs and demands to ensure profitable growth. Tools like Medallia and Qualtrics can analyze customer feedback across all business channels, helping you understand what customers are saying and feeling. As you leverage these tools, you will be able to predict customer behavior, identify at-risk accounts before they churn, and personalize your service approach based on nuanced insights.

Finally, when it comes to risk management, platforms such as RiskThinking.AI and Logic Manager can serve as early warning systems. They will help you identify potential risks across your operations, assess likelihood and potential impact, and suggest mitigation strategies. When you use AI for a proactive approach to risk management, you can avoid costly surprises and maintain business stability while having different variables analyzed to ensure you have the full picture.

As you can see, the prospects of AI tools for your company are vast and will depend on what you are looking for. To make the most of your selection, you must focus on three key areas:

1. Ensure your data is clean and well-integrated, especially since these systems are only as good as the data they work with.

2. Maintain appropriate human oversight. AI is valuable and can be very powerful, but your judgment and industry expertise remain crucial.

3. Invest in training for your team to ensure they can use these tools effectively and interpret their outputs.

As AI continues to evolve, it is more than likely these tools will continue to become even more powerful and sophisticated. Soon, they will be able to integrate data from more sources, provide clearer explanations for their recommendations, and adjust their analysis in real time, perhaps without even needing to upload data. This increase in capacity will lead to increased automation of routine decisions, thus allowing you to focus on more strategic parts of the business.

But how do I know the best tool to choose for me? The key to success is to carry out the necessary due diligence and understand their capabilities and features. Doing so will allow you to see which the right ones for your specific needs are and implement them thoughtfully. Start by identifying your most pressing analytical needs and the area your company needs the most insight. These can include market intelligence, financial analysis, risk assessment, customer insights, or any other area that you believe needs more information. Then, you should look for tools that will meet those needs and integrate well with your existing systems and processes.

While these tools will give you a significant advantage over other companies that do not have them, you must remember that it is your experience, judgment, and understanding of the business context that will turn the insights you derive from these tools into effective decisions. By embracing these AI-powered analytical tools, you are positioning yourself to make more informed decisions, respond quicker to changing conditions, and identify opportunities that otherwise might go unnoticed. The future of business decision-making is here, and it is augmented by AI.

OTHER INDUSTRY-SPECIFIC TOOLS

One of the most significant benefits of industry-specific AI tools is their ability to improve efficiency and reduce costs. As routine tasks are automated, human resources are freed for more strategic work. In industries such as healthcare and legal services, where documentation and compliance are critical, AI-driven tools significantly reduce administrative burdens. Similarly, in logistics and retail, real-time data analysis allows businesses to adapt quickly to changing conditions, improving their operations.

Implementing AI in an operational company brings significant change, especially for small and medium businesses. While large companies are investing in these tools with near-limitless budgets, smaller organizations need to be more objective on how they will leverage the technology. Many of these are built on top of LLMs, and it is those specialized to cater to specific industry needs by offering tailored solutions that the impact can be seen. By improving efficiency, decreasing costs, and enhancing customer satisfaction, many of these companies can compete with larger organizations with heftier investments.

Here are 10 examples for you to consider:

- **Healthcare:** Clinical documentation management tools such as Dragon Medical One leverage LLMs to transcribe doctor–patient interactions in real time. These tools reduce the burden of paperwork on healthcare professionals by automating note-taking, allowing them to focus more on patient care. Additionally, with these tools, you can ensure accuracy in medical records and improve compliance with industry regulations. Automating routine tasks ultimately allows for these professionals to save time, increase diagnosis and treatment rates, and reduce administrative costs.

- **Education:** Many examples could be named for adaptive learning platforms that can be leveraged in education. Tools such as ScribeSense use LLMs to personalize the learning experience for students and streamline educator work by analyzing performance data and adjusting content delivery accordingly. By using the correct prompts, you could provide tailored lesson plans and exercises, ensuring that students receive support based on their learning pace and style. For schools and organizations dedicated to learning practices, tools such as these can reduce teacher workload and improve student outcomes.

- **Logistics:** Tools such as Wise System can help optimize delivery routes by analyzing traffic patterns, weather conditions, and package constraints as they are being delivered. Using these tools allows the company to reduce fuel costs and improve delivery time, ultimately leading to customer satisfaction. Companies can benefit from this application in logistics and transportation to manage fleets more efficiently and deliver with fewer resources. Companies such as FedEx and UPS have already started implementing tools such as these to manage their vehicles, obtaining significant results since doing so.

- **Legal services:** Legal research and document review tools like Casetext's CoCounsel use LLMs to analyze large volumes of legal documents quickly and accurately. These tools can identify relevant case law, draft legal memos, and even spot inconsistencies in contracts. For small law firms, these tools reduce time spent on research and improve accuracy, enabling more clients to be served without increasing costs or hiring more personnel.

- **Retail:** Popular retailers are turning to AI-powered marketing assistants, such as Phrasee, to create personalized email campaigns and social media posts. Tools such as these analyze customer behavior data and generate content that will resonate with the desired audience according to their characteristics, needs, and demands. From increased customer engagement to higher conversion rates, these companies usually see increased profits and a stronger community without the need for large marketing teams or hefty advertising investments.

- **Sports:** One of the most popular applications of LLMs is in the sports industry, with applications such as Zone7 being used to analyze player performance data to predict injuries and recommend training adjustments. Large datasets are processed from wearable devices and training logs, which you will often see players use underneath their jerseys or wrapped around their arms. These tools allow coaches and training staff to analyze performance and make data-driven decisions. This proves to be a critical application of the technology, especially since coaches can create targeted performance analytics to improve athlete outcomes and reduce costly injury-related downtime.

- **Real estate:** Property valuation tools such as Zillow's Zestimate use AI technology and ML algorithms to provide accurate property price estimates. These tools analyze historical sales data, market trends, and property features to predict fair market values. Additionally, by leveraging LLMs for this purpose, realtors can improve decision-making when buying or selling properties and enhance client trust by offering data-backed insights. Although these tools can be used by larger organizations, they can also be leveraged by smaller companies and real estate agents to gain a competitive edge and remain aligned with market practices and expectations.

- **Human resources:** AI and LLMs have been increasingly adopted in the human resources business, helping companies analyze resumes and matching them with job descriptions and openings. This is the case of platforms such as Eightfold AI, which uses the technology to match candidates to open positions and predict their success on the job. Other capacities tools such as these often include a comprehensive analysis to suggest upskilling opportunities and professional enhancement. Finally, HR and recruitment areas can benefit from AI by reducing hiring time, improving candidate fit, and enhancing employee retention.

- **Financial services:** Financial firms are leveraging tools like ThetaRay for anti-money laundering and fraud detection. Tools such as these analyze transaction data to identify suspicious patterns and flag potential compliance risks. As real-time analysis and monitoring are implemented, there are reduced regulatory risks for these organizations, ensuring they remain compliant without hiring large compliance teams.

- **Agriculture:** Tools such as Granular are helping farmers make data-driven decisions about planting, irrigation, and harvesting. These tools analyze weather data, solid conditions, and crop health to optimize yields and costs. By associating AI technology with satellite images and incredible processing power as conditions change, you can increase productivity and profitability by adopting precision farming techniques without hiring large teams or needing a lot of resources and by having an all-in-one approach to decision-making.

While these AI tools offer several benefits, it is also important to consider the challenges they may pose. Some of these include implementation costs, data privacy concerns, and the need for human oversight, as often stated. It is also crucial to ensure that these AI tools are ethically used and free from bias, especially in areas that deal with sensitive information, requiring the need for a balance between leveraging technology and maintaining ethical practices.

As you explore these different applications, it is natural that you have doubts about other uses and applications in your business. For these reasons, in the final section of this chapter, you will read about case studies, applications, and prompts you can use for diverse purposes. As you will see, it is only a matter of starting—once you get the hang of it, you will be able to unleash the full power of AI tools within your professional life.

CASE STUDIES AND APPLICATIONS

Successfully implementing LLMs in the industry you work for will depend on how these tools will be leveraged. By understanding how larger companies have incorporated them into their businesses, you can obtain a road map that will help you find the best alternatives for your organization. In this final section of the chapter, you will explore how these versatile tools are being applied to solve specific challenges and lessons learned from their experiences. Additionally, you will see different prompt examples that might help you achieve similar results in your own business.

Case Study 1: eBay

eBay developed a framework that integrates different AI models to assist its staff in coding and marketing tasks. This system automates complex processes, enhancing operational efficiency. Using AI, eBay streamlined operations, allowing the company to handle tasks more efficiently and allocate human resources to strategic initiatives (Lin, 2025). eBay saw that integrating AI models into the business to automate complex tasks is feasible, but human oversight remains essential to ensure alignment with business objectives and handle nuanced scenarios.

Prompt example: "Generate a product description for a vintage 1960s jacket, highlighting its unique features and appeal to fashion enthusiasts."

Case Study 2: HubSpot

HubSpot introduced an AI-powered content creation tool to help marketers generate blog posts, social media content, and email campaigns quickly. By inputting a brief description, users can generate high-quality search engine optimization (SEO) content. The tool helped marketers increase content production by 40% while maintaining quality (Bodiroza, 2023). It also reduced time spent on first drafts, allowing teams to focus on strategy and refinement.

Prompt example: "Write a 500-word blog post on the benefits of email marketing for small businesses."

Case Study 3: Johnson & Johnson

Johnson & Johnson uses AI to enhance its drug discovery process, specifically in optimizing chemical synthesis. These models automate complex tasks, streamlining the development of new pharmaceuticals. With its implementation, it could now speed up the drug development process, enabling the company to bring new medication to the market more efficiently (Lin, 2025). When pharmaceutical companies can implement these programs in their processes, it allows for a more nuanced and monitored activity, ensuring they operate within the desired parameters and contribute effectively to research objectives.

Prompt example: "Develop an AI-driven strategy to optimize chemical synthesis processes in pharmaceutical research, focusing on reducing time and resource consumption."

Case Study 4: Cosentino

The Spanish brand Cosentino adopted AI to create agents that operate as a digital workforce to manage customer orders and operational tasks. These agents autonomously handle functions such as credit management, processing blocked orders, and enabling credit managers to process up to five times more orders without additional risk. This adoption led to increased operational efficiency, allowing humans to focus on more strategic business areas (Lin, 2025). When companies treat AI as digital employees with complete foundational skills, it becomes easier to adhere to company processes and compliance standards.

Prompt example: "Design an AI agent to autonomously manage customer order processing in a manufacturing company, ensuring compliance with credit policies and enhancing operational efficiency."

Case Study 5: Best Buy

The retail company partnered with Google to develop an AI-powered virtual assistant to help customers with self-service options. The idea is for the assistant to help customers troubleshoot product issues, modify order deliveries and schedules, and manage subscriptions. The company wants customers and human customer care agents to have AI-enabled tools that will help with real-time assistance, analyzing customer interactions, offering relevant recommendations, summarizing sentiment, and using call data to prevent future issues (Tilzer, 2024). Companies are implementing these solutions to ensure that there is a more personalized and efficient customer support experience, as well as streamline operations and allow employees to focus on complex customer needs.

Prompt example: "Design a generative AI-driven virtual assistant for a retail company that can handle customer inquiries, manage orders, and provide personalized product recommendations."

Other Useful Prompts

Here are 10 useful prompts you might want to consider using depending on your industry:

- **Marketing:** "Generate a 500-word blog post that explains the benefits of using social media marketing for small businesses. Ensure the tone is professional yet approachable, include three specific examples, and suggest a call-to-action at the end."

- **Sales:** "Write a personalized cold email for a B2B SaaS company offering project management software. Address the recipient's pain points of collaboration inefficiency and suggest a free demo. Keep the email concise, persuasive, and under 200 words."

- **Customer support:** "Create a professional response template for a customer service team addressing delayed product shipments. Apologize sincerely, explain potential causes briefly, and offer a discount code as compensation."

- **HR:** "Draft a job description for a Senior Data Analyst role. Include required skills (e.g., SQL, Python, and data visualization), experience (5+ years), and a brief description of the company culture."

- **Finance:** "Summarize the key financial metrics of a quarterly earnings report, including revenue, profit margin, and year-over-year growth. Provide a brief analysis highlighting significant trends or concerns."

- **Legal:** "Analyze the following nondisclosure agreement and highlight any clauses that may present legal risks for a small startup. Suggest modifications if necessary."

- **Education:** "Design a 60-minute lesson plan for a high school history class about the Industrial Revolution. Include a brief lecture outline, an interactive activity, and discussion questions to encourage critical thinking."

- **Product development:** "Based on the following user feedback, prioritize three new features for a mobile banking app. Justify the selection using criteria such as user demand, implementation complexity, and potential impact."

- **Logistics:** "Suggest an optimal delivery route for a logistics company with 10 drop-off points in a metropolitan area. Assume traffic data and delivery time windows are critical factors."

- **Real estate:** "Write a compelling property listing for a 3-bedroom, 2-bathroom suburban house. Highlight key selling points, such as a recently renovated kitchen, proximity to schools, and a large backyard."

Using these prompts as examples and adjusting them to your business, you will be able to start practicing and seeing the results that the LLM will provide you. However, while understanding and implementing AI tools is a significant step, the real potential lies in turning innovative ideas into sustainable income streams.

In the next chapter, you will understand how professionals and entrepreneurs are making money with AI by creatively leveraging these tools. Whether you are aiming to create a passive income stream, launch a new business, or enhance an existing one, the following two chapters will guide you through the practical steps of transforming AI-driven innovation into profitable ventures.

CHAPTER 7:
TURNING IDEAS INTO INCOME

As you might imagine, AI has created unprecedented opportunities for entrepreneurs and professionals to transform their expertise and ideas into successful businesses. Unlike previous technological revolutions, AI tools are unique since they allow you to amplify your capabilities. This usually means delivering higher-quality services and solving complex problems more efficiently.

In this chapter, you will see some of the practical steps of leveraging AI tools to create active income streams. You will see why AI is such an incredible opportunity for new business ventures, and how it can be used to enhance your services or create new ones. As you read, you will find different business models that are well-suited for AI integration, from consulting services to specialized solutions for specific industries.

Through real-world case studies, you will see how others have successfully built AI-enhanced businesses and examine the strategies used to overcome challenges. Whether you are a professional looking to start a side business or an entrepreneur ready to launch a full-scale venture, you will obtain all the information you need to build your own business and achieve financial success. Are you ready to discover how?

WHY USE AI FOR A NEW OPPORTUNITY?

While many might discuss the negative implications of AI in the market today, others are using this opportunity of an evolving market to leverage the technology to their advantage. With LLMs becoming more accessible to the market and easier to work with, they have become a powerful ally for those who want to look at new opportunities. Along with their increasingly enhancing features and capabilities, more people are resorting to these models to help them move out of the ordinary and bring new value to businesses.

AI is an incredible tool that can help entrepreneurs and professionals achieve success in areas never imagined before. Its capacity to generate new ideas and to interact with a human with the machine's processing capability allowed it to transform the business environment in revolutionary ways. *But can AI really help me develop new opportunities and increase my income?* Yes, and not only this, but it can help you turn that idea that was left inside the drawer into a real income stream if used correctly.

Here are eight reasons to start using AI LLMs as soon as you close this book:

- **Scale and efficiency:** AI's ability to handle massive amounts of data and automate tasks creates opportunities that traditional exclusively human-operating businesses cannot match. Consider a solo entrepreneur who recently adopted an AI-powered legal document review service or an accountant who subscribed to accounting software that recognizes invoices. By leveraging AI, they can analyze hundreds of contracts and documents at the same time, offering a high-level service at a fraction of traditional costs. This kind of scale would usually require a team of professionals, but AI enables a single professional to deliver equivalent or better results.

- **Personalization at scale:** One of AI's most powerful aspects is its ability to provide personalized experiences without the traditional trade-off between customization and scalability. Suppose you are a fitness instructor who uses an AI-powered platform that creates individually tailored workout programs based on each user's fitness level, goals, available equipment, and even daily energy levels. The system would adapt in real time to user feedback and progress, providing a level of personalization that would be impossible for a human professional to maintain across thousands of clients.

- **Innovative problem-solving approach:** Solving traditional problems is sometimes easier when you adopt AI into your workflow. In this case, you can imagine an urban farmer who adopted an AI program to optimize their indoor growing conditions. The system allows them to monitor traditional metrics like humidity and temperature, analyze plant growth patterns through computer analysis, predict crop yields, and adjust growing conditions to maximize production. This level of precision and automation allows urban farming to be economically feasible in spaces previously unsuited for agriculture.

- **Market gap identification:** In the past, companies used to carry out extensive market research to identify new market opportunities and identify the potential of new products. With AI, marketers and researchers can identify untapped opportunities by analyzing vast amounts of data to spot patterns and trends. In this case, a social media analyst could use AI to analyze conversations and online reviews across multiple industries to identify specific pain points that were not being addressed by existing solutions. A successful venture would lead to the development of a widely accepted niche product that larger companies might have overlooked.

- **Enhanced decision-making:** As you have seen in previous chapters, AI's ability to analyze large volumes of data allows professionals to have greater insight than would be impossible through traditional methods. In this case, a realtor who adopted AI into their work processes would be able to analyze hundreds of factors that affect the value of a property, from social media sentiment to satellite images showing neighborhood changes. This would allow them to identify up-and-coming areas before property prices rise and allow for more informed investment decisions and higher returns.

- **Rapid prototype and testing:** Another advantage of AI programs, especially LLMs, is that they accelerate the product development cycle by allowing rapid testing and idea iteration. In this case, you can carry out a "conversation" with the machine and refine ideas until the optimal solution is reached. Professionals in the fashion industry, for example, could use AI to generate and test thousands of designs and products with variations and gather feedback through virtual try-ons without producing any physical items. This process helps reduce waste, cut costs, and ensures a better market fit for their products, ultimately increasing profits and revenue.

- **Creating new value from existing resources:** Due to its ability to analyze and identify patterns invisible to the human eye, AI models can extract value from existing assets or data that were previously hidden. Business consultants, for example, could subscribe to an AI app that would analyze a client's historical business data to identify operational inefficiencies and growth opportunities that at first were not visible through traditional analysis. This could open up new opportunities and revenue streams from data the business already had but was not fully used to its best advantage.

- **Removal of barriers to market entry:** In many markets, the most frequent barrier faced by professionals is the need to have expertise and experience to work in it. However, with AI, the need for these, and even resources, has significantly reduced, allowing professionals with less experience to remove the initial barriers. Translators, for example, could use specialized translation services for medical documents, combining AI's speed with human expertise for the final check. This hybrid approach allows them to compete with larger translation services while maintaining high accuracy and lower costs.

The opportunity to create value with AI is not just about using the technology; it is also about identifying where the technology can solve real problems in real ways. To successfully leverage these tools, professionals must focus on value creation, identifying specific problems where AI can provide unique solutions and add value. Similarly, it is essential to start with clear use cases, meaning there must be well-defined problems that AI is suited to solve and that will build on the expertise you have in the industry.

At the same time, while implementing AI to generate new income is not uncommon, precautions must be taken to ensure it is a profitable venture. This means, for example maintaining the human connection with clients and using the technology to augment rather than replace your expertise. Generally, hybrid solutions offer customers a higher level of comfort, especially for those who are more resistant to change. Finally, you must remain adaptable and be prepared to evolve your approach as AI capabilities advance. Continuously learn and adjust your business model based on market feedback and the changes that happen in the market.

BUSINESS OPPORTUNITIES WITH LLMS

Whether you are looking to start a side business or launch a full-time venture, LLMs can help you create valuable services that meet real market needs. This section will explore real-life implementations of how technology can significantly change the way you work and generate income. Read on to discover 10 ways you can use AI and LLMs for a business opportunity:

- Sarah, a language teacher, transformed her traditional tutoring business by incorporating AI tools. She now offers personalized language learning experiences that were previously impossible to scale. With the use of LLMs, she can generate custom lesson plans and track student progress while focusing on providing high-value guidance and conversation practice. As a result, her students progress faster, and she can charge premium rates for this enhanced service.

- Marcus used LLMs to build a consulting practice, associating his knowledge with the tool's capabilities. He helps businesses analyze their content performance across platforms, predict trending topics, and create data-driven content calendars. What sets his service apart is how he uses AI to process market data while applying his human insight to craft strategies that resonate with specific audiences.

- Elena launched a modern career coaching service that goes beyond traditional resume writing. By using AI-enhanced systems, she optimizes professional documents for specific industries, while providing personalized coaching on interview techniques and career strategy. The combination of AI efficiency and human experience allowed her to help more clients and charge above market values for the insights that human knowledge associated with technology capacity offers.

- David used AI to enter the world of small business analytics, something that was before the domain of large firms. He created a service that helps small businesses understand their customers' behaviors, predict inventory needs, and optimize pricing strategies. By automating the data analysis process, he can offer sophisticated insights at prices that small businesses can afford and increase his customer base and income.

- Patricia's innovative approach to event planning by using AI took her business to another level. She developed an AI-enhanced service that generates creative event concepts and optimizes venue layouts. Additionally, the program helps her predict attendance patterns, offering significant savings to her clients and allowing them to cut costs. This technical edge allows her to create more memorable events while managing resources more efficiently.

- Dr. Chen found a different niche to work within the academic world. By leveraging AI tools, he helps researchers enhance their scientific papers by improving paper structure, checking methodology consistency, and generating compelling visual aids. What started as a side project for alternate income grew into a full-time business serving researchers worldwide.

- James, a real estate entrepreneur, started to adopt AI to provide services that go beyond market analysis. By using these systems, he can predict neighborhood trends, estimate renovation costs, and generate rental income forecasts. This approach allowed him to increase his client base and expand the market he works in, making him a valued advisor to property investors.

- Michelle, a writer, found that with the help of AI tools, she can enhance her creative writing workshop services. She uses LLMs to generate unique story prompts, analyze plot structures, and provide character development insights while offering personal mentoring to help writers develop their craft. Associating technology and personal guidance allowed her to create a unique learning experience that writers are eager to join.

- Carlos is an independent consultant in the sports business and uses AI to enhance player performance. As he combined his knowledge with technology, he was able to analyze player movement and generate personalized training programs. His service helps athletes optimize their performance while minimizing injury risks, creating value that traditional coaching alone would not provide.

The key to success in any of these ventures is not just about leveraging the right AI tools, but also understanding how the technology can be combined with human expertise to enhance services and create something truly valuable. When you are looking for the same opportunities for yourself, start by identifying areas where you have domain knowledge and can meaningfully enhance traditional approaches with AI capabilities. Focus on building scalable systems while maintaining quality by using your expertise.

Finally, you must also remember to price your services strategically, considering the value you provide, the market's willingness to pay, and the costs that you have associated with the business. Offer tiered service levels that allow clients to choose the level of support they need, and always include premium options for those who want service at the highest level. The opportunity to create value with AI is fast and growing. Reflecting on all probabilities will allow you to build a sustainable business that serves clients while providing you with rewarding work and financial returns.

REAL-WORLD CASE STUDIES

In the previous section, you saw some examples of how AI can be leveraged in different industries. However, while these are merely fictional examples to show that technology can be associated with your profession, some businesses and companies are already using them in the real world. Let's explore five examples of where the association between LLMs and humans in business has proven to be a success and led to corporate transformation.

- **Nakie** produces hammocks from recycled materials and faced a challenge as demand for its eco-friendly products increased. By adopting an AI-driven inventory management powered by LLMs, the company automated its supply chain operations, ensuring that stock levels were always optimized based on real-time demand forecasts. This technology enabled the company to manage a growing product line while reducing manual workload. As a result, it improved order accuracy, reduced stockouts, and scaled its operations without a significant increase in staff, maintaining its competitive edge in the market (Boyer, 2024).

- **Sprinklr** is a medium-sized social media management platform that offers services to enterprise clients. It adopted LLMs to enhance its social media listening and sentiment analysis capabilities. With AI models capable of processing huge amounts of data, it provided customers with real-time insights into customer behavior and emerging trends. This allows marketing teams to make data-driven decisions and tailor their campaigns more effectively. Doing so allowed the company to increase its product offering and strengthened client retention by delivering more precise and actionable intelligence (ODSC - Open Data Science, 2023).

- **Randy Speckman Design** is a boutique design agency that uses AI-powered tools to automate content creation for client proposals, presentations, and marketing collateral. In the company's systems, AI handles routine tasks like drafting design briefs and generating ideas, while employees focus on creative execution and client interaction. This adoption of the technology allowed the firm to deliver high-quality projects faster while keeping operational costs low. As a result, it expanded its client base and increased revenue without needing to hire additional staff (Anderson, 2024).

- **CMY Cubes**, a small business offering interactive science, technology, engineering, arts, and math toys, leveraged a custom-built GPT-powered tool to supercharge its content marketing strategy. It automated the generation of SEO-friendly blog posts, product descriptions, and social media content, achieving significant cost savings and improving its online visibility. The AI model also provided actionable insights by analyzing customer feedback and performance data, helping the company optimize its marketing campaigns. As a result, there was a significant increase in organic traffic and customer engagement, boosting sales and increasing revenue (Boyer, 2024).

- **Notice Ninja** is a tech-driven business offering tax compliance solutions that faced challenges managing the constant changes in tax regulations. The issue was solved when they integrated AI-enabled tools based on LLMs to automate key processes like document review, compliance checks, and reporting, leading to reduced human error, accelerated turnaround times, and improved client satisfaction. Additionally, the AI allowed the company to handle a larger client base without compromising service quality, leading to increased revenue and market share (Anderson, 2024).

These success stories demonstrate that AI is not just for large companies with massive budgets. Strategically implementing AI into your company can transform your business, regardless of its size. The lesson that should remain here is that successful AI integration requires a clear understanding of business needs, careful tool selection, and a commitment to learning and adaptation. These companies did not just adopt AI for its own sake; they identified specific challenges and found ways to leverage tools to solve them effectively.

At the same time, while these stories are inspiring, they also raise important questions about responsible AI monetization. As you consider your own AI-powered business ventures, it is crucial to understand how to create sustainable revenue streams while maintaining ethical practices. Read on to explore how you can use AI and still generate profit and contribute positively to society, maintaining long-term viability for the business.

ETHICAL AND SUSTAINABLE AI MONETIZATION STRATEGIES

As professionals and entrepreneurs find new ways to leverage AI to enhance their businesses, the questions regarding ethical and sustainable concerns are growing at the same level. Responsible AI use is not just a question of doing what is right; it is essential for long-term trust, sustainability, and growth. As you explore some of the considerations to keep in mind, remember that the AI world encompasses much more than this, which will be further explored in Chapter 9.

Transparency

For any business leveraging AI, trust is invaluable. Customers want to know how AI is being used, what data is being collected, and whether human oversight is present. Being transparent about your AI operations creates a sense of accountability and builds trust with users, meaning it is not enough to offer the latest technology. You must also clearly communicate how AI powers your service, if and why personal data is being collected, the known limitations of the model, and where humans are involved.

Responsible Data Use

As you know, AI models are powered by data, and without access to these datasets, the models cannot deliver accurate and meaningful results. However, it is the business's job to ensure that data collection and handling is done responsibly to ensure user trust. You must adopt clear policies on data collection, use, and storage, including giving users control over what they provide. This might mean offering opt-in or opt-out choices, access to account data, and maintaining strict security protocols to prevent breaches.

Addressing Bias and Ensuring Fairness

When AI systems are trained on biased data, they can produce discriminatory or unfair outcomes. These have consequences in daily life, meaning that when adopting these tools, you must test the model periodically for unintended biases, ensure diverse and representative training sets, and create feedback mechanisms that allow users to report unfair behavior. By prioritizing fairness, you can mitigate risk and appeal to more customers, as they will trust the content you are providing.

Minimizing Environmental Footprint

Environmental costs are one of the most significant when considering AI use, especially due to the significant amount of energy that is consumed during the training and deployment phases. Businesses must adopt sustainability as a key part of their strategy, choosing energy-efficient models, optimizing AI operations to minimize waste, using green hosting solutions powered by renewable energy, and offsetting carbon footprints by investing in environmental projects, where possible, to stand out in an increasingly sustainability-driven market.

Developing Customer-Centric Solutions

The last consideration is that while AI can be a valuable tool, you must ensure that it is not only about automating tasks and enhancing efficiency. You should look for AI implementation where it genuinely improves the customer experience and solves real problems rather than creating unnecessary complexities or removing all human interaction. This connection must be enhanced, and not replaced, including offering human assistance when needed and regularly collecting user feedback to improve AI interaction. Doing so will allow you to enhance user satisfaction and differentiate your business from competitors that are only looking for automation and cost reduction.

It is also essential to keep up-to-date with ethical guidelines and best practices, ensuring your business is adaptable to the changes in the market. This can mean staying informed about new developments, industry standards, and regulatory changes. Creating an ethical AI framework should not be something that is done once, but an ongoing process that is regularly updated and reviewed.

As you move forward, it is time to explore the other side of AI businesses that will require little to no input from your side: earning passive income. From automated content creation to AI-driven affiliate marketing and digital product sales, you will see some strategies to generate revenue with minimum hands-on effort. Are you ready to learn how to turn into A self-sustaining engine of profit? Keep on going to find out how!

CHAPTER 8:
BUILDING AN AI-POWERED
BUSINESS

It is not uncommon to find individuals who are looking for different ways to earn an extra income but struggle to find the time. Between demanding jobs, family responsibilities, and personal commitments, there is little room left to start a side hustle or new venture. This is where AI comes in: It does not only need to be used for income sources you will work with, like you have seen in the previous chapter. It also offers solutions for those seeking to generate passive income with minimal ongoing efforts. With LLMs and AI, creating tools that work for you even as you sleep is possible!

From developing automated products and services to building digital solutions that require little maintenance, you can find an AI solution that will help you achieve this goal. Among the options are automated content creation, AI customer-driven support, and selling customized AI tools, all within a few strokes on the keyboard. To help you understand this process, this chapter will help you see the alternatives to launching your own AI-powered business.

You will also explore open-source LLMs that can be tailored to fit specific niches, giving you more control and creativity in your business model. Also within this chapter are insights into potential challenges and pitfalls, which you must be aware of so they can be addressed effectively. If you are looking for a new way to grow your income without sacrificing your time, AI offers exciting solutions that will help you turn time constraints into financial freedom.

USING AI FOR PASSIVE INCOME

One of the main advantages of integrating AI into business ventures is that the model will do most of the heavy lifting while you collect on top of its success. Regardless of the industry applying it to, those looking for extra income will find that knowing how to leverage these tools will open up new—and even multiple—opportunities for some extra cash at the end of the month. The best part is that once the business model is designed, they can let the technology handle most of the work, requiring minimal input.

- **Automated content creation:** Using LLMs to create content allows you to reduce the time required to create content from hours to just a few minutes. You can use AI tools to generate articles, schedule posts, and even respond to comments. You can even create a monetized blog or YouTube channel using AI-generated content, allowing you to earn from revenue, affiliate links, or sponsored content.

  - *Example:* Some entrepreneurs use AI to run niche blogs on topics like travel, technology, or fitness. Once the AI produces high-quality posts, the blog earns passive income through ads and affiliate programs.

- **Affiliate marketing:** AI can also be used to supercharge your strategy of earning money by promoting other people's products and earning a commission on sales. LLMs will allow you to create targeted content faster, identify high-converting products, and optimize marketing campaigns. Strategies like using driven keyword analyzers and content generators can significantly enhance the process.

  - *Example:* An affiliate marketer could use AI to build a website focused on reviewing tech gadgets. With AI generating product reviews and optimizing SEO, the site can consistently drive traffic and passive income without requiring constant attention.

- **Subscription-based services:** Another lucrative passive income stream you can benefit from is offering AI-powered subscription-based services. These could include chatbots, AI financial advisors, and other tasks that can be automated. Once developed, customers pay a recurring fee to access these services, generating consistent revenue.

  o *Example:* You can create an AI-powered writing assistant tailored for legal professionals. Once the tool is built and marketed, it could continue generating passive income through monthly or annual subscriptions.

- **Stock analysis tools:** If you are interested in finance, it might interest you to know that you can create an AI-driven stock analysis tool to generate passive income. These programs use ML algorithms to predict stock trends and offer investment insights to companies and traders. You can earn money from these tools through subscription services or premium access to advanced features.

  o *Example:* Financial entrepreneurs developed AI platforms that analyze market data and provide automated trading signals. Once users subscribe to these platforms, the owner earns a steady income.

- **Chatbots for businesses:** Commonly used for customer support, lead generation, and user engagement, AI tools also allow you to build chatbots specific to certain industries. Once they are ready, you can license them out for recurring fees and even create subscription tiers. Since the chatbots operate 24/7, they will provide consistent value with little maintenance.

  o *Example:* You can develop a chatbot that is specifically designed for real estate agents. The bot can handle inquiries, schedule viewings, and answer common questions. The tool could be offered on a subscription basis and generate passive income.

- **Online courses:** Education today is widely accessible, and you can automate the full process of course development with AI tools. This means creating the content, posting updates, grading activities, and even setting personalized tutoring. Other possibilities are course material, quizzes, and interactive content, reducing the manual workload. Once the course is live, income can come from course sales, subscriptions, and certificates.

  - ○ *Example:* A teacher could use AI to create a series of courses on their subject of expertise. They would use the tool to automate most of the development and the delivery process, ensuring that passive income is generated long after the initial launch. As a bonus, they could also use AI to translate the content and sell or caption it in other languages.

- **Ecommerce stores:** AI can help run automated ecommerce stores by managing inventory, setting prices, and even handling customer service. With tools that predict demand and optimize pricing strategies, you can minimize your involvement while maximizing profits.

  - ○ *Example:* Online store owners today use AI-driven tools to print-on-demand businesses such as customized T-shirts and products. The AI manages product listings, optimizes ads, and handles customer interactions, leaving the owner to do little beyond the occasional oversight.

- **Licensing AI models:** If you have the technical skills to develop your own AI models, licensing them to other businesses can generate passive income. For example, you might create a model that predicts customer churn or optimizes supply chain operations and license it to companies in relevant industries.

- *Example:* A developer builds an AI model that helps retailers predict inventory needs. After licensing it to multiple businesses, they earn recurring fees for its usage.

- **Social media management:** For many businesses, social media management is a time-consuming task. However, with AI, this process can be streamlined and significantly simplified. Using AI tools, you can create a social media scheduler or content generator and charge a monthly fee for using your tool.

  - *Example:* Some marketing companies are working with platforms that generate and schedule posts based on trending topics. Once businesses sign up, you will have an active business in which AI handles most of the work.

- **Virtual assistants:** AI-powered virtual personal assistants can help individuals manage their daily tasks, such as scheduling meetings, setting reminders, and managing emails. You could create a subscription service that would monetize the work and bring you extra income.

  - *Example:* Some startups have created virtual assistants specifically designed for entrepreneurs. Once users subscribe, the AI handles repetitive tasks, providing value while generating income for the creator.

As you can see, there are numerous ways to generate passive income with AI, and it will all depend on your creativity! The key is identifying a niche or area where AI can deliver real value and create systems requiring minimal maintenance. To help you understand this development process and how to achieve the best outcomes, the guide you will see next will be the road map for your future ventures.

ROAD MAP TO CREATING AN AI-POWERED BUSINESS

Starting an AI-powered business requires diligence and a systematic approach that balances technological capabilities with market needs. Here is a road map to help you determine if the business you are considering is a good fit and the steps you will need to take to increase the chances of success.

1. **Identify and validate market problems***: Identify the specific pain points or inefficiencies that your LLM will target. Focus on problems where humanlike text processing, analysis, or generation could create significant value. Validate your identified problem through direct conversations with potential customers, online research of industry forums and communities, analysis of existing solutions and their limitations, and surveys or interviews with industry specialists.

2. **Define your value proposition:** In a document, clearly articulate how your AI solution will solve the identified problem better than the existing alternatives. The value proposition should include the specific business outcome you want to achieve, offer measurable improvements (time saved, cost reduced, quality improved), be easily understandable by nontechnical stakeholders, and differentiate your solution from conventional approaches.

3. **Develop a business model:** Define how your AI solution will generate revenue. This could mean it is a subscription product for ongoing access, usage-based pricing for specific operations, enterprise licensing for larger deployments, and hybrid models combining different pricing approaches. You will need to know exactly what the business you are developing is to identify the later characteristics of the tool and build it accordingly.

4. **Select your technical stack:** Carry out the necessary research and choose the best tools and technologies based on your requirements. This process should include looking at API solutions for quick deployment and scalability, cloud infrastructure providers, development frameworks and libraries for AI integration, and the technologies that will be used for your application. **Note:** For many of the existing tools today, such as GPT, you will need minimal technical intervention to create an app. You must also remember to verify the cost structure and pricing models, technical capabilities and limitations, integration requirements, and data privacy and security needs.

5. **Build a minimum viable product (MVP):** Create a basic working prototype that demonstrates what you are offering to the market. The MVP should focus on one core function that solves the main problem, has basic error handling and user feedback mechanisms integrated, offers an intuitive and user-friendly interface, and includes analytics to track usage and performance metrics.

6. **Test and iterate with users:** Find and engage early adopters to validate your solution. This can include 5–10 potential users willing to test the prototype and create a structured feedback collection process. It is also important to focus on monitoring the key metrics like usage patterns and error rates and document your findings, common issues, and user suggestions.

7. **Address technical and ethical considerations:** Ensure your solution is built responsibly. This means implementing proper data handling and privacy measures, considering bias and fairness in the implementation, developing transparent policies about AI use, and planning for model updates, reviews, and maintenance.

8. **Create a go-to-market strategy:** Plan how you will launch the product into the market by identifying initial target

segments and developing marketing messages that resonate with the audience. You should also remember to create educational content about your AI solution and build partnerships with industry influencers or complementary businesses to ensure increased engagement and reach.

9. **Prepare for scaling:** Plan for the tool to grow and increase use in the future. This means you must take into account technical infrastructure scalability, customer support processes, documentation and training materials, and team expansion needs. The tool must have all its information documented to ensure that others can consult information if necessary.

10. **Establish success metrics:** Finally, define key performance metrics (KPIs) that are relevant to the business you are developing. These include user adoption and retention rates, customer satisfaction scores, technical performance metrics, and financial indicators.

During the process, especially if you are new to managing these tools, it is normal and acceptable to feel frustrated. If this happens, you must remember that starting a business is an iterative process, where you will need to start small, focus on solving a specific problem, and continuously gather user feedback. At the same time, as mentioned earlier, several of these tools already come with built-in features that will allow you to integrate them into a website, for example, if necessary.

During the research process, you might be surprised at the cost these tools can come at. Do not feel hindered by this, as there are many options in the market. Some of them are just as powerful as paid tools, and you might not even need premium subscriptions, depending on what you plan to use them for. Regardless of the case, the following section will explore open-source LLM options, which can provide additional flexibility and cost advantages for what you are trying to build.

EXPLORING OPEN-SOURCE LLMS FOR BUSINESS

When thinking about leveraging LLMs, our first reaction is usually to think about ChatGPT. This is only natural, as it was the first tool and still serves, in many ways, as a benchmark for how AI tools would work. However, as you have seen in Chapter 4, the market does not only have licensed AI programs but also a world of open-source language models that could save you a significant amount of cash every month. While recurring to the most widely known tool is usually the first option we resort to, it is important to know there are several others that can help you achieve the same goals at a more reasonable price.

These are called open-source LLMs and include tools such as Llama, Mistral, and BLOOM, all of which represent an interesting alternative to proprietary solutions. Think of these models as customizable engines you can modify to fit your specific business needs. Just as you might customize a vehicle for specific purposes, these models can be tailored to your industry's unique requirements.

But what about technical expertise? you might ask. That is the topic that has probably been on your mind as you are reading these chapters. The good news is that while some technical knowledge helps, it is not always necessary. You can start off with friendly platforms such as Hugging Face's Space platform, which allows you to experiment with AI without writing a single line of code.

The process of building your custom tool will happen in stages. You might begin with prebuilt solutions that require no coding, similar to using a website builder instead of writing the code from scratch. As your needs grow, you could either invest in learning basic technical skills or bring in expertise through hiring or partnerships. Many successful AI businesses started this way, gradually building their technical capabilities as their needs evolved.

The cost–benefit comparison can be alarming. Unlike proprietary solutions that charge per token or API call, open-source models can be run on your own equipment. This is similar to buying a coffee machine instead of paying per cup at a café: There is an upfront investment, but it often pays for itself over time. In some cases, depending on the use and frequency, the cost of using open-source platforms can be as minimal as 10% when compared to tools such as Gemini, ChatGPT, and even Claude.

However, it is the customizability where there is the main difference. Using these models allows you to train the machine to understand your industry's specific jargon, adapt to your brand's voice, or handle specialized tasks. For those starting out, a practical path includes being with hosted solutions that offer user-friendly interfaces. As your understanding grows, you can explore more customized solutions and scale as you continue.

The secret is to match your approach and capabilities while keeping an eye on future needs. You can start with simple applications and gradually increase complexity. As AI tools evolve, it means that AI technology is no longer limited to tech giants or well-funded startups. Small businesses and independent entrepreneurs can now adopt and adapt AI solutions without breaking the bank. As new tools come to the market and others such as Llama mature, they will open up new opportunities for all kinds of businesses.

Nonetheless, this does not mean that the process will be without its challenges. There might be some, and you must be ready to tackle them head on to ensure that you can continue with your project. When you are informed about the obstacles that might be in the way of increasing your income, it makes it easier to manage the difficulties and prepare for what you have to do next.

CHALLENGES TO EXPECT

As someone looking to build a passive income stream with AI, you should keep in mind that you will face challenges that need careful consideration. While the rewards can be significant, it is important to know the elements that might hinder the process. Knowing these potential obstacles in advance will help you plan and execute your AI business more effectively and understand that if you do face difficulties, it is a part of the learning curve, not a reason to feel frustrated.

Here are eight of the most common challenges faced by those who are starting out in the AI business:

- **Technical complexity and infrastructure:** Even with today's user-friendly tools, you will need to manage the technical aspects of your system. Focus on solutions that automate as much of the technical aspect as possible, allowing you to maintain your passive income stream without constant intervention.

- **Need for human oversight:** While the goal is to create passive income, some level of human oversight remains necessary. Plan for periodic reviews of your AI's performance and regular quality checks. As you establish efficient monitoring processes, ensure that these don't demand too much of your time while ensuring your service maintains high standards.

- **Dataset challenges:** Your AI system will need quality data to perform well. As a small operator, you may face challenges in accessing or creating suitable datasets. Consider starting in niches where publicly available data is accessible and vast or in those where you can gradually build your own dataset during the operation.

- **Model customization and performance:** Getting your AI to perform exactly as needed for your specific use case will take time and effort. While the initial period will be active rather than passive, investing this time upfront can lead to more automated operations later.

- **Technical expertise requirements:** You do not need to become an AI expert, but you will need enough understanding to make informed business decisions. Focus on learning the essential aspects that directly impact your specific application while leveraging existing tools and platforms for more complex tasks.

- **Staying competitive:** The AI field moves quickly, and your passive income stream could dry up if you don't stay current. Carry out regular market research and updates to your system. The goal is to create a business that is sustainable with minimal intervention while remaining competitive.

- **Managing client expectations:** Clear communication about what your AI service can and cannot do will save you time and headaches later. Set up automated systems for managing client expectations and handling common questions or issues.

- **Cost management:** Start with solutions that have predictable costs and clear scaling paths. Your goal is to maintain healthy profit margins while keeping the business as automated as possible. Consider starting with lower-cost options and reinvesting profits as you grow.

The path to creating passive income streams with AI requires careful planning and initial setup, but with the right approach, you can build a sustainable automated business. While complete passivity might be challenging to achieve, you can create a system that runs smoothly with minimal oversight. Still, this does not mean there aren't other constraints you will need to face that could impact your AI business. These include data privacy and security, AI bias and fairness, and even hallucinations, which we have explored previously but will take a closer look at in the next chapter.

CHAPTER 9:

ETHICAL AI AND FUTURE TRENDS

When dealing with AI, it is not enough to present good and functional programs. Ethical considerations must also be addressed, meaning they cannot be optional add-ons, but an elementary factor to the tool's success. As creators, deployers, and users of these programs, it is up to us to use these programs responsibly and ensure that what we bring to the market enhances rather than harms society.

In this chapter, we will explore more on what these considerations are, adding to what you have read about so far in the book. You will also catch a glimpse of what to expect regarding the development of technology. If you are worried about technology taking over, rest assured this will not happen in the near future, as you are about to see. The future of AI is promising and exciting, and it will be up to you to know how to best leverage these tools to your advantage.

THE IMPORTANCE OF ETHICAL AI USE

Ethical standards in AI go beyond being transparent about its use and assuming accountability for the information it generates. With an alarmingly high amount of misinformation on the internet today from different channels, it is essential to use this technology responsibly, ensuring that you are not propagating bias or spreading harmful content. The power of AI brings with it considerable ethical responsibilities. Unlike traditional technologies, it can make decisions that affect countless lives in different ways. In the end, it is not *only* about preventing harmful outcomes—it is also about how the future will be shaped so that technology is used for good.

Consider the impact that AI has in our world today: It influences the information we see, the opportunities we are offered, and even how we interact with each other. This significant influence means that we have the responsibility to ensure these systems operate in ways that respect dignity, promote fairness, and protect individual rights. This is not just about compliance or risk management but also about using AI in a manner that sustains human development and social well-being.

If you consider the risks to which we could be exposed, this is even more important. Because AI can rapidly scale, it can amplify its benefits and harms, especially when one simple application can affect millions of lives within days or hours. This reach means that even ethical oversights have consequences. Both the negative and positive impacts can promote communities and create opportunities at an unimaginable scale. At the same time, using AI ethically is not about restricting innovation but ensuring its development moves in the right direction. When ethical considerations are prioritized, we are preventing problems and creating technology that better serves human needs. This approach leads to more sustainable, trustworthy, and successful AI implementations.

The challenge, in this case, is recognizing that ethical AI development is a path that must be trailed and adjusted along the way. As AI capabilities expand and society evolves, new ethical considerations are likely to appear. What seemed acceptable yesterday might raise eyebrows tomorrow. This dynamic requires us to maintain constant vigilance and adaptation to the current conditions, especially if we want to remain relevant in the market. It is also important to acknowledge that responsible AI is a collective responsibility. While individual developers and companies make specific decisions, the impact of these choices helps shape our future. Every choice we make regarding AI carries implications.

For AI technology users, ethical responsibility extends beyond all the companies and individuals who are developing the technology. As AI becomes more integrated into our lives, it is important to approach these tools with awareness and responsibility. This means understanding its limitations, verifying important information, and using these tools in ways that respect others' rights and privacy.

Users should be mindful of how they use AI-generated content, especially in professional and academic contexts. Maintaining transparency is essential, particularly when it affects others. Just as ethical frameworks were developed for other technologies, the same should be done regarding AI use. The shared responsibility between creators and users helps ensure that technology works positively in our society.

Finally, remember the impact that AI has already had on our lives. It is shaping our future and how we interact with one another. The ethical choices we make today will determine what it will be like in the future. Therefore, ethical AI is not the right thing, but the *best* *thing* to do. The commitment to ethical AI is more than just preventing harm. It is also about actively working to create a future in which humans and machines can work together.

HOW TO BE TRANSPARENT WITH AI PRACTICES

As you might imagine, transparency has become one of the most important elements in AI use and development, leading companies to create standards and countries to develop regulations. Although ethical implementations are guiding the way AI should be used, being transparent is essential to ensure that the technology remains accessible to others and that decisions can be explained. This transparency will allow us to communicate, implement, and maintain dialogue on these models and systems.

Transparency when using and developing AI systems requires a systematic approach regarding documentation and communication. However, this means more than just informing users that you are using the technology but also providing the necessary details so users can understand, question, and engage with it. To do this, you must ensure that the necessary documentation is available, and the decision-making process is clear. Additionally, stakeholders must be able to understand when the system is updated, and when there are changes, they can provide feedback when necessary.

Providing users with training and information allows you to have a transparent approach to AI systems and allows stakeholders to feel more trust in its use and development process. While this might seem like too much work to take on for the implementation of a program, the process should not be seen as a burden. It should be identified as an opportunity to build relationships with users and improve system performance.

Finally, remember that these protocols, documentation, and procedures should be updated, reviewed, and communicated regularly. This will allow your model to remain effective and relevant, creating a sustainable approach to AI development. When this process is carried out correctly, it becomes a competitive advantage, allowing for continuous improvement in AI implementations and increased customer loyalty.

FUTURE TRENDS: WHAT TO EXPECT NEXT?

As AI continues to evolve, it is only natural that you start to question yourself on what are the next trends and developments that will happen in the market. Some consider that we are going too fast, while others are working tirelessly to ensure the next big development is available soon. To understand where we are and where we are going next, you must remember what you read about in Chapter 1, about the different types of AI. By understanding where we are and what is expected from these machines, you can see the next phase of AI development more clearly, as well as its potential impacts on business and society.

Multimodal AI

Today, most of the AI models we have are limited to one function. Think about how ChatGPT works mostly with text or Dall·E with images. These are just two examples that can be named, but this is the situation for almost all AI applications. The idea is that in the future, these models will work with different types of information: text, images, audio, and video. When this happens, we will have reached what is called multimodal AI. Different from the other types of AI systems that will work with only one type of data, these AI models can simultaneously integrate and analyze different types of data, leading to a more nuanced understanding.

One example of this multimodal AI in action would be a system that can analyze a video conference by processing not only the spoken words, but also facial expressions, voice tone, and body language. If AI can have this capability, it will open up new opportunities in fields such as healthcare and education, allowing a more comprehensive understanding for professionals using the tools. In this multidimensional approach, AI would still be limited to understanding the data without becoming general AI, but it would increase human capability to better understand situations by using machine insight.

The Increasing Reach of LLMs

Throughout the book, you have seen the different ways that LLMs are being incorporated into different tools. You have seen how Google is adding Gemini to its suite, just as Microsoft is doing the same with its applications. This is the next step where LLMs are moving on from standalone tools into integrated components of larger systems. When this happens, the AI model will work with other tools such as databases and non-AI software, creating powerful and versatile systems that can handle complex tasks.

As these systems become more sophisticated, they will be able to understand the context and maintain long-term memory of their interactions. They will also get better at carrying out specialized tasks within their industries. Today, many of the solutions offered on the market are going in that direction, allowing companies and individuals to leverage AI for better outcomes.

Explainable AI

As you have already seen in the previous section, the concept of ethical and transparent AI is gaining momentum. As these programs become more complex and influential in our daily activities, it becomes essential to understand how the decisions are made. This explains the growth of explainable AI (xAI) as a field working to make AI systems more transparent, understandable, and interpretable to nontechnical stakeholders.

Currently, we have companies and individuals who have their content on the internet questioning how the information was collected and used, and even if there is authorization to do so. Lawsuits have been filed to ensure that content is not used to train AI systems, especially due to accountability. This movement is especially important in regulated industries like healthcare and finance, where decision transparency is often legally required.

Regulatory and Compliance Landscape

Speaking of regulation and compliance, the world is now seeing an increase in regulations and frameworks to govern AI. One of the pioneers in this implementation was the European Union, which published legislation in 2024 regarding how AI should and should not be used within its borders. Frameworks such as these aim to address concerns regarding privacy, fairness, transparency, and ethical use of these tools.

In the future, we are likely to see other countries following suit. There will be new data protection regulations, requirements for transparency, and standards for AI testing and validation. International cooperation among countries regarding AI use and development is also expected. Organizations such as the International Association of Privacy Professionals and others have created maps and trackers to identify how legislation and regulations are being developed and implemented as well as their current status.

Technology Democratization

One of the most discussed topics regarding AI is how the technology is reaching different people. While those with more financial power have access to the latest tools, others with limited budgets struggle to adopt the technology due to its cost. This offers large organizations and those who are wealthier access to models and AI programs that are not immediately available to smaller businesses and those with less money. While this was a reality in the past, the future seems to bring promising opportunities to democratize technology.

User-friendly tools and platforms are making it easier for individuals and small businesses to leverage AI capabilities that were once exclusive to large tech companies. This is leading to more accessible development tools and platforms, as well as lower costs for AI implementation. With more companies using the technology, there is increased competition and innovation, greater diversity in AI applications, and new opportunities for entrepreneurs like yourself, who consider using AI to make money.

Impact on Global Industries

Different markets are expected to see a significant impact with the increased use of AI. Traditional industries are being transformed, and new ones are being created. Manufacturing, for example, is becoming more automated and efficient through predictive maintenance and smart robotics. Healthcare is seeing advances in diagnosis and drug development. Financial services are being revolutionized by AI-driven analysis and personalized services.

However, it is not only these industries that will be impacted. This transformation also creates new job categories at the same pace as eliminating or changing others. Today, we have a growing demand for AI specialists and the evolution of traditional roles to incorporate

AI skills. Professionals with human skills that complement AI are being highly valued in the market, leading to significant shifts in workforce distribution across industries.

In this new market, companies that incorporate professionals with AI knowledge will become more diverse and competitive. As large companies continue to drive innovations, we are expected to see the rise of specialized AI service providers and a growth in AI consulting and implementation services. You should also expect to see an increased development of industry-specific AI solutions and an increased focus on regional and local AI applications, designed to meet specific and targeted needs.

Those who want to remain relevant in the market must stay informed and adaptable to the changes to come. Those who leverage these advances in their personal and professional lives will be more valuable to the market, especially if they maintain ethical standards and ensure human values. The next few years are promising and exciting, but it is essential that we remain conscious and aware that it is our job to guide its development to ensure it is beneficial to society.

PREDICTIONS FOR AI IN THE NEXT DECADE

Looking into the future, it is likely that AI and technology will continue to shape the way we live. In the next ten years, it is probable we will have a convergence of technologies that will become more powerful and personalized. With the increased processing power and computer capabilities, you could say that we are on the brink of transformation. Here are some of the expectations for the next years regarding AI and how it will relate to other technologies:

- **Evolution of AI technology:** AI technology is expected to achieve new levels of sophistication, blurring the lines between machine and human knowledge. These systems are expected to develop a more nuanced understanding of content and cultural events and better reasoning capabilities and logical thinking. In addition, researchers are working to create programs that have improved emotional intelligence and empathy with an increased capacity to solve complex problems. As machines develop a greater capacity to think like humans, they are expected to have a deeper understanding of human behavior and motivations (*The AI Index Report*, 2024).

- **The Internet of Things (IoT) and AI integration:** With the increase of technologies such as IoT, billions of devices are expected to be connected to AI technologies, decreasing 30% in energy consumption in smart homes and increasing customer satisfaction numbers by 25% (Rawjani, 2023). This integration will also allow the system to learn from real-time data across different sources, optimizing systems at all levels. Additionally, we will be able to predict and prevent problems before they happen. Finally, we will be able to create more efficient and sustainable environments, allowing smart cities and homes to work for us.

- **Personalization and collaboration:** Throughout the next few years, we will see AI becoming more personalized according to user needs. This means we should see AI assistants that learn and adopt personal preferences more than they do now, and see healthcare become personalized with targeted approaches and education tailored to individual learning styles. It is also expected to have work environments adjusting to personal productivity patterns and according to each industry.

- **Automation and workforce:** Research has shown that 70% of CEOs believe that AI will change how their companies work and that there will be significant automation in work processes (*Artificial Intelligence*, 2023). AI is expected to change how companies interact with customers and modify the shopping experience for most of them. High-volume tasks are expected to be automated, including communications and software development tasks. Furthermore, we will see new professions appear and increased collaboration between humans and AI technology, with humans providing the necessary creativity and emotional intelligence these machines do not have.

- **Societal expectations and challenges:** As AI becomes a more significant part of our lives, it is normal that more details and explanations on how these machines make decisions are required. This means companies are expected to generate more transparent and explainable AI systems, create better privacy protection and data control, and implement ethical standards for their use. The market is in constant change and the need for more fair and unbiased AI systems is growing, just as more human control in the decision-making and output processes. In the next decade, companies are expected to increase their investments in xAI to make the technology more transparent and accessible.

- **Need for governance:** While tech companies are working at maximum capacity to increase their AI capabilities, governments are struggling to keep up with the industry's pace. At the same time, several countries have already started taking the necessary steps to regulate the industry and ensure that these systems are not harmful to society. In the next decade, we are likely to see an increase in global AI governance frameworks and international standards for AI development. Expect to see new regulatory bodies, oversight mechanisms, and ethics boards for AI development.

Looking ahead, you can see that we are not going to witness just technological evolution but also how our relationships in almost all life aspects will be changed. The decisions we make and the skills that we will need to develop in the coming years will determine how we will succeed in this new reality and approach the job industry.

After all these considerations, you might be asking yourself, *How can I prepare for this AI-powered future?* This is one of the most important questions that should be asked right now. To help you understand the next steps and how to best prepare for this new reality, as we move on to the last chapter of this book, you will see a road map that will help you develop skills, knowledge, and a mindset to develop in an AI-driven world. Shall we get ready and start preparing for the future? If your answer is *yes*, read on!

CHAPTER 10:
YOUR PERSONAL ACTION PLAN TO MASTER AI

Throughout this book, different concepts regarding AI were explored, including its transformative potential and how it can be used to enhance your daily activities. You learned about the differences between AI systems and the ethical considerations that must be taken into account regarding them. LLMs are reshaping businesses, creating new opportunities for entrepreneurs, and allowing companies to leverage their power to become more competitive. As AI becomes more accessible to smaller organizations, we will see an increased use of the technology in everyday activities.

This final chapter serves as your practical guide to implementing AI in your professional life. Regardless of whether you are looking to integrate AI into an existing business, create a new AI income source, or optimize your activities, with all the information you are about to see all these options are possible. The concepts you have explored throughout this book will now be transformed into actionable steps to help you leverage the technology and ensure you remain updated and current with new AI developments. You will see how to

- assess your current AI knowledge and identify opportunities for AI integration

- select the right AI tools and platforms for your specific needs

- develop a realistic implementation timeline
- create sustainable AI-powered income streams
- build the necessary skills and knowledge
- address potential challenges and obstacles

As you read each of these steps, keep in mind that you do not have to become a technical expert to work and achieve success with AI. As you have seen, the secret is to know how to effectively leverage tools and platforms via the technology while remaining ethical. By implementing these steps, you will find that even for those with minimal AI and LLM knowledge, they can achieve the best results, without the need for specific details. No matter what industry you work in and what your objectives are with AI, you will see how to achieve your goals with real-life examples. Let's take a look at how this can be done!

STEPS TO INTEGRATE AI INTO DIFFERENT LIFE AREAS

Actioning what you have seen throughout this book might seem overwhelming, but you should not feel that way! In this step-by-step section, you will see how you can enhance your personal and professional life using AI. To do this, instead of viewing AI as a complex technology, think of it as a powerful assistant ready to help you achieve goals more efficiently.

AI for Personal Development

To start off, think about how you currently learn new skills or manage information. Now, consider a project or an area that you want to improve and that you feel could benefit from AI interaction. If this project refers to a personal development area you want to enhance, follow these steps:

1. Choose a topic you want more information on.

2. Open your preferred LLM (such as ChatGPT, Claude, or Gemini).

3. Instead of asking board questions, be specific, such as, "Create a structured 30-day learning plan for [*topic*], breaking it down into daily 1-hour sessions."

4. Use the AI to generate practice exercises and provide feedback.

5. As for explanations when the concepts are not clear, such as, "Explain [*concept*] using analogies from [*your field of interest*]."

In this case, if you are learning Spanish, for example, you might prompt the machine with the following, "I am a beginner learning Spanish. Create a conversation scenario about ordering food, then play the role of a waiter while I practice as a customer. Correct my grammar and pronunciation guidelines as we go."

AI for Professional Enhancement

To use AI for professional enhancement, you might need a little more time. This is because you will need to track your activities and then identify which ones you can automate. You will need to start small, with one task at a time, and only move to the next one once you are satisfied with the automation for the first. To carry out this process, follow these steps:

1. Track your daily tasks for a week and write them down.

2. After one week, identify the repetitive tasks, which can include replying to emails, report writing, and data analysis, among others.

3. For each of the tasks you identify, ask yourself, *Can AI help me automate this?*

4. Select one of the tasks to start with the automation.

5. Once you are satisfied and fully grasp the automation process for this task, move on to the next one.

An example of this process would be to automate the emails you send out. In this case, you can create an AI prompt that says, "I need to write professional emails for these common situations [*list situations*]." Create templates that maintain a consistent tone while being adaptable to different recipients.

Business Integration Strategy

Entrepreneurs and business owners looking to implement AI into their organizations can also achieve the objective by following a strategy. In this case, since it might mean significantly disrupting how business is carried out, you might need a timeframe of approximately 30 days to ensure that critical operations are not negatively impacted. If this is your idea, here is a structured approach to leverage the power of AI technology into your company:

- **Week 1:** Create an assessment of your company's processes. List all the relevant tasks and identify those that are the most time-consuming. Evaluate the current systems and tools in use and see if any could use an enhancement.

- **Week 2:** Research AI tools for your specific needs. Shortlist the most interesting tools and those who can help you optimize your tasks. During this process, you should take advantage of those tools that offer free trials. After carrying out the tests, calculate the potential return on investment with its implementation.

- **Weeks 3 and 4:** Implement the new tools to one specific task. You should take the integration process slowly, ensuring that one process is taken care of at a time. This should be carried out simultaneously with training team members.

- **After implementation:** Monitor results with established KPIs and adjust as needed.

This action plan will allow you to gradually evaluate the impact of AI on your company's processes and help you effectively monitor them. You should ensure that these processes are independently monitored and that the results are satisfactory, such as reducing costs or time to carry out an activity. Only when you have the expected results, should you move on to the next task, as you will have a better view of how AI can help you.

Creating Passive Income With AI

If you are interested in creating passive income using AI, this is certainly possible! You can use the practical approach you will see next to identify potential areas where you can create these opportunities and develop an automated side hustle. This process includes the following steps:

1. Identify your niche or the area in which you would like to work in. This means identifying the knowledge you have and that others might value, solutions AI programs can offer, or creating digital products.

2. Start small with a few cases, such as one product or service. You can test different options and AI applications to see how they develop and answer the requests you are making.

3. Use beta testers to see if your solution works or if any changes must be made. Having three to four potential customers who will use the product and obtaining feedback will be valuable to see if you need to modify anything.

4. After all changes are made, go live with the content. This could mean building a website or blog to deliver the content or offering your services to potential customers.

5. Market your initiative and ensure that it is working properly.

6. Refine and review results periodically to ensure there are no flaws in the process or the information.

These steps should take around one to six weeks, during which you will slowly implement each stage. In a simulated timeframe, this is what it would look like:

- **Weeks 1–2:** Research your target market, use AI to analyze competitor offerings, see where you can add value and be different, and create a prototype of your product or service.

- **Weeks 3–4:** Test your product or service with a small audience and gather feedback. Refine your offering so that it meets customer needs.

- **Weeks 5–6:** Develop your marketing strategy and create supporting materials. Launch your product and see how it performs in the market. Create relevant KPIs to monitor your product's performance and reach.

- **After launch:** Iterate and verify if the service or product is working. Ensure there are no deviations in the output process and that the results are acceptable.

As you implement these solutions, remember that you must carefully analyze what you are going to offer. In some cases, implementation might take more time, but it will be worthwhile if this means you are ethically developing your solution and that you are going step-by-step. In many cases, it is better to go slow than to revolutionize everything at once. So, start with one area, perfect your approach, and then expand to others.

TOOLS AND PLATFORMS

When searching for the best AI tool to use, you will find there are several options in the market. This means you will need to carry out at least some research to see if what the tool provides you with caters to your needs and meets expectations. Once again, before you sign up for any of these, you should take advantage of the trial period to ensure it really fulfills your needs. In many cases, some of the tools you will see in this section also offer a free version you can test and experiment with to evaluate performance.

Content Creation

- **ChatGPT:** Creates written content, from marketing copy to blog posts with humanlike understanding.

- **Jasper:** Specializes in generating marketing content and brand-specific messaging.

- **Midjourney:** Generates high-quality images and visual content from text descriptions.

- **Pictory:** Automatically converts long-form videos into short social media snippets.

Logistics

- **Lineal:** Optimizes delivery routes and predicts demand patterns for efficient distribution.

- **Flexport:** Automates shipping documentation and provides real-time cargo tracking.

- **6 River Systems:** Manages warehouse operations with collaborative robots and AI.

- **Shipwell:** Offers predictive analysis for freight management and carrier selection.

Customer Management

- **Zendesk AI:** Automatically handles customer queries and routes complex issues to human agents.

- **Persado:** Personalizes customer communications using emotional AI.

- **Gong.io:** Analyzes customer calls to provide insights and improve sales conversations.

- **Drift:** Provides conversational AI for website visitor engagement and lead qualification.

Sales and Marketing

- **Salesforce Einstein:** Predicts sales opportunities and automates customer relationship management tasks.

- **Mailchimp AI:** Optimizes email marketing campaigns and segment audiences.

- **Albert:** Manages digital advertising campaigns across multiple platforms.

- **Crayon:** Tracks competitors and automatically provides market intelligence.

Financial Management

- **Xero AI:** Automated bookkeeping and categorizes transactions.

- **Stripe Radar:** Detects fraudulent transactions using ML

- **Freshbooks AI:** Manages invoicing and expense tracking with smart automation.

- **Sage AI:** Predicts cash flow and provides financial forecasting.

HR and Recruitment

- **HiredScore:** Screens resumes and matches candidates to job requirements.

- **Pymetrics:** Assesses job candidates through AI-powered games and exercises.

- **BreezyHR:** Automates interview scheduling and candidate communication.

- **Ideal:** Screens and grades candidates while reducing hiring bias.

Project Management

- **Monday.ai:** Suggests task prioritization and resource allocation.

- **Asana Intelligence:** Predicts project bottlenecks and suggests workflow improvements.

- **ClickUp AI:** Automates task creation and provides workload management.

- **Wrike Analyze:** Offers predictive project analysis and risk assessments.

Data Analysis

- **Tableau AI:** Creates automated visual insights from complex datasets.

- **Power BI AI:** Generates natural language insights from business data.

- **ThoughtSpot:** Provides AI-driven search-based analytics.

- **DataRobot:** Automates the process of building and deploying ML models.

These are only some of the examples of tools you will find on the market. With some research, you will find other tools that might be suitable for your business. Remember, this process will require some time and attention until you find the best solution. If you work with more people in your company, you can ask them to help you test these tools to see if they meet their demands and needs, as well as ensure that what you want to implement is useful.

It is usually ideal to start with one or two tools in the areas where you face the most immediate challenges. After you understand their suitability and how they can be used, you can expand your AI implementation throughout other areas. Finally, consider that most of these tools can work together with others, creating a better integration process for your business. For example, content creation tools can provide information for marketing automation, while customer management AI can inform sales strategies and logistics planning.

BUSINESS CASE

In the final part of this book, you will look into a fictional brand business case to understand how AI can help you develop your own business. In this case, the LLM being used is ChatGPT. Although the outputs presented in this section are a copy of what the machine has prompted, please remember that the results may not be the same when you insert them into your computer.

Project: Creating a fashion brand.

Prompt 1: *Generate 3 innovative business ideas at the intersection of sustainability, fashion, and sharing economy. Include market potential and key differentiators.*

Output 1: This is the output provided by ChatGPT, without modifications:

1. Circular Fashion Rental Platform

Concept: A peer-to-peer fashion rental marketplace for sustainable and ethically produced clothing. Users can rent out high-quality pieces they own or rent items for special occasions, minimizing waste and promoting reusability.

Market Potential: The global online clothing rental market is expected to reach $4.4 billion by 2028, driven by eco-conscious millennials and Gen Z.

Key Differentiators:

- Focus exclusively on sustainable and ethically certified brands.
- AI-powered recommendations for styles based on user preferences and events.
- Carbon offset program to make rentals 100% carbon-neutral.

2. Upcycled Fashion Co-op

Concept: A platform where independent designers can collaboratively upcycle used garments and sell them as unique, eco-friendly pieces. Consumers can donate unwanted clothes and receive discounts on purchases.

Market Potential: Upcycling aligns with the $6 billion sustainable fashion market and appeals to eco-conscious consumers seeking one-of-a-kind designs.

Key Differentiators:

- Direct collaboration between donors and designers for personalized upcycled creations.
- Community-based model supporting local artisans.
- Subscription option for regular "upcycled drops" tailored to individual styles.

3. Sustainable Fashion Subscription Box

Concept: A subscription service that curates eco-friendly, ethically sourced wardrobe staples for customers, focusing on timeless, high-quality pieces. Customers can return items they no longer use for resale or recycling.

Market Potential: The subscription box market is projected to grow at a 20% CAGR by 2030, with sustainability-focused niches attracting loyal customer bases.

Key Differentiators:

- Transparency on brand sourcing and production practices.
- Items tailored to each customer's climate and lifestyle to reduce wardrobe clutter.
- Gamification: Reward points for recycling or referring friends.

3. Sustainable Fashion Subscription Box

Concept: A subscription service that curates eco-friendly, ethically sourced wardrobe staples for customers, focusing on timeless, high-quality pieces. Customers can return items they no longer use for resale or recycling.

Market Potential: The subscription box market is projected to grow at a 20% CAGR by 2030, with sustainability-focused niches attracting loyal customer bases.

Key Differentiators:

- Transparency on brand sourcing and production practices.

- Items tailored to each customer's climate and lifestyle to reduce wardrobe clutter.

- Gamification: Reward points for recycling or referring friends.

Prompt 2: *I like option number 1, on the circular fashion rental platform. Can you help me create 5 names for this brand?*

Output 2:

- **LoopWardrobe:** Emphasizing the circular economy, "LoopWardrobe" conveys the idea of sharing and reusing clothing within a continuous loop.

- **StyleCycle:** A catchy, easy-to-remember name that highlights sustainability and the recurring use of fashionable items.

- **ReFash:** Short for "Refashion," this sleek name represents giving clothes a new life while staying trendy.

- **EcoThread:** Combining "eco" for sustainability and "thread" for fashion, this name speaks to the platform's core mission of eco-conscious clothing.

- **GreenCloset:** A warm, relatable name that evokes the image of an environmentally friendly wardrobe ready to be shared.

Prompt 3: *Now help me create a tagline that goes with the name ReFash, which is the name I selected among the options.*

Output 3:

"ReFash: Where Style Meets Sustainability." It succinctly conveys the platform's mission of blending trendy fashion with eco-conscious practices.

If you'd like alternatives, here are a few more options:

- "ReFash: Renew. Rewear. Redefine."
- "ReFash: Fashion Forward, Planet Friendly."
- "ReFash: Share the Style, Save the Planet."
- "ReFash: Modern Style, Sustainable Choice."
- "ReFash: Fashion with a Future."

Prompt 4: *What are the best channels to promote this product and what kind of content should I create to attract more customers?*

Output 4:

Promoting **ReFash**, a circular fashion rental platform, requires leveraging channels and content that resonate with your eco-conscious and fashion-savvy audience. Here's a tailored plan:

Best Channels to Promote ReFash

1. **Instagram**
   - **Why:** Highly visual platform, ideal for showcasing fashion styles and sustainable living content.
   - **What to Share:** Short reels of styling tips, before-and-after transformations, and eco-friendly lifestyle posts. Partner with influencers passionate about sustainability and fashion.

2. **TikTok**

   o **Why:** Popular among younger demographics, known for driving trends.

   o **What to Share:** Quick, engaging videos like "Outfit of the Day" (OOTD) challenges, creative unboxing of rental items, or fun skits emphasizing sustainability.

3. **Pinterest**

   o **Why:** A go-to for inspiration in fashion and lifestyle.

   o **What to Share:** Curated boards with outfit ideas, sustainability tips, and rental fashion hacks.

4. **YouTube**

   o **Why:** Perfect for long-form storytelling and tutorials.

   o **What to Share:** Mini-documentaries on sustainability in fashion, customer testimonials, and styling tutorials using ReFash items.

5. **Email Marketing**

   o **Why:** Great for nurturing leads and encouraging repeat customers.

   o **What to Share:** Exclusive discounts, styling newsletters, and updates about new inventory or sustainability milestones.

6. **Sustainability and Fashion Blogs**

   o **Why:** Reach an audience already interested in your niche.

   o **What to Share:** Guest posts or sponsored content about circular fashion and the benefits of renting over buying.

7. **Local Community Events**

   o **Why:** Personal connections foster trust and loyalty.

   o **What to Do:** Host pop-up styling events or workshops on sustainable living.

Content Ideas to Attract Customers

1. **Educational Content**

   o Explain how circular fashion works and its environmental impact.

   o Create infographics showing how renting fashion reduces waste.

   o Share "Did You Know?" posts about the fashion industry's carbon footprint.

2. **User-Generated Content (UGC)**

   o Encourage customers to share photos of their rented outfits with a branded hashtag (e.g., #ReFashStyle).

   o Feature UGC on your social media channels and website.

3. **Storytelling**

   o Share the origin story of ReFash to build a connection.

   o Highlight the journey of an item on the platform, from listing to rental.

4. **Lifestyle Integration**

   o Create content that shows how rental fashion fits into everyday life, such as weddings, parties, or work events.

5. **Exclusive Offers and Challenges**

   o Offer discounts for first-time renters.

   o Run challenges like "1 Month, 10 Outfits: Sustainable Style with ReFash."

6. **Sustainability Progress Reports**

   ○ Regularly update followers on how much waste your platform has saved.

   ○ Share testimonials from users about how ReFash changed their perspective on fashion.

7. **Behind-the-Scenes**

   ○ Post videos showing how you clean and prepare clothes for the next rental.

   ○ Highlight your team's commitment to sustainability.

8. **Partnership Content**

   ○ Collaborate with eco-friendly brands, influencers, or stylists.

   ○ Co-create content that ties their products/services with your rentals.

9. **Interactive Content**

   ○ Host live Q&A sessions on Instagram or TikTok about sustainable fashion.

   ○ Use polls and quizzes to engage your audience (e.g., "What's Your Sustainable Style Personality?").

10. **Case Studies and Success Stories**

    ○ Showcase how customers used ReFash for special occasions and loved the experience.

    ○ Share data on how renting fashion helps reduce environmental impact.

Additional Tips

- Focus on authenticity. Consumers value transparency and genuine efforts toward sustainability.

- Tailor content for each channel while maintaining consistent branding.

- Use analytics tools to track performance and refine your strategy.

Would you like assistance developing a more detailed content calendar or marketing strategy?

As you can see, you will be able to refine the outputs and build on the previous prompt in the same conversation, allowing you to create a cohesive and all-around strategy for your business. The more prompts you add and the more feedback you provide to the program, the better it will become at understanding your needs and tailoring its responses. By iterating on the same project within the same prompt, it will be able to continue the conversation with context in the future.

CONCLUSION

" AI is the future." How many times have you heard a phrase like this in the middle of a discussion at work or between friends? The truth is that the technology has come to stay, even if its consequences and development in the future are still unknown. As it becomes more accessible and powerful, it presents early adopters with an opportunity to leverage its potential and create value in ways that were not possible a few years ago.

While some might still discuss the ethical ramifications the technology might have, such as job displacement and digital segregation, others are using this opportunity to create extraordinary things. If your condition fits the first, you are not wrong but missing out on being part of the change. As these applications continue to evolve and expand, it is up to those using them to ensure they foster an inclusive, ethical, and safe environment. Consider: *What better way than to do this by implementing AI thoughtfully and responsibly in your own ventures?*

With the information you have received and the road maps you have seen throughout this book, you can start using AI *right now* to change your business or your personal life. From understanding foundational concepts to ideas on how to create passive income, you can now see that the possibilities are endless, allowing you to make an impact in whichever area you choose. Use your creativity, determination, and commitment to ensure that you have the best options that align technology with ethical and transparent practices.

Finally, remember the tools you use are just *tools*, meaning you will need to bring your mindset and ideas to the table. AI is not a magical solution but a means and an enabler to help you make your ideas come true. To ensure you stay updated on the latest information on the market, follow technology blogs; new solutions are being presented daily, and it will be up to you not to stay behind!

To help you start working with these AI tools and practice prompting, you will see that following this conclusion, there is a *bonus chapter* with a few market prompts you can use to leverage LLMs. They have been crafted to help entrepreneurs and business owners inspire and provide practical ways to integrate AI into their business strategies. Use them to spark your creativity, refine business workflows, and discover innovative opportunities.

Yes, AI is the future, but the technology does not survive on its own. It is also about the people who use it and its impact. If you are ready to lead the way and change how business works, there is no better time to start than now! It is time to turn these ideas into income and be a part of the change, not just a spectator. It is now up to you: Are you prepared to change your life by leveraging AI?

BONUS CHAPTER: BUSINESS PROMPTS FOR EVERYDAY USE

The prompts you will see in this section were created for specific purposes and have placeholders for you to add your specific area. They have also been optimized by ChatGPT to bring you the best outcome, ensuring they are effective and deliver the expected results. You can use these prompts for your business or even to create a new income source. Feel free to modify them and change them according to your needs and demands! Remember that as you create and modify each prompt, you should provide the machine with some context to ensure it understands your needs.

EXISTING BUSINESSES

Here are a few prompts you can use if you have an existing business and want to optimize your operations using AI.

Marketing and Customer Engagement

- Write a [type of marketing copy] promoting a [product/service] that emphasizes [unique selling point]. The tone should appeal to [target audience].

- Create a content calendar for a [specific platform] for a [type of business] targeting [specific demographic] over the next [timeframe].

- Draft a [type of campaign] for a [type of business]. Include three key messages and a call-to-action to drive [specific result].

- Generate three tagline options for a [product/service] that convey [core value] to [target audience].

- Develop a creative strategy for a [type of ad] to attract [specific audience] and achieve [specific goal].

Product Design and Development

- Brainstorm ideas for a [type of product] that addresses [specific problem or trend]. The design should appeal to [target audience] and emphasize [specific features].

- Suggest five improvements for an existing [product/service] in a [specific industry] to meet the needs of [specific customer group].

- Draft a development roadmap for a [new product/service] targeting [specific market]. Include milestones for [specific phases].

- Propose three features for a [software, app, tool] that would differentiate it in the [specific market] and meet [specific user needs].

- Generate ideas for packaging a [type of product] that is [adjective] and aligns with [brand values].

Customer Service and Support

- Draft responses for frequently asked questions in [specific format] for a [type of business]. Prioritize clarity and helpfulness.

- Create a script for a [specific customer service scenario] in a [type of business] that ensures a positive customer experience.

- Design a chatbot flow for a [specific purpose] in a [type of industry]. The tone should be [adjective].

- Suggest ways to improve customer feedback collection for a [type of business]. Focus on [specific goals].

- Generate three personalized email templates for following up with [specific customer actions]. Emphasize [specific outcome].

Data Analysis and Reporting

- Analyze [specific dataset or metric] for a [type of business]. Identify trends and suggest actionable insights to improve [specific area].

- Generate a report outline for [specific performance metric] with key sections focusing on [specific aspects].

- Provide predictions for [specific trend or behavior] based on [type of historical data] to guide [specific decision].

- Suggest KPIs for tracking the success of a [specific initiative] in a [type of business].

- Draft a presentation summarizing the [specific analysis] for stakeholders, highlighting [specific focus areas].

HR and Team Development

- Develop an onboarding plan for [specific role] in a [type of business]. Include training modules and milestones for the first [timeframe].

- Create a job description for a [specific role] emphasizing [specific qualifications, skills, or company values].

- Generate three icebreaker activities for [specific event] in a [type of team].

- Suggest a performance review framework for evaluating [specific employee type] in a [type of organization]. Focus on [specific metrics].

- Draft a diversity and inclusion training agenda for employees in a [specific industry or company size]. Address [specific challenges].

Finance and Budgeting

- Create a monthly budget template for a [type of business] focused on [specific priorities].

- Generate financial projections for [specific initiative or new product] over the next [timeframe]. Include key assumptions.

- Propose cost-saving strategies for a [type of business] without compromising [specific goal].

- Draft a pitch deck slide explaining the ROI of investing in [specific product/service] for [specific audience].

- Create a financial risk assessment for [specific business decision].

Sustainability Initiatives

- Propose eco-friendly practices for a [type of business] to minimize [specific impact] and appeal to [specific customer segment].

- Develop a plan for achieving [specific sustainability certification] for a [type of project or business].

- Suggest ways to incorporate sustainability messaging into the branding of a [specific product/service].

- Create a green supply chain strategy for a [type of business] to meet [specific sustainability goals].

- Draft an internal sustainability report framework for [specific industry or company size].

DEVELOPING PASSIVE INCOME SOURCES

Use the prompts you will see in this section to help you create a passive income source and leverage LLMs to help you identify the strategy and the action plan for how it will be launched.

Content Creation

- Generate a list of [specific type of content] targeting [specific audience]. The content should focus on [specific niche] and be designed for [monetization method].

- Write a step-by-step guide on [specific topic] that is optimized for SEO, targeting [specific keywords] and aimed at [specific audience]. Include actionable tips and a call-to-action for [specific purpose].

- Create a week-long social media content calendar for [specific platform] focused on [specific topic or niche]. Include captions, hashtags, and post ideas for engagement.

- Draft a long-form article or e-book on [specific subject] aimed at [specific goal]. Provide sections that detail [specific subtopics].

- Generate ideas for a YouTube channel targeting [specific demographic] in the [specific industry/niche]. Suggest themes, episode formats, and monetization strategies.

Ecommerce and Dropshipping

- Create product descriptions and marketing copy for a [specific type of product] sold through a [specific platform]. Ensure the tone appeals to [target audience] and includes [specific features] to increase conversions.

- Identify trending products in [specific industry] that could perform well in a dropshipping business targeting [specific audience]. Provide potential suppliers and pricing strategies.

- Write an email marketing sequence to promote a flash sale for [specific product] on [specific platform]. Include subject lines and call-to-action phrases to maximize conversions.

- Generate ideas for bundling [specific types of products] to increase average order value. Suggest pricing and promotion strategies for [specific audience].

- Draft a compelling FAQ section for a product page selling [specific item], addressing common concerns like [specific issues].

Online Courses and Digital Products

- Outline the curriculum for an online course teaching [specific skill] aimed at [specific audience]. Include engaging lesson ideas, exercises, and potential upsell opportunities like [specific add-ons].

- Design an engaging webinar outline on [specific skill or subject] that serves as a lead magnet for an online course. Include key talking points and interactive elements.

- Create a sales page for a digital product, such as [specific type], targeting [specific audience]. Highlight benefits, testimonials, and a call-to-action.

- Generate email templates to promote an upcoming online course launch on [specific subject]. Include urgency tactics like early bird discounts.

- Outline a content strategy for a podcast aimed at promoting a digital product related to [specific niche]. Suggest episode themes and guest ideas.

AI-Powered Subscription Services

- Design an AI-powered subscription service for [specific use case]. List the key features and benefits that would appeal to [specific customer base] and outline a plan for pricing and scaling the service to generate recurring revenue.

- Develop a pricing strategy for an AI-powered subscription service in [specific field]. Suggest tiers and corresponding features for different customer segments.

- Create a landing page copy for an AI service offering [specific feature]. Focus on clear value propositions and customer testimonials.

- Draft a customer retention email series for a subscription service in [specific industry], aiming to reduce churn and improve engagement.

- Generate a list of partnership opportunities for a subscription service focused on [specific niche]. Suggest cross-promotions and cobranded campaigns.

Affiliate Marketing Automation

- Generate a series of automated email sequences promoting [specific affiliate products]. Each email should focus on [specific benefits] and include calls-to-action to drive traffic to [specific platform or website]. Tailor the tone to resonate with [specific audience].

- Write a script for a YouTube video promoting [specific affiliate product]. Focus on storytelling and how the product solves a common problem.

- Generate blog content ideas that naturally incorporate affiliate links for [specific type of product] aimed at [specific audience].

- Develop a social media campaign plan to promote affiliate products in [specific niche]. Include post themes and ad copy ideas.

- Draft an automated chatbot flow to recommend affiliate products based on user preferences in [specific industry].

NEW BUSINESS IDEAS

If you are looking to start a business, AI might help you find the ideal niche and customers for it! You can use the examples you will see below to develop a customized service based on your abilities and skills, allowing you to start something new or even a side hustle. Use and adapt the information below to become an entrepreneur.

Personalized Wellness Coach

- Design an AI-powered daily wellness program for [specific demographic]. Include features like meal planning, fitness tracking, and stress management tips.

- Generate a series of app notifications for a personalized wellness AI targeting [specific goal]. Ensure they are motivational and actionable.

- Draft a landing page for an AI wellness coach app, highlighting how it adapts to user behavior over time to deliver personalized results.

- Develop an onboarding sequence for new users of a wellness AI app, ensuring they set clear goals and understand key features.

- Create a content marketing strategy for a blog promoting an AI wellness coach, focused on [specific topic].

AI-Powered Language Tutoring

- Create a curriculum for an AI-powered language tutoring app for [specific language]. Include interactive lessons and real-time practice suggestions.

- Draft a social media campaign promoting an AI language tutor, targeting [specific audience].

- Write an FAQ section for a website offering AI-powered language lessons, addressing common concerns like [specific concerns].

- Generate a gamification strategy for an AI language learning app, incorporating rewards for milestones like [specific goals].

- Create a series of emails to engage and retain users of an AI-powered language tutoring service, focusing on their progress and achievements.

Sustainable AI-Powered Fashion Recommendations

- Generate a recommendation engine for sustainable fashion, suggesting [specific type of items] based on user preferences and eco-friendliness ratings.

- Draft a blog post about how AI is revolutionizing sustainable fashion, aimed at attracting environmentally conscious consumers.

- Write ad copy for a campaign promoting an AI-powered sustainable fashion platform, emphasizing [specific benefits].

- Create an email series targeting users of a sustainable fashion AI tool, highlighting new eco-friendly products and how they align with their preferences.

- Design an AI-powered style quiz for a sustainable fashion platform, helping users discover their style while focusing on eco-friendly options.

AI-Powered Virtual Interior Designer Assistant

- Create an AI-powered virtual interior design assistant that helps users redesign a room by suggesting furniture, color palettes, and layouts based on their style preferences and budget.

- Develop a system where users can upload photos of their rooms, and the AI recommends design changes, offering links to purchase suggested items.

- Generate marketing content for an AI interior design tool that targets first-time homeowners, offering them personalized design solutions and cost estimates.

- Write a blog post outlining the benefits of using an AI virtual interior design assistant, focusing on convenience, affordability, and time-saving features.

- Create a chatbot script that helps users choose the right furniture and decor based on their space size, personal preferences, and budget.

Custom Meal Planning and Recipe Service With AI

- Design an AI-powered meal planning service that generates custom weekly menus based on dietary preferences, nutritional needs, and available ingredients.

- Generate a subscription service for personalized AI meal plans, where users receive recipes and grocery shopping lists tailored to their taste and health goals.

- Create an AI chatbot that helps users find recipes based on what they currently have in their fridge or pantry, reducing food waste and offering alternatives.

- Write a content marketing strategy for a website promoting AI-driven meal plans and recipes, aimed at busy professionals and health-conscious individuals.

- Generate a targeted email campaign for an AI meal planning service, highlighting customer testimonials and showing how the service saves time and improves meal variety.

Digital Marketing Automation Service

- Develop an AI-powered marketing automation tool for small businesses that creates personalized email sequences, social media posts, and ad campaigns based on customer behavior.

- Create an AI system that can analyze customer data and automatically generate content and ad campaigns to boost engagement and conversion rates for ecommerce businesses.

- Design a system where users can input their business goals, and the AI suggests the best marketing strategies, channels, and content ideas to implement.

- Write a tutorial for small business owners on how to use an AI-driven marketing automation tool to enhance customer engagement and boost sales.

- Develop a marketing campaign plan for an AI digital marketing service targeting small business owners, emphasizing ease of use, cost-effectiveness, and measurable results.

REFERENCES

AI in education market worth $32.27 billion by 2030. (2024, November). Grand View Research. https://www.grandviewresearch.com/press-release/global-artificial-intelligence-ai-education-market

The AI index report – Artificial intelligence index. (2024). Stanford University. https://aiindex.stanford.edu/report/

Anderson, M. (2024, September 24). *Almost all small businesses are using a software tool that is enabled by AI.* AP News. https://apnews.com/article/small-business-artificial-intelligence-productivity-f6fa7b2a1ce0a9f2e5b8b48670b3098a

Artemakis A. (2024, January 12). *Large language models (LLMs) and their impact on everyday technology.* LinkedIn. https://www.linkedin.com/pulse/large-language-models-llms-impact-everyday-technology-artemiou-84def/

Artificial intelligence. (2023). PwC. https://www.pwc.com/gx/en/issues/artificial-intelligence.html

Artificial intelligence statistics 2024 - AI facts & stats report. (2024). AIPRM. https://www.aiprm.com/ai-statistics/

Bodiroza, M. (2023, September 6). The power of AI: HubSpot's generative AI content tools and ChatSpot. *New Perspective.* https://www.npws.net/blog/hubspot-generative-ai-tools

Boyer, D. (2024, November 4). *Case studies: How SMEs are using AI to compete with big players.* Inside Small Business.

https://insidesmallbusiness.com.au/people-hr/productivity/case-studies-how-smes-are-using-ai-to-compete-with-big-players

ChatGPT. (2024). OpenAI. https://openai.com/chatgpt/overview/

51 artificial intelligence statistics to know in 2024. (2024). DigitalOcean. https://www.digitalocean.com/resources/articles/artificial-intelligence-statistics

Gemini. (n.d.). Google DeepMind. https://deepmind.google/technologies/gemini/

Introducing Meta Llama 3: The most capable openly available LLM to date. (2024, April 18). Meta. https://ai.meta.com/blog/meta-llama-3/

Kavanagh, K. (2023, December 22). *How artificial intelligence is revolutionizing diagnosis in health care*. Infection Control Today. https://www.infectioncontroltoday.com/view/how-artificial-intelligence-is-revolutionizing-diagnosis-health-care

Khan, A. (2024, June 20). *Conversational AI unveils $11 billion savings, 28.5% growth, and 91% business adoption*. TDM. https://www.thedevmasters.com/ai/conversational-ai-unveils-11-billion-savings-28.5-growth-and-91-business-adoption

Khan, J. (2024, August 24). *91+ eye-opening generative AI facts and stats (2024)*. Learning Revolution. https://www.learningrevolution.net/generative-ai-facts-and-stats/

Lin, B. (2025, January 6). *How are companies using AI agents? Here's a look at five early users of the bots*. The Wall Street Journal. https://www.wsj.com/articles/how-are-companies-using-ai-agents-heres-a-look-at-five-early-users-of-the-bots-26f87845

Linacre, R. (2024, December 29). *The emerging impact of LLMs on my productivity*. RobinLinacre. https://www.robinlinacre.com/two_years_of_llms/

Llama. (2024). Meta Llama. https://www.llama.com/

Matleena S., & Brian. (2024, December 16). *AI statistics and trends: New research for 2025*. Hostinger. https://www.hostinger.com/tutorials/ai-statistics

Meet Claude. (2024). Anthropic. https://www.anthropic.com/claude

Merchant, B. (2024, July 23). *AI is already taking jobs in the video game industry*. Wired. https://www.wired.com/story/ai-is-already-taking-jobs-in-the-video-game-industry/

Ms. Byte Dev. (2024, November 28). The impact of large language models (LLM) on everyday technology. *Stackademic*. https://blog.stackademic.com/the-impact-of-large-language-models-llm-on-everyday-technology-be391f2f134d

ODSC - Open Data Science. (2023, March 31). *5 practical business use cases for large language models*. Medium. https://odsc.medium.com/5-practical-business-use-cases-for-large-language-models-7b21b0059554

Rangarajan, K. (2024, January 1). *The impact of LLMs on learning and education*. Medium. https://medium.com/@keshavarangarajan/the-impact-of-llms-on-learning-and-education-3cd2a8367c23

Rawjani, M. M. (2023, October 30). *AI and IoT integration: Synergy for the future*. Medium. https://medium.com/@muzammil.rawjani/ai-and-iot-integration-synergy-for-the-future-9115a1ec2caf

Research Graph. (2024, September 19). *What is Grok?* Medium. https://medium.com/@researchgraph/what-is-grok-3fc13cd61397

Revolutionising the legal world: The breakneck speed and pinpoint accuracy of AI technology for law firms. (2022, November 5). V500 Systems. https://www.v500.com/ai-advantage-how-law-firms-are-boosting-efficiency/

The state of AI in early 2024: Gen AI adoption spikes and starts to generate value. (2024, May 30). QuantumBlack.

https://www.mckinsey.com/capabilities/quantumblack/our-insights/the-state-of-ai

Thomas, D. (2021, October 28). *Facebook changes its name to Meta in major rebrand*. BBC News. https://www.bbc.com/news/technology-59083601

Tilzer, B. (2024, April 9). How Best Buy is using generative AI to create better customer experiences. *Google*. https://blog.google/products/google-cloud/google-generative-ai-best-buy/

12 hyper personalization statistics that demonstrate value. (2024, October 9). *Monetate*. https://monetate.com/resources/blog/12-hyper-personalization-statistics-that-demonstrate-value/

Understanding the impact of large language models (LLMs) on businesses: Evaluating uses and integrations. (2023, September 18). Gaper. https://gaper.io/impact-of-large-language-models-llms/

Uspenskyi, S. (2024, September 19). *Large language model statistics and numbers (2024)*. Springsapps. https://springsapps.com/knowledge/large-language-model-statistics-and-numbers-2024

xAI: Understand the universe. (2025). X.ai. https://x.ai/